THEORY AND INTERPRETATION OF NARRATIVE

*James Phelan, Peter J. Rabinowitz, and Katra Byram, Series Editors*

# NOVELIZATION

*From Film to Novel*

~

## JAN BAETENS

Translated by Mary Feeney

THE OHIO STATE UNIVERSITY PRESS

COLUMBUS

Library of Congress Cataloging-in-Publication Data
Names: Baetens, Jan, editor. | Feeney, Mary, translator.
Title: Novelization : from film to novel / Jan Baetens ; translated by Mary Feeney.
Other titles: Novellisation. English | Theory and interpretation of narrative series.
Description: Columbus : The Ohio State University Press, [2018] | Series: Theory and interpretation of narrative | Includes bibliographical references and index.
Identifiers: LCCN 2017056193 | ISBN 9780814213674 (cloth ; alk. paper) | ISBN 0814213677 (cloth ; alk. paper)
Subjects: LCSH: Film novelizations—History and criticism. | Motion pictures and literature.
Classification: LCC PN3448.F54 N6813 2018 | DDC 808.3—dc23
LC record available at https://lccn.loc.gov/2017056193

Cover design by Susan Zucker
Text design by Juliet Williams
Type set in Adobe Minion Pro

# CONTENTS

# ACKNOWLEDGMENTS

This volume would not have been possible without the support of many individuals and institutions.

First of all, I would like to thank Benoît Peeters, managing director of Les Impressions Nouvelles, where the first French edition of this book was published in 2008, for his continuous help and encouragements. These thanks must be extended to the translator of the book, Mary Feeney, the anonymous reviewers of the manuscript, whose observations were crucial for the writing of the complementary final chapter of this new version, and the series editors of "Theory and Interpretation of Narrative," James Phelan, Peter J. Rabinowitz, and Robyn Warhol. The reworking of the original version has strongly benefited from the collective work of the BELSPO-funded interuniversity research program on Literature and Media Innovation (2012–17), involving the universities of Leuven, Brussels, Louvain-la-Neuve, and Liège (all in Belgium) as well as the research groups FIGURA (Montréal) and Project Narrative (OSU-Columbus).

Over the years, I have had the opportunity to share my interest in novelization with many colleagues and students, whose critical feedback has been of vital importance for my work: Sémir Badir, Nadja Cohen, Dirk de Geest, Michel Delville, Bertrand Gervais, Sjef Houppermans, Marc Lits, Philippe Marion, David Martens, Donata Meneghelli, Heidi Peeters, Charlotte Pylyser, Anne Reverseau, Adelaide Russo, Domingo Sánchez-Mesa, Steven Surdiacourt, and Thomas Van Parys. My debts to all of them are great.

～

# A Universe to Discover

What do these books have in common: *King Kong* (Delos W. Lovelace), *La Règle du jeu* [*The Rules of the Game*] (Raymond Varinot), *La Dolce Vita* [*The Sweet Life*] (Lo Duca), *Les Vacances de Monsieur Hulot* [*Monsieur Hulot's Holiday*] (Jean-Claude Carrière), *Les 400 coups* [*The 400 Blows*] (François Truffaut and Marcel Moussy), *Jabberwocky* (Ralph Hoover), *Basic Instinct* (Richard Osborne), *The Full Monty* (Wendy Holden), *Saving Private Ryan* (Max Allan Collins), *eXistenZ* (John Luther Novak), or even as a further example, *Agents secrets* [*Secret Agents*] (Olivier Douyère)? Are they little-known novels that found a wider audience in their film versions, confirming the old stereotype that only bad literature makes good films, while the adaptation of a masterpiece remains a doomed undertaking? In fact the opposite is true: the volumes in question are novelizations, meaning that they translate into book form, generally as novels, a preexisting cinematic work, original or otherwise.

## IGNORANCE AND MISUNDERSTANDING OF THE GENRE

Novelization, which we shall see is *anything but a reverse adaptation,* represents one of the least-known aspects of literary production over the last century or more. This phenomenon's overwhelming richness and diversity have never been duly recognized, vital as it may be for anyone wishing to grasp the dynamics of the literary object in the complex media environment now surrounding it. Studying novelization means shedding light on a forgotten or repressed area of literature, yet also taking a new look at cultural production in general, impossible to reduce to a more or less distant dialogue between texts, authors, or techniques belonging to essentially independent literary or cinematic domains. In this way, novelization offers the chance to break with the study of cultural relations in terms of reciprocal adaptation or imitation, with cinema cannibalizing literature, and literature being rejuvenated by its contact with cinema, to review the most tenacious platitudes on the subject.

If nearly *universal,* since traces of it are found in every culture where the cinema appears, novelization is not, however, a *unique* phenomenon. It is, rather, a type of writing whose form, meaning, status, even whose basic issues vary distinctly over time and within the geographic or cultural contexts where it emerges. Novelization constitutes a veritable industry at the meeting point of film and book. Certain reference works list titles in the thousands[1] (mass production and standardization not being modern-day inventions), and more inclusive guidelines regarding the genre would multiply this figure tenfold.

There are good reasons to explain why novelization has gone unrecognized in its current form, at least until very recently. But several recent phenomena have given the genre new visibility. Among the factors that may have hindered wider knowledge of the genre, sociological deprecation is surely decisive. To many, novelization is of little consequence for the pure and simple reason that every category of professional book reviewers ignores it: critics, researchers, and historians. Here novelization suffers from several handicaps. It is associated with the popular sector of literature (paraliterature, mass literature, industrial literature), that is, a form of writing intimately tied not to an author's inspiration but to a publisher's strategy, hiring a writer to perform a more or less predetermined job. Novelization is often an "authorless" form of literature: most novelizations are published under a pseudonym or produced by ghostwriters (no one really believes that Steven Spielberg wrote the book based on *Close Encounters of the Third Kind,* or Hugo Pratt penned *The Ballad of the Salt Sea*). Furthermore, the policy of novelization inherently implies erasing the author from the process. Take the example of Spielberg's *Saving Private Ryan,* novelized by Max Allan Collins, a specialist in the genre. Since now the director has abandoned any pretense to being a fiction writer, he entrusts the novelization of his films to "professionals," that is, to authors unlikely to take themselves for "authors" and who agree to turn out

---

1. For instance, Larson, *Film into Books.* One further addition is specialized websites such as "Film-TV Tie Ins": www.film-tvtieins.com.

books that may undermine the cinematic work. The books in question appear directly in paperback, not always in top-quality collections (note the French series "J'ai Lu" [I have read]), and through distribution networks unlikely to reach the same public Spielberg might target in his films. Incompatible with our myths about writing, which value the originality of the text as well as the author's autonomy, the novelizer's seemingly money-making output is held at arm's length from the field of literature. What is more, novelization has never enjoyed the selective interest in certain areas of noncanonical production. Unlike crime fiction, graphic novels, or pornography, which have been assimilated into more or less legitimate sections of literature, novelization has followed a trajectory similar to that of photo novels, regional fiction, or pink-cover romances, never benefiting from the attention of model or professional readers (achieving real popular or critical success/a boost?). Novelization is treated like a lowbrow form of photo novel: the scorn attached to such byproducts of the cultural industry is so massive and lasting that any involvement at all in novelization, whether as a reader or (even worse) an author, is a losing proposition, even if there may be some redeeming qualities, as evident in Roland Barthes's weakness for the photo novel and its "touching" stupidity.[2]

Adding to this lack of legitimacy is the difficulty of constituting a *memory* of the genre, so important for the status of a cultural practice. Novelizations are seen as inferior products, severely limiting their shelf life. Prime examples of disposable literature (*romans de gare* in French, *airport novels* in the United States), they were neither kept by their readers, nor acquired by libraries, nor featured in publishers' catalogues, nor saved from oblivion by specialized bibliographies, nor even miraculously stockpiled for some brighter day by second-hand or remaindered booksellers. The historically variable from of novelizations (an example from the 1920s bearing little resemblance to today's offerings), as well as the perplexing confusion in publishing terminology (novelizations were not called "novelizations" in the interwar years, at least in France, and the terms utilized, such as "ciné-roman [film novel]," were hardly unequivocal in designating the genre's production) served to exacerbate the breakdown in memory, such that novelization is less an *unknown* continent than a *buried* continent.

In principle, the combination of sociological rejection of novelization on one hand and historical neglect of the books themselves on the other should have meant not the genre's death sentence but rather a marked reduction in its presence on the literary forefront. Yet instead of being eclipsed, novelization has begun to garner interest, if only quite recently. Obviously it would be

---

2. Barthes, "Third Meaning," 66.

absurd to credit only the first articles that began to appear,[3] then the colloquia that can today be organized (and published),[4] finally the uncovering of original sources, and, perhaps, their eventual republishing.[5] All these initiatives reflect a somewhat diffuse but still very real perception of the genre's existence, finally coming to light, as well as its henceforth less disputed importance.

Among the factors contributing to this turnaround, the most important are of the quantitative order. For the last ten years or so, novelization of big-budget films has once again[6] become so systematic that their presence in various retail outlets is inescapable, despite top-tier retailers' resistance to this type of book. In fact, if novelizations are more visible than they were twenty or thirty years ago, it is also because the way in which cinematic works are produced has itself undergone a metamorphosis. The "New Hollywood," a somewhat trite term, here referring to the reorientation of studio policy toward big-budget films and new marketing techniques[7], has ceased turning out mere films and latched on to *concepts* produced and sold simultaneously in the most diverse forms of media, from online trailers to television series, from DVDs to CD soundtracks, from video games to clothing, from the film itself, finally, to its novelization. The very distinction between the original film and its derivatives is blurred in this multimedia blitz, holding a reserved spot, and consequently a minimum of visibility, for novelization.

But this institutional factor is far from the only one that counts in the return of novelization. Indeed, the effect of digital publishing cannot be overestimated, more specifically the ever-growing access to online sellers such as Amazon or eBay, which offer a second life to many novelizations and tend to favor the emergence of reading communities. Little by little, a certain memory of the genre is being revived, and however incomplete and imprecise it may be, this is creating a groundswell that translates into greater curiosity about novelization and a greater appreciation of the books in question.

---

3. It seems that the first real articles date from the second half of the 1990s. In this regard, it is most instructive to compare two works by the same author on a more or less identical subject, and observe therein the spectacular growth of the space occupied by novelization: Clerc, *Littérature et cinéma,* and Clerc and Carcaud-Macaire, *L'Adaptation cinématographique.* For more details see the general bibliography at the end of this book.

4. See the proceedings of two conferences, one in Leuven, Baetens and Lits, *La Novellisation,* and one in Udine, Autelitano and Re, *Il Racconto del film.*

5. Just prior to his untimely death in 2008, Francis Lacassin, who rediscovered Georges Meirs's novelization of Feuillade's *Vampires* (see subsequent chapter on the genre's history), was working on a book entitled *La Société des ciné-romans, 1919–1930, ou la dernière chance.*

6. I say "once again" because during the 1920s, the golden age of the "ciné-roman," novelization was already widespread.

7. Schatz, "New Hollywood."

The appearance of more ambitious novelizations heads in the same direction. For alongside paraliterary novelizations, there exists, at the opposite end of the literary spectrum, a legitimate cultural variant, close to the forms and status of innovative literature. These more ambitious novels often diverge widely from their cinematic basis, and, unlike commercial novelizations, are informed by a deep knowledge of film culture. From the literary system of research, they adopt the tone, the style, the reading public, the publishers, the models, and the cultural ambition. Novels of this type adapt very different films than do commonplace novelizations: they generally draw their inspiration from cinematic *genres* rather than specific films, or from classic films, or from both (obsession with the past and mastery of film credits being the two hallmarks of the classic cinephile). Finally, these novels—whose authors have actually seen and studied the films they are reworking—are as a general rule more visual than novelizations for the broader market, more focused on narrative. At least within the confines of their text, they concentrate on being what they are, transpositions of films; and this is their distinguishing characteristic, while commercial novelizations remain confined to the peritextual zone (which, logically, is rather "blank" in the case of novelizations termed "literary").

The clichés surrounding the genre are gradually giving way thanks to the publication of less conventional novelizations. Here again it is important not to confuse cause and effect. If a book like Tanguy Viel's *Cinéma* [*Cinema*] (1999), to give an example that quickly became canonical, is cited today as an indication of novelization's literary emancipation, this is not only due to the novel's intrinsic merit but also thanks to the context of its reception, which has changed a great deal in a short time. Published ten years earlier, the same book would no doubt have received the same critical praise, but would be no more likely to be recognized for what it is, namely a novelization. That is what happened to older examples such as *Kiss of the Spider-Woman* by Manuel Puig (1976) or *A Night at the Movies* by Robert Coover (1987). These novels were hailed by critics, each in its own way, but never, except retrospectively, as actual novelizations, so great was the divide between appreciation of a serious novel (even a difficult one, in Coover's case) on the one hand and the disdain for intertextuality on the other. Yet Viel's book saw itself touted immediately, and even in the most official way possible,[8] as a rare but legitimate literary example of the hitherto unmentionable practice of novelization, which seems to prove that this time the label was very much in the spirit of the times.

---

8. In this instance, this cultural legitimization was all the stronger for coming from academic sources such as the above-cited book by Clerc and Carcaud-Sicaire, *L'adaptation cinématographique,* and the reference work by Vercier and Viart, *La Littérature française.*

## DANGEROUS SIMPLIFICATIONS

Like many genres of popular literature, novelization can barely write its own history, lacking an institutional framework. Thus there is the risk, when examining older forms, of overemphasizing the clichés of the times, while also misunderstanding the present. Novelization is very much in danger of being viewed only through the prism of contemporary stereotypes, which reduce the genre to a sort of reworked screenplay, trapped in the confines of young-adult science fiction (such as *Star Trek*). What secretly underlies these definitions, which moreover come from both sides of the Atlantic, is easy enough to see. They make novelization into a sort of subliterature, produced by nonwriters (often either ghostwriters or authors publishing under a pseudonym) for nonreaders (meaning mass consumers of nonbooks) in a purely mercantile and nonliterary context. Novelizations would be an impulse buy from a supermarket, a secondhand store, or perhaps a bland airport newsstand. By glancing at the title, or getting hooked by the cover art, the reader is drawn to spend some pleasant, mindless time with familiar material before tossing the book to the side, like a magazine or newspaper. As a corollary, the precited definitions are most instructive as to how people think novelizations are written, or rather ordered up by Hollywood studio headquarters, where launch campaigns for blockbusters are programmed years in advance. These multinational corporations have advertising strategies with a growing role for spin-offs: for some time now the paraphernalia (T-shirts, games, websites, to name a few) involved in motion picture promotion have been conceived less as products manufactured in the wake of a film's success than as an integral part of the actual publicity buy, and there is no reason to exclude novelization from this "package deal." Even before the first shot is filmed, a team of writers is put to work so that the "based on the film" book will be available in every major language once the cinematic work premieres, the lifespan of such a book being strictly identical to the film's box office success: once its run is over, the book is either sold for pulp or remaindered, where it might enjoy an afterlife, though always a much more modest one than a film's second life on video or DVD.

In our conception of "industrial" literature, one of the key factors is the status of the author, *dominant* in the system of "real" literature where the writer is the system's alpha and omega, but *dominated* in the plebian regime of mass nonliterature, where the writer is only one link in the chain, and a weak, interchangeable one at that (a writer can be changed as easily as a printer, for instance). In the classic literary system, the author is an *individual*; in the other, the author is a *function*. Formulaic ideas about novelization generalize a possible type of author. In this version, which corresponds to a real social practice, novelization is the outcome of a prior transaction between the film's legal department and a mercenary turning out words without ever engaging his or her writerly superego (if any). Thus novelization can operate in a legal stranglehold, with a cinematic work's rights of adaptation controlled by the film's producers and their assignees—so that it is impossible to novelize a film in any format other than industrial novelizations, which alone can guarantee producers the profit they desire.[9] It then follows, without further discussion, that there is no room for a more personal type of novelization, and that all those approaching the genre with higher ambitions must contend with these institutional constraints in the manner of Tanguy Viel, the inventor of "oblique" novelization (in his *Cinéma*, he tells the story though the protagonist's repeated visioning of it, creating a secondhand narration), or of certain poets, who leave behind narrative in favor of atmosphere.

In the United States, all these restrictions seem less traumatizing for writers than for their European counterparts, as witnessed by the way major novelizers are able to discuss their profession without boasting or false modesty.[10] Let us treat the term "major novelizer" in its quantitative sense: certain authors are veritable "factories," mass-producing books. In Europe, since the earliest days of novelization, pen names have been the rule, indicating how squeamish writers have been about "prostituting" themselves. Generalizations are nevertheless misleading. Personal unease and disgust with the cinematic book industry also exist in the United States, as confirmed by John August's fascinating account of the novelization of *Natural Born Killers*,[11] or in the a few disparaging lines from Woody Allen's *Manhattan*, where Diane Keaton earns a living writing novelizations, among other things ("It's easy and it pays well."). Inversely, professional and literary pride are apparent in declarations by some European writers, as evident in this Surrealist dispute:

> On sait malheureusement peu de choses sur les auteurs qui pratiquèrent ces adaptations, la plupart d'entre elles n'étant pas signées, ce qui prouve le peu d'estime où était tenu ce genre de travail. Georges Ribemont-Dessaignes

---

9. Moreover, it is clear that project leads always keep a close eye on the manuscript and that they can have it revised as many times as they wish, sometimes even entrusting the "rewrite" to another author, cf. Christopher Priest's account of the novelization of *eXistenZ* (first published under a pseudonym, then reissued under the author's own name), see Van Parys, Jansen, and Vanhoutte, "*eXistenZ*." Here we are in a rather extreme situation, as least in the realm of fiction, of what Souchier, in "Formes et pouvoirs," terms *editorial enunciation*.

10. Larson, *Film into Books*. The central section of the book (53–234) contains short interviews with some fifty (American) novelizers, full of the most "no nonsense" explanations and positions possible.

11. Available online: johnaugust.com/archives/2004/where-to-find-natural-born-killers-novelization.

raconte qu'André Breton lui reprocha violemment cette tâche "alimentaire" dont pourtant il avoue n'avoir pas accepté de rougir.

Unfortunately little is known about authors who turn out these adaptations, since most of them are unsigned, proof of the low esteem in which this genre was held. Georges Ribemont-Dessaignes relates that André Breton took him to task for this "hack job," although he claims not to have been embarrassed by it.[12]

Platitudes about the genre lead to instances of exclusion. Preconceived ideas about contemporary novelization ignore large sections of the genre's history (believing the genre is a recent one and that its emergence reveals the publishing industry's steep decline). They also lead to overlooking the relationships between various types of novelization (leaving aside ambitious works while reducing novelizations to their most mechanical aspect, instead of taking them for true creations). The link between these two proscriptions is obvious: the stubborn determination to confine novelization to its lowliest form accelerates the genre's lack of recognition, since the books most destined to last do not become associated with the genre, while the absence of recognition helps maintain the divide between *industrial-type* novelizations, where a screenplay's framework is more or less transcribed in novel form, and intentionally *creative* adaptations that are not generally branded as novelizations.

## BEYOND STUDIES OF ADAPTATION

One serious drawback to a better knowledge of the genre is the near-exclusion of the better-known and better-studied corpus of adaptations. Yet more and more voices are making themselves heard, rejecting the notion of adaptation as little furthering the intelligent dialogue or exchange between different forms and media.[13]

Many commentators have focused on the process of the transference from novel to film where often a well-known work of great literature is adapted for the cinema and expectations about the "fidelity" of the screen version

---

12. Clerc, *Littérature et cinéma,* 99.

13. For a critique of adaptation as a theoretical concept, see the influential work by Cartmell and Whelehan, *Adaptations.* All things considered, it is possible to compare this rejection with the debate, some decades earlier, about the concept of influence in literary studies and its replacement by the notion of intertextuality.

come to the fore. [. . .] These commentators have already charted the problems involved in such an exercise and the pitfalls created by the demands of authenticity and fidelity—not the least the intensely subjective criteria which must be applied in order to determine the degree to which the film is "successful" in extracting the "essence" of the fictional text. What we aim to offer here is an extension of this debate, but one which further destabilizes the tendency to believe that the origin text is of primary importance.[14]

Obviously, this wariness about adaptation extends even more easily to a genre such as novelization, suffering as it long did from being only a stepchild of adaptation, entirely dependent on the source text. The result is a more flexible appreciation of today's novelization, then a revaluing after the fact of the past corpus, henceforth better *recognized*, in both senses of the term. New perspectives become possible, such as the hypothesis of reading adaptations as if they were novelizations and vice versa. Such a suggestion, inspired by Jorge Luis Borges,[15] is quite symptomatic of contemporary approaches to the phenomenon of adaptation, simultaneously rejecting the cult of the original and the belief in a linear relationship between source text and target text. Over this traditional paradigm, reading the adaptation's cultural network is now preferred; the adaptation process is part of culture as a whole. In new studies on novelization, literature is no longer the prestigious source against which a film's failure or success is judged, the film inevitably trailing behind, both in time and in substance compared to the adapted material. The object of future analysis will be more the interaction between various texts (some visual, others literary) and contexts (the publishing world, the movie world) within a more complex and layered arena than is found in traditional approaches toward adaptation.

The study of novelization appertains to the recent interest in questions of intermediality, which define the reciprocal imbrication of works and mediums in media culture. Thus what changes is the orientation of new comparative studies of cinema and the novel. Instead of analyzing how the text of a novel is transformed into a cinematic work,[16] the preference is to study how texts and films participate in vaster cultural constellations that far exceed the equivocal, linear, and teleological relationships between any one novel and film, or film and novel. This is of course where novelization is very much at home, as evi-

14. Ibid., 3.

15. As suggested in Baetens, " . . . aboutir à un livre?," 13–14.

16. The key work on the subject remains McFarlane, *Novel to Film,* which imposed the fundamental split between "transfer" (or the conversion of elements likely to be maintained from one medium to the next) and "adaptation" (or the invention of equivalent or new forms where transfer is deemed impossible). This theory is not unrelated to the practice of French "cinema of quality" adaptors, as discussed in the chapter on *Monsieur Hulot's Holiday.*

denced by its strong new presence in the latest summary work on the subject: Linda Hutcheon's 2006 *A Theory of Adaptation*.[17]

## AN INITIAL RESEARCH OUTLINE

The present volume is purposely limited to a very precise type of novelization. The emphasis will be on French productions, with preference given to novelizations aimed at a general readership. This necessarily excludes novelizations of television series or other origin texts (theoretically speaking, everything lends itself to novelization: plays, video games, radio broadcasts, comics, etc.), as well as novels for children or young adults (where little seems to separate "juvenile" adaptations from the even more prevalent "condensed books" for adults). These restrictions are necessary, given the many faces of novelization past and present, as well as its breadth and depth. But they should not prevent a systematic treatment of the chosen domain. We shall first propose an overview of the genre's major aspects: the *historical* evolution of its principal classes and occurrences, from the beginnings to its current incarnations; the *theoretical* definition of novelization; the *practical* importance of its material presentation to readers. The second part will offer a series of six micro-readings, each dealing with the outer limits of the film-book relationship. With this in mind, we will approach the transcription of a silent film (Carl T. Dreyer's *Joan of Arc,* novelization by Pierre Bost); the "straightforward" novelization of an original cinematic work (*Monsieur Hulot's Holiday,* film by Jacques Tati, novelization by Jean-Claude Carrière); the renovelization of a film originally adapted from a novel (the case file on Vernon Sullivan/ Boris Vian's *J'irai cracher sur vos tombes* [*I Spit on Your Graves*], culminating in Françoise d'Eaubonne's novelization); a translated novelization based on a remake (*Breathless* by Leonore Fleischer); an exploration of the boundaries between novelization and scenario (essentially via Bruno Dumont's *Life of Jesus*); and finally the singular instance of an illustrated self-novelization (Olivier Smolders's *La Part de l'ombre* [*The Shadows Share*]). After that, we will discuss some aspects of what is no doubt the least-known part of the corpus: novelization in poetry. The final chapter of this book, specially written for this edition, offers a survey of the most important work done in the field since its initial publication in French in 2008.

---

17. For a presentation of the enlarged version of this work, Hutcheon and O'Flynn, *Theory of Adaptation,* see the final chapter of this book.

# PART I

## On the Genre of Novelization

CHAPTER 1

∿

# Establishing Landmarks in the Genre's History

## WHY THERE IS (AS YET) NO HISTORY OF NOVELIZATION

(Re)constructing a genre's evolution is no easy task, especially when trying to do justice to its production as well as its reception. Many aspects of novelization remain poorly known due to lack of documentation. These gaps are real and cannot be ignored when attempting to write a history of the genre, something that has only been done in a fragmentary fashion to this point. The film historians who have looked into the problem, from Francis Lacassin to Alain and Odette Virmaux, from André Gaudreault and Philippe Marion to Jeanne-Marie Clerc, to cite only the most influential voices[1], have not been immune to this fragmentation. The result has been a mosaic of representation: evocative and multifaceted, but also incomplete, full of holes, unfinished.

Reconstitutions of genre's history generally labor under a triple handicap. First come terminological hesitations: failing to use a single term to describe examples from the distant past may conceal similarities; conversely, one generic label may paper over vastly divergent approaches. Next is how the cor-

---

1. Here we rely essentially on: Clerc, *Littérature et cinéma*; Gaudreault and Marion, "Les catalogues"; Lacassin, *Pour une contre-histoire*; Virmaux and Virmaux, *Le Ciné-roman,* and *Du film à l'écrit* (a short summary of Alain and Odette Virmaux's research is given by Marc Melon in his entry "Cinéma" in Aron, Saint-Jacques, and Viala, *Dictionnaire*). To which we should add: Autelitano and Re, *Il Racconto del film.*

pus is viewed with a selective eye, only a portion coming under consideration, not always attached to a broader perspective. Finally, the study of novelization may be relegated to fields of secondary interest, diverging from the genre or using it as a springboard for discussion of different questions.

## FROM CATALOGUE DESCRIPTIONS TO PROTONOVELIZATIONS

The notion that history "begins" rather than "continues" something that already exists, in a movement without beginning or end, is one of our culture's fundamental myths, found in many writings on novelization. Versions circulating about the origin of the genre are legion, and often contradictory. Nonetheless, unlike more accepted practices such as photography, graphic novels, or cinema, where it is possible to pinpoint the very beginnings, disputed and controversial as they may be, it would seem that novelization has not yet identified its starting point. Mention is made of George Meirs, the novelizer of Feuillade's *Vampires* (in 1916, soon after the first films launched in 1915), and before him, Robert Carlton Brown and *What Happened to Mary* (in 1913, an Edison movie adapted from a women's magazine series dating from 1912), and no doubt future research will bring to light even older examples,[2] especially if one delves, as Anne-Marie Thiesse or Véronique Elefteriou-Perrin has done, into the missing links between nineteenth-century serial novels and the first film "serials."[3]

As it is, this quest for origins might still be mistaken, approaching the past with the help of today's presuppositions. To put it another way: any treasure hunt with the aim of localizing the "first" novelization is perhaps doomed to fail, for it starts from the representation of what novelization will later become—namely a fictional text with a more or less literary mission—instead of closely following the trail of its formation. Thus the capital importance of André Gaudreault and Philippe Marion's work: in a series of articles on the

2. In his *Introduction à la paralittérature*, Daniel Couégnas mentions a few examples of novelization, including *Mystéria* [*Mysteria*] (1921) and *L'Héritière de l'île perdue* [*The Heiress of the Lost Island*] by Gustave Le Rouge. He dates the latter novel to 1912; unfortunately for us and for the precedence of French over American novelization, this is a misprint, since the book dates from 1922. This is even more regrettable since the author in question played anything but a secondary role in the history of exchanges between text and image in the twentieth century. We also know, thanks to Francis Lacassin's research, that the eighteen monthly installments of *Le Mystérieux Docteur Cornélius* [*The Mysterious Doctor Cornelius*] were the basis for Blaise Cendrars's collection *Kodak* (1924), a manner of "advance" *sampling* or *cutup,* as OULIPO might have put it.

3. Thiesse, *Le Roman du quotidien,* and Elefteriou-Perrin, "Film-feuilleton, guerres et propagande."

question, they consider novelization as the more evolved form of an earlier type of discourse, that is, descriptions of films in producers' catalogues, which the authors claim contain a strong element of what they call "protonovelization." Particularly representative of the trend is this entry for George Méliès's *L'Homme-orchestre* [*The One-Man Band*]:

> *Scène à transformations.* . . . Cette vue est un des trucs les plus extraordinaires et les plus incompréhensibles qui aient jamais été exécutés. Le même personnage se dédouble 7 fois. . . . [C]hacun des personnages qui sort du précédent, [*sic*] ayant entre les mains un instrument de musique différent, ils arrivent à former un orchestre; le personnage du milieu bat la mesure tandis que les autres jouent avec des contorsions comiques. Enfin tous les personnages rentrent pour finir les uns dans les autres.

> *Transformation scene.* . . . This is one of the most extraordinary and incomprehensible tricks ever seen. The same person splits into 7. . . . [E]ach character that comes out of the last one [*sic*], holding a different musical instrument, to make up a band; the man in the middle conducts while the others play with comical contortions. Finally, all the characters step back inside the bandleader.[4]

Gaudreault and Marion's basic idea is not to show that these catalogue entries, which describe the earliest films to those who might rent them for public picture shows, are already novelizations but rather to analyze the new genre's cultural genealogy. For novelization to become thinkable, this type of writing had to steer clear of two pitfalls: submission to the film, which remains present through the description given, and indifference to the literary effects of this description, whose ends are journalistic and commercial. Once this double handicap is overcome, the way is cleared for real novelization, taking off from the protonovelisitic daubs of catalogue entries (or, aside from these texts, the earliest movie reviews).

From these first analyses, it can already be concluded that novelization is not readily confined to the limitations of "literature." The study of protonovelization reveals that the genre can also include paranovelization, a grouping of nonfiction forms of varying literary ambition. A certain journalistic language is certainly part of this, as seen in the "filmatics" of the Flemish author Johan Daisne, novelist and film critic, who intended his weekly columns during the 1950s and 1960s as a way of saving films from oblivion (this was the era before rebroadcasts on television and more especially video or DVD reproduction),

---

4. Gaudreault and Marion, "Les Catalogues," 43.

all the while offering a literarily improved or ennobled version (Daisne tried to seize the true meaning of the films he loved, which in his view meant a broad interpretation of what was actually on the screen). But paranovelization is also present in the work of certain film theorists, who likewise talk about the cinema with a mixture of description and invention. That is, in any case, Roger Odin's position when, in Christian Metz's work, he finds forms of "description" that he likens to novelization:

> L'exemple le plus développé se trouve dans les *Essais sur la signification au cinéma,* tome 1, avec la présentation sur plus de vingt pages des segments autonomes du film de Jacques Rozier, *Adieu Philippine* (1963), suivie d'une étude syntagmatique du film. Il s'agit donc, ici, de la novellisation d'un film entier.

> The most developed example is found in *Essais sur la signification du cinema,* volume I, with the presentation of more than twenty pages of independent segments of Jacques Rozier's film *Adieu Philippine* (1963), followed by a syntagmatic study. This, then, represents the novelization of an entire film.[5]

The corpus of paranovelization further includes a series of "lesser" cinematic genres whose importance is anything but negligible, from trailers (audiovisual paratext) to the synopses found on DVD cases (verbal paratext), through the commentary, analysis, rewrites, and sequels that abound in movie fanzines and fan websites (*Star Trek* being the prime example, but we also know how much the offshoots of Ridley Scott's *Blade Runner,* based on an original novel by Philip K. Dick, owe to discussions of the film's structure and meanings[6]). A history of the genre could hardly sidestep the intertwined analysis of novelization and the avatars of its shadow, paranovelization.

## THE GOLDEN AGE OF "FILM-NOVELS" AND "RETOLD FILMS"

The leap from protonovelization to novelization did not arise from any internal dynamic, at least not primarily. On the contrary, the impetus came from an important mutation in the film industry: not from the move away from nov-

---

5. Odin, "La Novellisation du théoricien," 399–400.

6. Saint-Gelais, "La Novellisation en régime polytextuel," 131–40. A more "upscale" example would be Salman Rushdie's work *The Wizard of Oz,* where the author invents "an auction of the ruby slippers."

elty to narrative films but rather the introduction of a new cinematic "format" on one hand and new forms of marketing on the other. The "serial" would bring film into contact with a known but waning literary genre: the popular novel, generally published in installments. The shared interests of press barons and film production companies would broaden novelization's sphere and open the door to newspapers, magazines, and books.

Thanks to research by several film studies historians, it is now possible to form a rather precise idea of the chain of events. In the years around 1910, novelization is a highly commercial phenomenon, linked to advertising— French companies hardly differing from their American counterparts from this point of view. In the already highly globalized cinema market, America and France were direct competitors. Large French companies such as Pathé had American subsidiaries turning out films on site, then exporting them to Europe. The publication structures of the earliest novelizations bear witness to the unparalleled industrial, commercial, and cultural ferment surrounding the cinema, for the first examples emerged around 1910 either as serials in major newspapers, as inexpensive magazines, or as *book* collections aimed at a very general public.

The three types appeared in succession, or more exactly one on top of the other, over time. It all began in the United States. As Francis Lacassin writes:

> Mais le public américain ne se passionnera vraiment pour le "film en séries" qu'après 1913, lorsqu'il prendra appui sur un phénomène littéraire précis. Ainsi Edison remue-t-il l'opinion en 1912 avec les péripéties successives de *What Happened to Mary?* qui procède du feuilleton à succès d'un journal pour dames *The Ladies World*. Mais le coup d'envoi est indiscutablement donné par la Selig en 1913, avec The *Adventures of Kathlyn*, série de films indépendants les uns des autres mais hebdomadaires et accompagnés d'un feuilleton quotidien racontant les péripéties du film au fur et à mesure de la projection dans les salles. La rivalité des groupes de presse devait faire le reste.

But the "serial" craze did not take hold in America until after 1913, with the help of a specific literary phenomenon. Edison gained attention in 1912 with *What Happened to Mary?*, based on a popular serial melodrama in the women's magazine *The Ladies' World*. But the genre only really took off with the Selig Polyscope Company's *The Adventures of Kathlyn*, pairing weekly film episodes with a daily newspaper serial detailing the plot twists as each new film came out. A circulation war added to the drama.[7]

---

7. Lacassin, *Pour une contre-histoire*, 118–19. Certain information from this book is also found in the same author's *Georges Feuillade* (2005), published in Gallimard's "Découvertes"

This history is probably even more complex, since at least one of the titles Lacassin mentions also exists in book form, *What Happened to Mary?*, novelized in 1913 by Robert Carlton Brown. For the moment, however, let us concentrate on the coalescence of serial film and novelized serial.

In France, the fierce competition between Gaumont and Pathé gave rise to the serial. After the success of *Fantômas* (Gaumont) in 1913, Pathé shot back with *The Perils of Pauline* via its American subsidiary (unaffected by the World War I), serialized in William Randolph Hearst's daily papers. After this the "serial" (a series of films centered around a single character, with each episode relating a separate incident) gives way to the "chapter film" (the cinematic version of the serialized novel). Here is Lacassin on the subject:

> Cette nouvelle formule apparaît pour la première fois en France avec *Les Mystères de New York* version condensée en vingt-deux épisodes d'un ensemble de trois films réalisés par Gasnier et Georges B. Seitz. Pathé le présente en décembre 1915, une semaine après le début des *Vampires* (qui souffrira injustement de cette concurrence) après un matraquage publicitaire sans précédent: annonçant les exploits de Pearl White contre "La Main qui étreint" et son chef "L'homme au mouchoir rouge." Le feuilleton publié par le puissant quotidien *Le Matin* et divers journaux régionaux est dû à un feuilletoniste médiocre: Pierre Decourcelle, mais il tient un bon sujet.

> This new form appears for the first time in France with *Les Mystères de New York* (*The Exploits of Elaine*), a condensed version in twenty-two episodes of a group of three films directed by Louis Gasnier and George B. Seitz. Pathé presents it in December 1915, a week after the premiere of *Les Vampires* (which will suffer unjustly from the competition) after an unprecedented publicity barrage: announcing the exploits of Pearl White contending with "The Clutching Hand" and its overlord "The Man with the Red Handkerchief." The series published in the influential daily *Le Matin* and various regional papers comes from a second-rate writer, Pierre Decourcelle, but his source is excellent.[8]

The Pathé-Hearst alliance had paved the way for the novelization of serials. Gaumont and their artistic director Georges Feuillade would follow the example, not with *Fantômas*, which was itself adapted from a very recent novel in installments by Allain and Souvestre (Feuillade later reprising this method

---

collection, but also (aptly) offered as a bonus in *Les Vampires* boxed set (Gaumont, 2006, 4 DVDs).

8. Lacassin, *Pour une contre-histoire*, 119–20.

with the adaptation of Bernède's *Judex*), but with *Les Vampires* (1915–16), now widely considered one of silent film's great masterpieces. While *Fantômas,* an almost on-the-spot reinterpretation of what Allain and Souvestre delivered, was not novelized in any strict form of the term (it did, however, inspire a great many poems, which represent one of the genre's outer limits), *Les Vampires* was indeed novelized by Georges Meirs, not in daily tabloids but in book form, published by Tallandier in the "Librairie contemporaine" collection, in paperback form with garish covers, very much in the style of "sensational"[9] pulp novels of the times—it is easy enough to find marked similarities on the covers of *Les Vampires* and the *Harry Dickson* series, which had a longer shelf life than Meirs's adaptations.

The popularity of these texts arose from several factors, well-summarized by Jeanne-Marie Clerc:

> C'est ainsi que, marquant l'interpénétration indifférenciée qui les unissait, le terme de ciné-roman ou de roman-cinéma en vint à désigner, sans distinction, les films à épisodes imités du roman-feuilleton et les transpositions romanesques publiées parallèlement dans un triple but: d'une part, inciter le public à voir le film ou à acheter l'hebdomadaire et, plus tard, le volume correspondant; d'autre part, permettre au spectateur encore neuf devant ces images éphémères, de relire à loisir un film dont le défilement rapide ne lui avait pas permis de saisir parfois tous les détails signifiants; enfin, porter le cinéma ou son équivalent imparfait au fond des campagnes reculées où l'image n'avait pas encore accès.

> This is how, marking the undifferentiated interpenetration uniting them, the terms film-novel and novel-film came to designate, without distinction, films in episodes imitating serialized novels and the novelistic transpositions published simultaneously with a triple objective: first, to incite the public to see the film or buy the weekly magazine, and eventually the entire book; next, to let the moviegoer, still unaccustomed to fleeting onscreen images, revisit at leisure a film whose rapid action sometimes meant that significant details were missed; and finally, to bring the cinema or its imperfect equivalent to distant venues that moving pictures could not yet reach.[10]

These mass-market novels met with stunning success, as witnessed by the colossal numbers put out by certain publishers (Tallandier alone counted

---

9. On the "sensational novel," see Nicholas Daily, *Literature, Technology, and Modernity.*

10. Clerc, *Littérature et cinema,* 98–99. Comparable analyses are found in Virmaux and Virmaux, *Du film à l'écrit,* 8, and Leonardi, "La Vie passionnée des *Cousins.*"

more than three hundred such works, and others were working in the same niche) as well as the publication, in 1919, of the first takeoff on the genre. In *Le Copiste indiscret* [*The Curious Copier*],[11] the poet Jean Pellerin offered clever imitations of classic authors (Hugo and Vigny, among others) and literary stars of the day (notably Claudel and Giraudoux), but also included a satire of a "typical" film-novel.[12]

The triumph of the film-novel was short-lived. As Francis Lacassin explains, serials and chapter films remained in vogue during the 1920s. A key moment came in 1922, when the daily paper *Le Matin* joined forces with Pathé to form the "Société des ciné-romans" or "Film-Novel Company." But it was a Pyrrhic victory: the genre was losing steam and would disappear with the advent of talking pictures. Beyond these few titles, dates, and authors, the literary and cultural reasons behind this early success are worth exploring. Working from initial suggestions by Clerc and others, just as for the commercial aims of novelization, it is possible to sort out three principal reasons why this type of writing swiftly became so widespread.

First is the symbiosis between the worlds of cinema and literature. In search of new material, movies quickly tapped the literary reservoir, borrowing from the national heritage while also pressing successful contemporary authors into service. This media symbiosis is hardly surprising, and without overgeneralizing, it is possible to say that the back-and-forth between early twentieth-century cinema and literature mirrors theatrical adaptations of well-received novels in the century beforehand. (Balzac had complained bitterly about this, since novelists, their sales already undermined by imitations, made no profit from these adaptations.) We can broadly state that there is a "meeting of the minds" between cinema and literature, yet it is never a one-sided exchange from book to film or film to book.[13]

The second point is satisfying a series of public demands. If the earliest novelizations found instantaneous and resounding success, it was because they met a real need in the viewing and reading public. Complex needs, which historians relate to the advent of moving pictures and to serial films. To begin with, the rudimentary nature of silent film led many viewers to the supplementary information that film-novels offered, the most attractive of which was "complete" dialogue (since intertitles only hinted at the verbal exchanges seen on film, which the viewing public tried hard to figure out).[14] Similarly,

---

11. Pellerin, *Le Copiste*.

12. The rediscovery of this text, specifically the chapter on novelization, is due to Alain and Odette Virmaux, who further reproduce it in an appendix to their booklet *Du film à l'écrit*.

13. See Charles Grivel's illuminating remarks in his article "Photocinématographication," 30.

14. For an analysis of this phenomenon, see Raynaud, "Dialogue in Early Silent Screenplays."

readers sought any type of psychological clarification, because it sometimes proved difficult to deduce any clear and distinct character motivations from the playacting, histrionic and subject to many gestural conventions as it was.[15] Identical needs were also at play in regard to the genre of serial films itself: published at the same time as series were parceled out on the screen, film-novels served the goals of producers as well as moviegoers, eager to follow a story when they might have missed an episode, or impatient for a verbal guide to give clues for better understanding the narrative. Finally, in regard to the question of being allowed or denied admittance to view films in darkened theaters, novelization—combined with other specialized publications—provided an ideal solution for anyone unable to go to the movies, whether for geographical or sociological reasons.

Thirdly, the film-novel's phenomenal success was also tied to the fact that this type of narrative effortlessly fit the mold of a genre already well known to the movie-going public: the serialized novel, model of so-called "popular" fiction, which specialists place somewhere between "gothic" fiction of the romantic age and "romance writing" of the Harlequin variety. A rapid glance through "The Severed Head," the first installment of *Les Vampires* novelized by Georges Meirs reveals all the clichés, if not tics, of a largely codified genre.[16] The meeting between the protagonist, young reporter Philippe Guérande, with the newspaper's publisher, Monsieur de Villemont, takes place as follows:

> "Monsieur Guérande, M. le directeur vous prie de vouloir bien venir dans son cabinet."
>
> Le jeune homme se redressa brusquement, et la vue du garçon, dont la voix l'avait tiré de son rêve, le fit tressaillir.
>
> Machinalement il se leva, et ce mouvement lui rendit toute sa présence d'esprit.
>
> Une minute plus tard, il était introduit chez M. de Villemont, le sympathique et talentueux directeur du *Mondial*.
>
> Fort accueillant, quasi-paternel, le vieux journaliste, qui avait dû deviner dès longtemps chez son jeune collaborateur l'esprit d'observation et de méthode qui devait un jour consacrer sa renommée, lui tendit affectueusement la main.
>
> "J'ai besoin de vous, mon cher enfant."

---

15. For an analysis of hand gestures, notably the codification of the "Delsarte Method," see Jacqueline Nacache, *L'Acteur de cinema*, 105–8.

16. Feuillade and Meirs, *Les Vampires. Vol. 1. La Tête coupée* [*The Vampires. 1. The Severed Head*]. This 188-page book has three parts, each corresponding to an episode of Feuillade's film: "The Severed Head," "The Ring That Kills," and "The Red Codebook."

Philippe Guérande s'inclina.

Ce n'était jamais sans une réelle émotion que le hardi et audacieux reporter se trouvait en présent de son vénéré directeur.

Il ne pouvait oublier, en considérant le visage affable et spirituel de ce parisien-né, la carrière remarquablement brillante et rapide qui avait été la sienne. Et il se défendait mal d'un sentiment de naïf orgueil quand l'éminent publiciste en usait à son égard avec cette familiarité condescendante qu'il avait accoutumée.[17]

"Mr. Guérande, the publisher will see you now."

The young man sat bolt upright. The boy had jolted him out of a daydream. He automatically got to his feet, and the movement restored his presence of mind.

A minute later he was shown into the publisher's office. So this was Villemont, the kindly and talented head of *The Paris Chronicle*.

Gracious, almost fatherly, the older journalist, already familiar with his young reporter's gifts of observation and organization that were sure one day to bring him renown, proffered a friendly hand.

"I need your help, my dear boy."

Philippe Guérande inclined his head slightly; intrepid he might be, he was not unmoved to be meeting with his idol.

He could not forget, when considering this quintessential Parisian's wise and affable face, how brilliant and swift his rise had been. And he could barely repress the swell of pride when the great man treated him with easy familiarity.

In the progressive institutionalization of a genre, it makes sense for the movement from newspaper to (pulp) magazines to continue on to book-length publication (the editorial history of other popular genres, such as photo-novels or comics, followed a parallel trajectory). This shift occurred during the 1920s with the appearance, in the wake of collections inspired by Fayard's success with high-volume, low-priced books, of novelizations that took the form of real books, not mere booklets. The *film raconté* or film retelling then came to the fore, often illustrated with images from the film (generally set photographs), with writing that strove to "outdo" the omnipresent film-novel. These efforts to legitimize and enhance the genre were not limited to material questions regarding the publishing format. Care was also taken in the choice of authors asked to write a *film raconté*. Gallimard, for instance,

---

17. Ibid., 13.

took a leading role, regularly announcing novelizations by noted authors during the late 1920s, while never publishing any. The new emphasis on the genre also affected the output of publishing houses, with some trying to set themselves apart from the competition (this point will be reexamined as we discuss Jacques Bost's interpretation of Dreyer's *The Passion of Joan of Arc*). Finally, attempts toward legitimation would be expressed as a series of formal and stylistic innovations whose aim was to broaden the scope of novelization's discourse, as the movement from silent to talking films made it possible or inevitable. Just as it was no longer very useful to supply textually what was missing from the screen in the silent era (either with extended dialogue or a clearer and more explicit psychological motivation), some of the most highly rated novelizations of the period tried to invent new specifications.

One priority in this regard seems to have been offering the reader a sort of expansion of the film's subject matter, less within its plot line (such liberties would have been seen as too radical a departure from the norms in force) than in moving boundaries at the beginning or end of the story. Thus novelizations might open with a "prequel," then continue, with multiple detours, far beyond the book's eventual end. This process—which we shall see at work in the novelization of Dreyer's *The Passion of Joan of Arc*, a key transition between the silent and talking eras—was to be spectacularly illustrated by Raymond Varinot, who wrote the novel of Jean Renoir's *The Rules of the Game*.[18] Far from thrilling the reader with the famous Le Bourget airstrip landing that opens the movie, with its daring montage and unprecedented use of close and long shots, the start of the novel (a six-page, double-columned "Prologue") in the stilted prose of popular fiction, details the near-complete biography of the main characters. And rather than ending where the film does, Varinot adds a moralizing three-page "Epilogue" that must have left Renoir scratching his head:

> Le soir, au premier dîner qui réunit tous les hôtes du château, le général qui occupe la droite de la marquise prend la parole, selon la tradition. Son discours est toujours à peu près le même et s'il s'arrêtait, Christine pourrait poursuivre. . . . Elle l'écoute vaguement sans l'entendre. . . . Elle se rappelle le même cérémonial d'un soir lointain déjà. . . . Nulle amertume dans son âme. . . . Elle ne souffre plus à l'évoquer.

---

18. Varinot, *La Règle du jeu* [*The Rules of the Game*]. The same author novelized a number of cinematic works, including a *David Copperfield* (after Dickens) and *Lac-aux-Dames* (adapted from a novel by Vicky Baum, *Hell in Frauensee* [*Martin's Summer*]). His novelization of *L'Alibi* [*The Alibi*] (after Marcel Achard, 1938) is still occasionally cited in specialized studies on the relationship between literature and film.

Dans la monotonie d'une existence qu'elle a acceptée auprès de son mari, elle garde le souvenir radieux de l'amour d'André Jurieux, héros de légende, qu'un destin aveugle a misérablement fauché, une claire nuit de novembre, étendant un bras impuissant vers un but qu'il ne pouvait plus atteindre.
FIN

That evening, with all the guests at the castle gathered for dinner, the General, seated to the right of the Marquise, made the customary opening remarks. His speech was always more or less the same and if he stopped Christine could supply the rest. . . . She only half-listened. . . . She remembered the same proceedings on an already distant evening. . . . No bitterness in her soul. . . . It no longer hurt to think of it.

Down through the monotonous existence she'd accepted with her husband, she held onto the shining memory of her love for André Jurieux, the legendary hero, cut down by cruel fate on a clear November night, one powerless arm outstretched toward a goal he could no longer reach.
THE END

It is certainly not easy to speculate about the erosion of the French-style film-novel, but instead of emphasizing the relationship between the short-lived serial film and the particular type of novelization linked to it, we should inquire about more global metamorphoses. Readers had flocked to the film-novel because it brought them something—details, explanations, retellings—that they needed. But in the talking era, this function was no longer imperative, which no doubt explains the diminished desire for novelizations (especially on the part of the general reading public). In an even more radical manner, upheavals in the world of literature itself probably led to this loss of interest. Novel writing began to trend more toward a possible cinematic transposition, as in the American "hard-boiled" vein, and authors were less often hired hands from the movie world dreaming of "great literature" than writers hoping for screen adaptations. In such a context, the quest for a cinematic type of writing no longer needed novelizations to be complete: henceforth it was all literature, whether or not it admitted its relationship to cinema, which *virtually* presented itself in terms of novelization.[19] Every novel written is done so with an eye toward cinematic adaptation and is modeled on a scenario ("shorten, simplify, dramatize"). It is not absurd to suppose that the production of novelizations is essentially due to that transformation, which goes far

---

19. See for instance André Bazin's remarks on "hard-boiled" novelists at the beginning of his article "Pour un cinéma impur" [For an Impure Cinema/In Defense of Mixed Cinema], 81–82.

beyond the domain of one-on-one relationships between books and films, toward completely overhauling literary production.

## ALONGSIDE THE FILM-NOVEL

The film-novel, less monolithic than it might seem at first glance, was not the only contender on the novelization scene in the interwar period. On the margins of popular novelization, more ambitious literary variants appeared throughout this time, but especially during the 1920s.

Once again, transformations in the broader cultural field determine these developments. There is obviously the omnipresent phenomenon of cinematic adaptations of literary works, like *Fantômas* or *Judex*. These borrowings contribute to resolving the conflict between verbal and visual expression. But the demand for cinema also existed within literature, starting from the silent era. In 1917, Apollinaire had issued his famous manifesto "L'Esprit nouveau et les poètes" ["The New Spirit and the Poets"]:

> Il eût été étrange qu'à une époque où l'art populaire par excellence, le cinéma, est un livre d'images, les poëtes n'eussent pas essayé de composer des images pour les esprits méditatifs et plus raffinés qui ne se contentent point des imaginations grossières des fabricants de films. Ceux-ci se raffineront, et l'on peut prévoir le jour où le phonographe et le cinéma étant devenus les seules formes d'impression en usage, les poëtes auront une liberté inconnue jusqu'à présent.

> It would have been strange if in an epoch when the popular art *par excellence,* the cinema, is a book of pictures, the poets had not tried to compose pictures for meditative and refined minds which are not content with the crude imaginings of makers of films. These last will become more perceptive, and one can predict the day when, the photograph and the cinema having become the only forms of publication in use, the poet will have a freedom heretofore unknown.[20]

The impact of these lines would be real, if not immediate: if there was a great deal of writing on cinema, there was as yet little for cinema. After the First World War, we witness the earliest attempts at considering the cinema

---

20. Apollinaire, "L'Esprit nouveau et les poëtes." Translation by Roger Shattuck, *Selected Writings of Guillaume Apollinaire,* as cited in Jon Cook, *Poetry in Theory, An Anthology 1900–2000.*

as an independent art form. To be sure, these attempts to legitimize the cinema are not entirely new, but for the first time they go through a consideration of cinematic "language" itself, rather than focusing on the context of projection, like the first analyses beginning in 1905 through 1910 (examining the new central-city "temples" to cinema, modeled after and competing with the bourgeois theater) or on the elevated nature of what was filmed (as was the case during the "art film" years, a futile effort to reproduce the world of classical theater repertory). Symbolically, it was the very critic who came up with the label "The Seventh Art," Ricciotto Canudo, who decided to favor the "Impressionist" cinema (namely French avant-garde cinema of the 1920s, the first avatar of what was later conceived as the typically French model of "art house cinema") with an appropriate literary equivalent. In 1923 he published a fictionalized version of *La Roue* [*The Wheel*] "after the film by Abel Gance," which opens with a preface revealing the author's ambitions:

> Il faut compter trois moments qu'un seul cerveau doit concevoir tant ils sont liés étroitement ensemble:
> —la première vision de l'œuvre,
> —la conception du développement,
> —enfin l'expression écrite, ou peinte, ou sculptée, ou jouable.
> À de rares cas près, tel celui d'écrivains issus du même sang familial ou de même milieu de culture et d'âme, la collaboration n'a jamais donné d'authentiques chefs d'œuvre.
>
> Mais on peut admettre ce travail en commun, et en sentir toute la joie la plus intime, *lorsque la "vision" de l'œuvre d'un autre répond à nos propres penchants esthétiques.*
>
> C'est mon cas à propos de *La Roue* d'Abel Gance.

> A single brain must conceive of three closely linked points:
> —the first vision of the work,
> —the conception of its development,
> —at last the written, painted, sculpted, or acted expression.
> With rare exceptions, such as writers from the same bloodlines or the same cultural and intellectual milieu, collaboration has never produced authentic masterpieces.
>
> But there is room for this joint work, and all its satisfactions, *when the "vision" of another's work melds with one's own esthetic leanings.*
>
> This is the case with my response to Abel Gance's *La Roue.*[21]

---

21. Canudo, *La Roue* [*The Wheel*]. Quoted by François Albera in "*La Roue* roman de Ricciotto Canudo," 89. Albera's article contains a most enlightening comparison of several variants of the work: film, screenplay, novel.

Whatever the merits or faults of this type of novelizations, and it cannot be said that Canudo's text made much of a mark on the genre's history, having real writers take control of the genre is a striking characteristic of this period; "real writers" in the agreed sense of the term, authors who write on their own initiative rather than doing work for hire. In fact, what we are witnessing is a role reversal, with filmmakers becoming writers and vice versa. Abel Gance, who published a written version of his film *Napoléon,* is an example of the first case. The Surrealists, though not alone, are the prime example of the second.[22] The true meeting point between cinema and "great" literature in the silent era would be due to this new generation's breakthrough, quickly finding publication by Gallimard and passed on to the *NRF* (*Nouvelle Revue française*) by its new editor, Jean Paulhan, who succeeded Jacques Rivière in 1925. The Surrealists wrote on but also for the cinema, trying to invent new forms of writing that could simultaneously function as real texts as well as real screenplays (in itself an absolute contradiction in terms: a screenplay is anything but a text, and if it seeks to become one is rendered unusable).[23]

Nothing reveals this ambiguity better than the emergence of the scenario as a literary form; it is not always obvious whether these texts were supposed to be filmed (thus superseded by a new form) or if in contrast they represented a new and original literary form, independent of any consideration related to filming, and requiring an inherently literary evaluation (somewhat in the manner of "closet drama"). In short, these new projects written "for the cinema" burst on the scene and certain publishers actively supported this trend, intense but fleeting, given the rush toward production at the time. But many Surrealist texts proved too radical, in form as well as in content, to translate without undue "loss." And the arrival of talking films, which multiplied production costs by a factor of ten, would mean the death sentence for many projects" . . .

As much as the growing split between these two categories of novelization, one geared toward a very general public, the other addressing an audience of peers (meaning reader-writers or writer-readers), the unstable side of this equation should be examined. Unlike the situation we know only too well today, with its rather sharply drawn boundaries between "expanded" and "restricted" markets, the transformations in the field of novelization during the 1920s show how many gateways were still open between the worlds of avant-garde and popular literature.

This lack of a real rupture was evident in publishing output as well as reader demand: the film-novel was not the sole prerogative of popular literature but

---

22. See Kyrou, *Le Surréalisme au cinéma* [*Surrealist Cinema*], and Virmaux and Virmaux, *Les Surrealistes et le cinéma* [*The Surrealists and Cinema*].

23. See Delllisse, *L'Invention du scénario* [*The Invention of the Screenplay*].

also attracted the attention of serious publishers; educated readers were not indifferent to the film-novel's faded charms, and inversely, general readers willingly returned to classics adapted for the screen. But the greatest indicator of how porous the border between these registers can be was the career of novelizing writers or paranovelizers. A noteworthy case is Robert Carlton Brown, a now-forgotten trailblazer, whom a recent study characterizes as follows:

> For a good part of his life, Brown was little more than a hack writer, turning out jingles, advertisements, news stories, and popular novels, one of which, *What Happened to Mary,* was perhaps the very first film novelization, adapted from the very first serial movie, issued by Edison in 1912.[24]

What makes Brown such an interesting character is the systematic mixture, even if relatively common in the days when more than one Surrealist did work for hire (often under an assumed name, it is true), of blatantly boilerplate writing with the most intrepid literary experiments or enterprises. In Brown's case, there is also mention of a postfuturist "reading machine," pushing the idea of *freed speech,* the scrolling of printed text on film. Crossing diverse technologies, Brown foresaw literature on microfilm[25] as well as "sculpted" holopoetry with moving 3-D letters by cyberartists like Eduardo Kac. Yet Brown was well and truly the author of the "first" film novelization and much other writing that was probably held in the greatest disdain by the contemporary intelligentsia.

Cases like Brown's were not isolated, for some on the fringes of "high culture" literature were not afraid to "lower" themselves. Consider the Surrealists, Aragon and Desnos in the lead, who drew inspiration from popular films as well as from the then-emerging avant-garde cinema. Consider further the approach of writers adapting film-novels, generally very prominent authors in their own right, who would never in the world have stopped using what they thought was "real" style or producing "real" literature while rewriting cinematic series.[26]

In hindsight, we cannot help but be struck by the connections between the film-novel and experimental forms of writing. Mainstream novelization

---

24. North, *Camera Works,* 74.

25. Around the same time, another marginal "inventor," the Belgian bibliographer and utopian Paul Otlet, would propose various means of distributing written sources with the aid of photography and cinema in his *Traité de documentation* (1934), see Levie, *L'Homme qui voulait classer le monde.*

26. As Jeanne-Marie Clerc notes: "It seems that the most sought-after authors were still popular novelists, which explains the, most often, very conventional character of these texts, promoted as highly literary and visibly wary of allowing the Seventh Art to adulterate the received norms of fiction" (*Littérature et cinéma,* 99).

at the time seemed to be less in conflict with other forms of cinema writing (essentially the screenplay, a new genre that had not as yet found the form or status we think of today, whence the attempts to craft it as a freestanding genre, without production concerns). As we draw nearer the present day, we can observe the most commercial and popular forms of film writing, diverging from experimental forms to blend in with highly standardized fictional canons. Or so things appear; the rest of the story will provide a more circumspect interpretation.

## NOVELIZATION IN THE AGE OF THE "CAMÉRA-STYLO" AND "AUTEUR THEORY"

The immediate postwar years saw the return of novelization, but not in a relatively unique or unified form, as during the film-novel's prime. While the book format now seemed to dominate, at the expense of the proto-book[27] or pulp magazine format, novelization became even more prone to foreign influences, especially American and Italian. A few years later, internal changes in the French system would be the basis for an unprecedented national and international advancement.

Overseas, meanwhile, the equivalent of the film-novel had been less monopolized by the world of popular literature. According to the historian Charles Musser, the American film industry's vertical buildup had allowed studios during the Golden Age (1930–48) to control almost every aspect of film production, distribution, and projection. Hollywood had also found a way to give novelization a specific place in its global strategy of "cannibalizing" literature. The genre thus found itself shelved between two other new cinema-related genres: on the one hand, celebrity journalism, via the specialized magazines and fanzines that regularly featured some form of novelization or paranovelization; and on the other, the Hollywood Novel,[28] a contemporary variant of the artistic novel, more or less representing the literary side of new types of film writing. While the Hollywood Novel was not novelization, per se,

27. This did not continue in France, but remained a thriving branch of publishing well into the 1960s in countries such as Spain or Portugal, more closed to market developments under the dictatorship of Franco or Salazar.

28. Some bibliographies give up to a thousand titles, and these lists are no doubt far from exhaustive, see Larson, *Film into Book*. European examples include *On tourne . . .* [*Si gira . . .*, (1915–17)], reprinted under the title *I quaderni di Serafino Gubbio, operatore* (1925) [*Shoot! The Notebooks of Serafino Gubbio, Cinematograph Operator*]) by Luigi Pirandello; certain works by Blaise Cendrars; or more recently, Jean-Jacques Schuhl, *Ingrid Caven* (Paris: Gallimard, 2000).

some examples may tend, however dubiously, in that direction.[29] The broader distribution of American cinema—starting with the liberation of Paris after years of embargo during the Nazi Occupation, and despite the French government's ongoing quota policy aimed at preserving its own cultural output—brought with it the growing presence of American novelizations, especially as the paperback trade took off during the 1950s. For the first time, these novelizations were truly translated rather than freely adapted to the local public's needs, as had been the case until then,[30] even if it is difficult to pinpoint when the change occurred. During the 1950s, it was not uncommon to find wide divergence in the novelizations of a single film, depending on the country or market where it ended up.[31] Whatever the case, American examples were not without influence on their French counterparts, if only in hastening the end of the clichéd cinema-novel.

During the 1950s, the most common novelizations are self-styled "modern" ones that might be mistaken for "real books" if their often highly stylized covers did not set them apart in a market that still prized the classic French "white cover." A book that took itself seriously would remain free of vulgar illustrations, inside or out. But the tone, the style, the rhythm of these works differ from those of serial novels that had survived within the confines of the film-novel. These novels are probably much more numerous than believed, even if efforts to expose the hidden part of this iceberg are hampered by the lack of specialized and mass-produced editions like those from Tallandier or Ferenczi in the interwar period.

Relatively speaking, the Italian influence was no less strongly felt, but the domain in which it operated was quite different. One of the great innovations of the new neorealism-based Italian cinema had been to hone marketing techniques that used a barrage of interconnected media, which might be termed multimedia before the fact. To reach an often preliterate public, Italian production companies aimed at wide-scale circulation of movie iconography through every possible type of still image—ranging from celebrity photos to specialized journalism, and including reworking of film content in the recent genre of photo-novels.[32] The changeover of the genre and its cinematic muta-

---

29. Charles Musser analyzes as implicit or unacknowledged examples of novelization two works by Horace McCoy, *They Shoot Horses, Don't They?* (1935) and *I Should Have Stayed Home* (1938), which he posits are based on the films *42nd Street* (Lloyd Bacon, 1933) and *Gold Diggers of '33* (Mervyn LeRoy, 1933), see Musser, "Devil's Parody."

30. Francis Lacassin's *Sur les chemins qui marchent.*

31. For one example, see De Berti, "'King Vidor Comes to Italy.'"

32. A fine example of these strategies is Titanus, the production company of Dino Risi's 1955 film *Scandal in Sorrento,* starring Sofia Loren and Vittorio De Sica; see the book edited by Giovanni Fiorentino, *Luci del Sud.* Federico Fellini gives indirect evidence of the photo-novel

tions was almost immediate in France, where novelization/photo-hybrids were anything but rare during the 1950s.[33] This quite singular and curiously underutilized form of novelization[34] was not simply an example of a "digest" (as it was nothing unusual for a full-length film to be represented by a limited number of prints). It also draws attention to a broader social context, the modernization of Western European societies. Yet this modernization was as much technical and technological as social and ideological. It went hand in hand with a redefinition of relationships between men and women as well as the status of the individual in what was becoming a consumer society at lightning speed. Such transformations must be kept in mind as we approach several very specific examples of novelization at the time.

American and Italian influences did nothing to diminish the energy and diversity of the French scene. The major trend of the times, the New Wave, was inarguably the invention (not too strong a term) of a burgeoning cinephile culture,[35] its two hallmarks being the *caméra-stylo* or camera-pen concept launched by Alexandre Astruc in 1948, then the "auteur theory" elaborated during the early 1950s by the *Cahiers du cinéma* group of writers and eventual filmmakers. These developments, which will be analyzed in detail in the ensuing chapters on Jacques Tati and Jean-Luc Godard, were the culmination of the growing intermingling of film and literature, then the increasing predominance of cinema. The strengthening of links between film and novel would be translated and validated through the respective relevance of the writer and the director. At first their status would equalize: as in literature, centered on the figure of the author, the film world gradually acknowledged the "auteur," and the cinematic author took the director's place.[36] The writer-filmmaker role then became interchangeable: the literary author was asked to write *for* the cinema, then *like* the cinema, while the director took on the definitive functions of "writing." They finally blended together: distinctions among media were blurred, and only the authorial function remained, whether in writing

---

industry in his *The White Sheik* (1952), which can be interpreted as a fictionalized documentary on the production of a photo novel. For an overview of Italian photo-novel/novelization hybrids during the 1950s, see Morreale, *Lo Schermo di Carta*.

33. See Leonardi, "La Vie passionnée des *Cousins*."

34. Yet a work such as *La Jetée/The Jetty* (New York: Zone Books, 1992), photo-novelization of the film by Chris Marker and Bruce Mau, would on its own justify the existence of this variant that some readers might dismiss out of hand as silly and vulgar. It may be appropriate, with all due caution, to compare such books to collections such as "The Library of Film Classics" (Balland publ.), which during the 1970s offered examples of visual recreations of films with a series of stills in a generally identical format, captioned with dialogue.

35. De Baecque, *La Cinéphilie* [Cinephilia].

36. See Jeancolas, Meusy, and Pinet, *L'Auteur du film* [*The Film Author*].

or filmmaking (but better to film than to write, after all) as long as an author was in charge.

The notion of the *caméra-stylo* or camera-pen means just that, positing that the modern writer can find expression through filmic images as well as in words. The same is true for the meaning of "auteur theory," which rethinks the cinema's complexity of roles and functions to the exclusive benefit of the filmmaker, while redefining the latter's intervention in directorial terms, creating a basic vision of the world, a privileged role traditionally reserved for the writer as "seer."

For novelization itself, this radically changed context—with the growing weight of the American film industry, the broadcast of new cinematographic images, the emergence of New Wave "auteurs"—would engender a fractured landscape, its heterogeneity concealed by the growing diversity of the viewing public and viewing modes. A mosaic now became the norm, and little by little communication between the various fields and subfields would break down.

What forms did this more differentiated market take by the mid-1950s, as American and Italian cinematic culture reached the height of their influence and the French New Wave was arriving on the scene? In short, three main types of novelization might be said to exist, corresponding more or less to categorizing readers as informed, average, or the general public: first, the most ambitious novelizations, written in emulation of true novels; then, commercial novelization, sometimes in paperback form; and finally, visual and photo-novel representations, often on the fringe of proper novelization, and paranovelizations that proliferated in a narrow sector of the press. A few years later, new markets would open up thanks to the growth of television, which would give rise to TV serials or miniseries, but also a series of novelizing adaptations for young readers. But the impact of these developments would become more obvious in recent times.

The singular thing about the arrival of New Wave novelizations was the deep uncertainty about the underlying theory. Far from establishing a direct connection between specific types of films and novelizations, a plethora of formats appeared. Certain works have an obvious place in the upper ranks: Jean-Claude Carrière's novelizations of Jacques Tati's films, for instance, which we shall return to; or Truffaut's *The 400 Blows,* coauthored by the director and his screenwriter, Moussy, and published by Gallimard. Others shamelessly adopted new American styles, like the novelization of *À Bout de souffle* [*Breathless*] by Claude Francolin and several other texts in Seghers's "Romans-choc" ("Shocker Novels") collection, which we shall have reason to revisit. This style, with its echoes of American thrillers, was a 1945 offshoot of Gallimard's "Série Noire" imprint. Several recurrent features of "hard-boiled" crime fiction (behaviorism, crude language, voiceovers, stock settings and characters: the private detective, the femme fatale, the crooked lawyer, a fast-paced narrative) were prevalent in these novelizations. This was in itself an illustration of the "auteur theory's" firm belief in the importance of genres. Young French filmmakers were able to show that being an "auteur" was not incompatible with the notion of genre work: far from rejecting a genre's rules, an "auteur" would bend those rules to his own purpose and style. Hence the priority given to genre films, essentially the thriller, and the predominance of an American tone in novelizations at the time. The choice of this American-style novelization, lowbrow but determinedly modern, is all the more significant for not being the unanimous choice of all New Wave auteurs. Truffaut, for instance, whose literary identity was more traditional, is said to have refused any association with the "Romans-choc" imprint, even when offered complete control over the novelization of his own work. Finally, still others play the visual card, to supplement other types of textual rewriting: Chabrol's *Les Cousins* [*The Cousins*], novelized and paranovelized in several genres and formats, remains an intriguing example of such fragmentation.[37]

Little by little, however, the New Wave and novelization began to head down different paths, even if an auteur like Truffaut would still self-adapt on occasion (though he was not immune to trends, and his self-novelizations would quickly become the exception and not the rule). A differentiation emerged, discrediting the novelization process itself. French cinephile culture began to proliferate unfamiliar forms of literature and types of books, reputedly more modern and serious than traditional novelizations. The filmmaker concerned with standing out as a writer therefore turned away from the novel to concentrate on three types of works: books of interviews, which would top off the intense journalistic outpouring of the early 1950s, the unsurpassed and unsurpassable example being *Hitchcock/Truffaut*; shooting scripts, deemed true literary productions under the *caméra-stylo* regime; and finally, many experimental forms that are often difficult to categorize, from "film-novels" by Alain Robbe-Grillet, Marguerite Duras, or Jean Cayrol to Guy Debord's *Oeuvres cinématographiques complètes, 1952–1978*[38] or even, many years later, an alien form like *Histoire(s) du cinéma* [*History/Histories of Cinema*] (which should one day be read with reference to Debord's book, but that, no pun intended, is another story).

Literary authors themselves reacted energetically to the loss of bearings caused by the *caméra-stylo* model. If the writing of a text or the making of

37. Leonardi, "La Vie passionnée des *Cousins*."

38. Debord, *Œuvres cinématographiques complètes, 1952–1978* [*Complete Filmographic Works, 1952–1978*] (1994; first edition 1978).

a film became interchangeable, this new situation pushed authors either to adopt an even more visual and behaviorist style, according to what they thought were the American novel's teachings,[39] or else to reemphasize the inalienable distinction between camera and pen. Jean Ricardou became the standard-bearer of the latter attitude with two milestone articles: "Plume et caméra" ["Pen and Camera"] and "Page, film, récit" ["Page, Film, Story"].[40] Here is an excerpt:

> Le succès du cinématographe incite certains à s'interroger avec inquiétude sur l'avenir du roman. Or, la réussite du film n'est peut-être pas exempte de fragilités. Il est permis de voir un film; nous sommes contraints de déchiffrer un livre. Sans doute les larges audiences que recueille le cinéma comportent-elles une majorité de spectateurs fascinés par l'image et une minorité active, comparable à celle qu'obtient la littérature et qui, prenant ses distances, sait déchiffrer les signes. Pour le roman et le cinéma, l'avenir réside sans doute dans l'établissement de leurs spécificités respectives, ou, si l'on préfère, dans la recherche, toujours élargie, reprise et précisée, de leur définition.

> The success of filmmakers leads some to wonder and worry about the future of the novel. However, film's predominance may not be exempt from weaknesses. We are allowed to see a film, but forced to decipher a book. No doubt the wide movie-going public contain a majority of spectators riveted by the image and an active minority, comparable to experienced readers, who take a longer view and are able to decipher cinema's signs. For the novel and the cinema, the future no doubt resides in the establishment of their respective specificities, or, if you wish, in their ever-widening, recast and refined definition.[41]

But rather than honing in on any one of these works, some of which will resurface in later discussions, let us take a closer look at the imprint that published several of the most important novelizations of the latter half of the 1950s: Seghers's "Romans-choc." No single imprint can claim responsibility for all the innovations in this new stage of the genre, yet the collection did clearly demonstrate what would distinguish novelization at the time from older and still influential incarnations. Americanization, however ambiguous and dan-

---

39. Edmond-Magny, *L'Âge d'or.*
40. Both reprinted in Ricardou, *Problèmes.*
41. Ibid., 88.

gerous the term remains, was undeniably present, at least if we take it to mean recourse to strong-arm marketing tactics, the use of a more direct tone (or more brutal, if you will), and finally an emphasis on scandal, as the detailed analysis of *J'irai cracher sur vos tombes* [*I Spit on Your Graves*] shall reveal.

"Romans-choc," which ran to ten volumes published between 1956 and 1960—namely two translated works, *La Fureur de vivre* [*Rebel Without a Cause*] and *Les Sentiers de la gloire* [*Paths of Glory*] in 1956, then eight original works in 1959 and 1960[42] (including several with New Wave ties)—was certainly not the imprint that rebooted novelization following World War II. After the deterioration of the "film-novel" variant common during the interwar period,[43] the genre had swiftly resurfaced. On one hand, it had joined in with new forms of popular press and literature, primarily the photo-novel, hugely popular during the 1950s and regularly pressed into service for novelization "in pictures." On the other hand, it had found its niche in the book world, superseding the pulp magazine format more commonly used for film-novels in the 1920s and 1930s. Even though the novelizing output of the times left no lasting mark, it was high in volume and widely available through newsstands as well as bookstores. Many publishers produced novelizations at a more or less steady pace, and the material form they took was like that of real books. Certainly, the publishers in question were not generally highbrow, yet it would be unfair to underestimate their importance or the spirit of innovation, especially on the commercial side, of publishing houses like Laffont or Seghers, although the authors they signed were often novices (like Jean-Claude Carrière) or unknowns. The latter were not always hack writers, but also well-known authors or at least up-and-coming writers, who used a pseudonym to pursue novelization for profit. All in all, the genre was accruing a certain legitimacy, especially when it appeared in the physical form of a book.

Driven by novelization's decided trend toward invading the territory of the true book, Seghers's new series was groundbreaking in the way it promoted its collection, while other publishers seemed to struggle with the concept of an imprint.

An imprint's first job is to make itself seen. During this period, when the arrival of paperbacks and the marketing strategy that went along with them

---

42. See below: Appendix 2.

43. See Virmaux and Virmaux, *Le Ciné-roman*, and *Du film à l'écrit*. Let us reiterate that Francis Lacassin, who had already published widely on this subject (essentially regarding Feuillade), was working on a book entitled *La Société des ciné-romans, 1919–1930 ou la dernière chance* before his untimely death in 2008.

was causing a deep divide in the French publishing industry,[44] the decision to group together similar publications in an unconventional yet easily recognizable format was not a given. The break with the classic French "white cover" favored by all major literary publishers may have been an attempt to bring paperbacks in line with the rest of the bookstore. The books in the "Romans-choc" collection were traditional in format, paper quality, number of pages, typography, and thickness, but their covers were quite a departure, both illustrated (with a large picture on the cover, sometimes an inset as well, and a series of smaller pictures on the inside flaps) and brightly colored (every volume had its own color scheme). The back cover was likewise turned into an advertising poster: the traditional publisher's blurb and author's biography were replaced with a selection of taglines from film reviews. These were always set in the same stylized way, no longer representing a conversation with a prospective reader, but instead a hard sell. Each quotation was prefaced with the words "they said," in bold and capitalized, and the list of these supposedly shocking proclamations was followed by the invitation "Jugez vous-mêmes [You Be the Judge]." By way of an example, here are the back covers of Jean-Luc Godard's *Breathless*[45] and Marcel Carné's *Young Sinners*.[46] Godard, of course, was the standard-bearer of the New Wave, and Carné the pride of prewar poetic realism. The comparison is instructive, since it shows to what extent a collection's internal logic tramples the differences between films.

ON A DIT que "Les Tricheurs" étaient l'image de la jeunesse française comme "La fureur de Vivre" était l'image de la jeunesse américaine.

ON A DIT que le thème de Marcel Carné était celui du refus de soi-même, du refus des autres, du refus de l'amour.

ON A DIT que le sujet des "Tricheurs" était non seulement psychologique, mais aussi métaphysique et même religieux (*Maurice Clavel—Combat*).

ON A DIT qu'il était navrant de voir des jeunes gens se livrer à la sexualité comme des grenouilles (*Tribune de Lausanne*).

ON A DIT que ces garçons et ces filles n'avaient pas d'idéal.

ON A DIT au contraire que c'est l'idéal qui les a menés jusqu'au bout, malgré eux.

---

44. On the extremely violent debates surrounding the emergence of paperbacks, a tool of democratization to some, cultural mass marketing to others, see Enzensberger, "La Culture considérée comme bien de consommation," and Damisch, *Ruptures, Cultures*.

45. Novelized by Claude Francolin in 1960.

46. Françoise d'Eaubonne signed on to novelize this film; her role will be examined in our study of *I Spit on Your Graves*. The adaptation of *Young Sinners* was published in 1959.

ON A DIT . . . Sur l'écran noir de notre mémoire, le petit visage fermé de Pascale Petit, tricheuse jusqu'à la mort, le faciès inquiétant de Laurent Terzieff, prince noir des truqueurs.

ON A DIT "Les Tricheurs: . . . un aspect essentiel de notre temps, dans la Babylone occidentale."

**JUGEZ VOUS-MÊMES**

THEY SAID . . . that "Young Sinners" was the portrait of today's French youth like "Rebel Without a Cause" was of Americans.

THEY SAID . . . that Marcel Carné's theme was the rejection of self, of others, of love.

THEY SAID . . . that the theme of "Young Sinners" was not only psychological, but also metaphysical and even religious (*Maurice Clavel—Combat*).

THEY SAID . . . that it was appalling to see young people indulge in sex like animals (*Tribune de Lausanne*).

THEY SAID . . . that these boys and girls had no ideals.

THEY SAID . . . that no, ideals were what drove them to extremes, in spite of themselves.

THEY SAID . . . on the blank screen of our memory is the imprint of Pascale Petit's hard little face, the face of a sinner unto death, and the troubling countenance of Laurent Terzieff, dark prince of impostors.

THEY SAID "Young Sinners: . . . an essential portrait of our times and Western materialism."

**YOU BE THE JUDGE!**

ON A DIT . . . "*À Bout de Souffle*, c'est peut-être l'histoire d'un assassin vendu par la fille qu'il aima et qui l'aime, c'est l'histoire de notre temps, la *Médée* d'Euripide plus la *Nouvelle histoire de Mouchette* de Bernanos."

ON A DIT . . . : "On peut être à la fois insolent et tendre, lâche et courageux: et voilà le voyou sympa, devenu un héros moderne!"

ON A DIT . . . : "Le vol idiot ne se pardonne pas. Volez haut. Insinuez-vous plutôt dans les affaires."

ON A DIT . . . : "De la distraction à l'action, il y a les trente étages qui vont de l'adulte à son fils: l'un s'amuse en spectateur devant un film de gangster, l'autre devient gangster lui-même. Les croulants ne s'incarnent plus."

ON A DIT . . . : "Si vos enfants jouent aux durs, ouvrez les yeux sur vos refoulements."

ON A DIT . . . : "Le film le plus tragique, le plus lucide sur le plan de la morale."

**JUGEZ VOUS-MÊME!**

THEY SAID . . . *Breathless* is more than the story of a killer sold out by his lover, it's also the story of our times, Euripides' *Medea* meets Bernanos' *Mouchette.*

THEY SAID . . . : "He can be insolent and gentle, cowardly and brave at the same time: today's appealing delinquent is the modern hero!"

THEY SAID . . . : "Stupid stealing is unforgivable. Set your sights higher. Go into business."

THEY SAID . . . : "From distraction to action, there are thirty floors down from adult to child: one of them enjoys watching gangster films, the other becomes a gangster. The young and the restless turn their backs on old fogeys."

THEY SAID . . . : "If your children pretend to be tough guys, check your own inhibitions."

THEY SAID . . . : "The most tragic, most lucid film in terms of morality."

**YOU BE THE JUDGE!**

Clearly, the "Romans-choc" collection represents a fine balance between a book posing as a paperback and a paperback as a serious book, a practice very common today but quite daring at the time.

Yet the "Romans-choc" are interesting for more than formal considerations. The attempt to break through market segments is also found in the imprint's content and outlook. It is no accident that Seghers, which will be discussed again in the chapter on Vian, does not mention the film-novel but goes straight for *screenplay* and *rewriting.* The first term, *screenplay,* plainly belongs to the higher reaches of production: in the 1950s, no doubt under the influence of the new cinephile culture and theories on the *caméra-stylo* concept, the publication of movie scripts became one of the hallmarks of auteur theory. A novelization aligned more closely with the script than the film itself is therefore less an easy solution than a sign of cultural ambition. Inversely, *rewriting* is a way to avoid alienating the general reader targeted by the collection (and, in the end, by the movie industry fueling it): "bare" film scripts are left to the most rarefied sectors of cinematic publishing (specialized film reviews, essentially), while novelization—obviously involved with script rewriting—tries to reconcile the vogue for scripts with the general reading public's continued preference for narrative. Even the form that rewriting takes in the collection goes in two directions at once, displaying innovation but remaining conservative in the books' appearance and the collection's outlook. Many volumes take certain liberties with the script and try for a lively, quick, "young" style of writing (a prime example is *Breathless,* novelized by Claude Francolin and heavily influenced by Gallimard's "Série noire"). However, this reworking never begins to touch the experimental forms that writers such as Duras and Robbe-Grillet were then exploring. The "Romans-choc" authors were struggling to pump new life into film-novel writing without being side-tracked by the hybrid forms at the limits of the "Nouveau Roman" and *Cahiers du Cinéma.*

## POSTMODERN DIVERSITIES

At first glance, the diversification under way in the 1950s and 1960s began to settle down toward the end of the 1970s, when the scope of novelization evolved toward the situation we know today. Hollywood novelization acquired an ever-growing market share, but without standing in the way of new variants (novelizing "expansions" of television series occupied an important position, especially when they had ties to the cinema world). A strong sign of this normalization is the stricter control of translations. It is not easy to say when the major studios began to tighten their policy, which had been rather liberal in the genre's first few decades, especially regarding coverage of nondomestic markets. Until the 1950s, the novelization of a film for a foreign audience did not necessarily involve translating the original text but rather a reinterpretation by local publishers, who novelized according to the taste of "their" reading public.[47] Even today, certain aspects of global novelizations, conceived as a part of the film's production, with translations appearing in print as the movie premieres in various locales, continue to reflect local preferences, even within the same linguistic market (it is not unusual for an English novelization to differ from the American version, or vice versa).

Continued yet moderating diversity and progressive yet uneven normalization are not the only elements that characterize the genre's postmodern period. First of all, we should definitely point out that diversity and normalization are not merely conjoined phenomena, but that each one directly influences the other. One indication of this mutual involvement is the high degree of fragmentation in the field, with exchanges between types of novelization becoming less intense. Between Hollywood, or more accurately commercial-style, novelization, at once (rigidly) standardized and (subtly) innovative, and attempts to explore the genre's possibilities in other contexts, including that of "real" literature, the connection seems less direct than in earlier days. The trend is toward a two-tiered system, with commercial novelizations on the one hand and quite isolated literary experiments on the other. In France,

---

47. For an example, see De Berti, "King Vidor Comes to Italy."

those in the first category reinvent or more properly update the old film-novel formulas, especially in the domain of television series novelizations, which veer off into a separate genre, distinct from Hollywood-style novelizations in terms of style as well as themes. Stylistically, series novelizers readily align with the popular tradition, notably the serialized novel, which is making a strong comeback in the contemporary literary landscape.[48] Thematically, it is clear that these authors draw from the double reservoir of history (French history, if possible) and local concerns. Authors like Jean Van Hamme, successfully juggling several pop-culture media (television, novel, graphic novel), or Michel Peyramaure, author of more than sixty historical novels including several novelizations, are characteristic of this fresh blend of "Made in France" film-novels. Alongside these novelizations that dust off the conventions of popular literature, attempts at literary novelization are not unheard of, but hardly stand a chance, if only because they are rarely identified as belonging to the same genre. Still, the number of these novelizations, paranovelizations, and literary near-novelizations has become so considerable that new interchanges seem likely in the not-too-distant future.

The skillfully intended or maintained consequence of this multiplication of "concepts" or "ideas," lending themselves to every possible treatment, is the blurring of boundaries between source material and derived or adapted products. As regards novelization, the distinction has always been somewhat unclear, with certain publishers mixing novelizations and adaptations together under one imprint, and using the same generic labels. One quite typical and very early case was *King Kong* (Delos W. Lovelace, 1932), which incorrectly passed for an adaptation: due to postproduction problems, the film came out well after the book although they were supposed to appear simultaneously. The time lag generated, then aggravated, a mistaken identity, even though the nature of the text was clearly indicated in the paratext, listing several layers of authorial input in traditional movie format: "Conceived by Edgar C. Wallace and Meriam C. Cooper, screenplay by James A. Creelman and Ruth Rose; novelization from the Radio Picture by Delos W. Lovelace."[49]

The intertwining of literature and film, which Charles Grivel aptly pointed out by means of the portmanteau word "photocinématographication," here

48. This includes the domain of "serious" literature, as in the case of Jacques Jouet. The principal reason for the return of serialization in this type of literature, however, is less the desire to capitalize on the fashion for mass media series than the diversity of distribution techniques for the written word, distribution that no longer takes place through books alone but through a multitude of channels, notably the Internet, with certain of these, such as blogs, "reprogramming" the serial novel format.

49. To avoid any misunderstanding: Christopher Golden's 2005 book from the *King Kong* remake is also a novelization.

reaches one of its nearly logical extremes, easily uncovered by an on-the-spot investigation: the average reader regularly confuses the difference between adaptation and novelization, mistaking for earlier what really came later or vice versa, and the format of various books plays an increasing role in the misunderstanding. Novelizations are made to seem like adaptations, or the opposite. But these misapprehensions no doubt play an integral part in how we watch and read: seeing a film based on a novel, why wouldn't we think of video game spinoffs, or bonus features and director's commentary that the DVD version will feature? If works change shape so quickly today, it is because even before their conception they are seen as all-encompassing.

CHAPTER 2

# Variations on a Definition

As its history shows, novelization encompasses very diverse practices.[1] Any too-narrow definition might exclude many examples whose analysis would be indispensable to a better understanding of the genre, a term we ought to interpret broadly and flexibly herein. In the case of novelization, such an approach is all the more interesting in that theories already abound. Novelization is something we think we know all about: a book "after the film," one everyone feels free to judge and categorize, a minor, commercial, disposable genre. Studying novelization as a genre will thus depart from preconceived notions, as much to critique them as to come up with substitute ideas, fairer and more forceful ones, where necessary. This chapter's intent is to examine the basic clichés that interfere with a direct approach to works themselves: on one hand, the fact that novelization is supposed to be a profoundly anachronistic, even reactionary, genre, and on the other hand, the fact that the relationships between film and book are reduced to a simple form of translating visual and textual signs.

---

1. An earlier version of this chapter appeared in *Poétique,* 138, 2004, and *Critical Inquiry,* vol. 32:1, 2005. The present text differs from these versions on several essential points.

# THE TEXT COUNTERATTACKS

Contemporary culture is visual, more precisely a culture marked by the "pictorial turn,"[2] that is, the move from a writing-based culture to an image-based one. No matter how we parse this phenomenon, all of whose implications we are no doubt far from understanding, we must recognize that new ways of conceptualizing the image often labor to move beyond the dichotomy between the verbal and visual domains. The theory of visual culture does not imply, however, the naive assumption of an "anti-verbal" or "anti-linguistic" culture. Instead, it finds its place at the intersection of two regimes, insisting on the imbrication of registers or purviews and on integrating text into a new semiosphere hitherto dominated by images.

What is, from this perspective, the status of novelization? In the long view, novelization initially appears as an anachronism. First because this cultural practice seems to go in the opposite direction from the visual influence over every form of writing in our times. Next because this paradoxical return to the written form seems to exist unapologetically, instead exacting a sort of revenge on the visual. To paraphrase an expression that was everywhere a few years back ("The Empire Writes Back"[3]), one might say that the recent novelization boom is one of the ways in which a now subjugated system, that of the written word, manages to "counterattack," making use of the dominant system's tools, even using those tools against visual culture: "The Text Writes Back." Considered more closely, this judgment must be qualified to some degree. Novelization is neither a genre shaped by the omnipresence of visual messages, nor a reactionary genre, hostile to the progression of visual culture. It is at once a genre opposed to the image (the very fact that such a genre exists reveals a form of resistance by written culture, also highlighting the limits of the movement from "logosphere" to "videosphere"[4]), and further, one that can only be imagined within a broader visual context (without movies no novelization is possible, the latter being the historical outgrowth of the

---

2. "Whatever the pictorial turn is, then, it should be clear that it is not a return to naïve mimesis, copy or correspondence theories of representation, or a renewed metaphysics of pictorial "presence": it is rather a postlinguistic, postsemiotic rediscovery of the picture as a complex interplay between visuality, apparatus, institutions, discourse, bodies, and figurality. It is the realization that *spectatorship* (the look, the gaze, the glance, the practices of observation, surveillance, and visual pleasure) may be as deep a problem as various forms of *reading* (decipherment, decoding, interpretation, etc.) and that visual experience or "visual literacy" might not be fully explicable on the model of textuality." Mitchell, *Picture Theory,* 16.

3. After the volume of the same name, edited by Ashcroft, Griffiths, and Tiffin.

4. To borrow Regis Debray's terminology in *Vie et mort de l'image* [*Life and Death of the Image*].

former). To designate this contradiction, we might speak of a textual genre's contamination by a visual practice, providing we recall that this type of contamination, rather than being lethal, can prove a source of cultural innovation.

## A FALSELY INDEPENDENT GENRE

For André Gaudreault and Philippe Marion, as we have seen, any novelization worthy of the name must conform to two characteristics. "Independent" novelization must first of all break free from its parent form of film. It must therefore repress, obliterate, reject the fact that the story it tells in fact comes from the cinema. Second, novelization must also cease to be a mere description with a utilitarian function and become a self-sufficient narrative, with all the dramatic and innovative possibilities that implies. Take the example of *Monsieur Hulot's Holiday,* Tati's film novelized by Jean-Claude Carrière: the novel does indeed refrain from mentioning its cinematic origins at the same time it manages, with no small amount of flair, to invent literary and narrative effects absent from the film, starting with the introduction of a first-person narrator.

Yet there is cause to wonder whether Gaudreault and Marion's definition holds for novelization as a whole. For instance, what about the solution of continuity between film and book which they hold so important? We must observe that "liberation" from the original medium is quite relative. There remain a great number of novelizations where mention of the film is still much in evidence, as is the case with the novelization often cited as the genre's prime contemporary example: Tanguy Viel's *Cinéma,* which flaunts its relationship to Mankiewicz's *Sleuth.* There is also an area, not in textual but in book terms, where mention of the parent form remains mandatory: the peritext. Take the film out of the text and it will only resurface in the peritext: cover art, copyright information, etc., all converge to proclaim what the text attempts to muzzle. One might further wonder about novelizations that extend this declaration of independence to the peritextual domain. It is a safe bet that they will go . . . unnoticed, as far as novelizations reach. No doubt there exists a vast category of implicit novelizations, one with unclear boundaries. We have already seen the example of Horace McCoy's two novels, which Charles Musser has analyzed as cases of *cryptonovelization* (even though he refrains from using this somewhat overblown word). For French literature, one might add a text such as *Le Malheur au Lido* [*Misfortune at the Lido*] by Louis-René Des Forêts.[5]

---

5. Des Forêts, *Le Malheur.* Yet again peritextual clues are not entirely absent, as with McCoy. What reader (meaning what reader of Des Forêts) will fail to think of Visconti?

## NOVELIZATION AS ANTIADAPTATION

Novelization is undeniably a form of adaptation. A second idea, however, is much less implicit, yet largely shared by those commenting upon the genre. Many would indeed consider novelizing adaptation as the inverse procedure of cinematic adaptation of a literary text: one goes from writing to image, the other from image to written text. This analogy is not simply misleading but also, if only one more attentively examines how novelizations are written, dead wrong. Novelizations are actually very different from film adaptations, not (or not only) as a result of their culturally less legitimate standing but also because of the lack of the two absolute requirements for a true cinematic adaptation.

On one side, novelizations are missing the *transmedial* nature that marks the passage from one medium to another[6] and that is at the heart of any book-to-film adaptation project, even though the film's images may very well feature in the book's inception. The majority of novelizations are based on one form or other of the screenplay, thus a *verbal* pretext,[7] meaning among other things that the problem of "translation" from one semiotic system to another is systematically eluded: novelization is not necessarily a series of images transposed into verbal units, for it often happens that the novelizer begins not from the film but rather from some stage of the screenplay.

On the other, by relying on an already prenovelized pretext (dare we say), novelizations sidestep the major challenge to any film adaptation, namely the equally problematic and exciting equilibrium between the two forces that Brian McFarlane[8] has termed "transfer" and "adaptation proper." Under the first heading, McFarlane includes all the aspects and mechanisms allowing one system of signs to "replicate" the other without difficulty; the second designates the opposing forces that impede such a transposition, requiring a "creative" effort on the part of the adaptor.[9] To the extent that novelization supposedly settles for transposing a piece of writing from a

---

6. For more details on transmedialization procedures in the literary field, see Genette, *Palimpsests*.

7. The screenplay can take the form of a "visual" script or storyboard. But with few exceptions, this is never the form that serves as intermediary between film and book. Later we will mention the case of visual novelizations (for example as picture-novels), which make up a separate genre.

8. McFarlane, *Novel to Film*.

9. To use the Groupe Mu's terminology, it might be said that "adaptation proper" can take four forms: suppression, adjunction, suppression-adjunction, and permutation, see Groupe Mu, *Rhétorique générale* [*General Rhetoric*]. The finest example of a discussion of these aspects remains François Truffaut's polemic against French cinema of quality in the 1950s, rightly founded on a very particular interpretation of the adaptation of literary texts, see Truffaut, "Certain Tendency." For more details, see the subsequent chapter on novelizing Tati.

script-related medium into text, and transposing an already highly narrative structure into a novel, the genre can afford the luxury of being spared almost all the classical problems of cinematic adaptation. Thus one can say that novelization is a false adaptation; indeed, in an even stronger sense and always in contrast to the traditional book-into-film adaptation model, it is an *antiadaptation*.

Historically speaking, it is interesting to recall that simply from the standpoint of origins, shooting a film and writing a novelization are carried out on a parallel track, to such an extent that in certain cases it is impossible to say which medium preceded the other. One deservedly famous example is Pier Paolo Pasolini's *Teorema* [*Theorem*], simultaneously begotten as both film and book. But essentially the situation is hardly different for the most commercial and mediocre novelization that might exist. The explanation for this synchronicity is simple: if the book is written before the film comes out, it is because the two arise from the same source, the screenplay. And, even more generally speaking, Charles Grivel has already drawn our attention to the fact that from the genre's earliest days novelization has been at once upstream and downstream from the film, since the first novelizations adapted films that were themselves based on books already written in script form.

However, despite the formal complexity or refinement of these examples, the thesis of novelization as antiadaptation can be defended without injury to the corpus in general. Novelizers sometimes tend to camouflage the typical aspects of adaptation, the specific difficulties or concerns of which are very rarely thematized or elucidated. The guiding thread of their work is incontestably the drive to minimize the tension between media and systems of discourse. Novelization claims to be less the film's *other* than its *double*. This strategy of conflict avoidance makes it an antiadaptation. The imaginary system novelization adopts for itself is that of *tracing*, that is, immediate transfer.

## NOVELIZATION AS ANTIREMEDIATION

In the common definitions of novelization, the film-book relationship is presented in transmedial terms: novelization in *book* form is meant to reproduce a *cinematic* work. These definitions result in comparative judgments: the *derived* product that is novelization is measured against the filmed *original*. To be sure, each of these dimensions is toned down to some extent, since novelization does not in principle seek to *rival* the film. All the same, the genre's overall horizon is clearly binary. Yet this binary and teleological vision of relations between media is swept aside by the hybrid character of contemporary visual culture where, in addition to the blurring of before and after, the genre's very autonomy tends to be fleeting as well:

> Phenomenologically, the field of visual images in everyday contemporary "Western" cultures (and others, such as that of Japan) is heterogeneous and hybrid. The consumer of images "flips" through endless magazines, "channel surfs" on waves of TV shows. The integrity of the semantic object is rarely, if ever, respected. Moreover, the boundaries of the "object" itself are expanded, made permeable or otherwise transformed. For example, a "film" may be encountered through posters, "blurbs," and other advertisements, such as trailers and television clips; it may be encountered through newspaper reviews, reference work synopses, and theoretical articles (with their "filmstrip" assemblages of still images); through production photographs, frame enlargements, memorabilia, and so on. Collecting such metonymic fragments in memory, we may come to feel familiar with a film we have not actually seen.[10]

This unbridled cross-pollination, supposedly postmodern, is hardly new. According to an author like John Storey, there are clear parallels with the structures of popular culture as they have evolved since at least the nineteenth century.[11] The *Industrial* Revolution was also a *cultural* revolution undermining the production as well as the reception of cultural heritage. Following the lead of Dominique Kalifa,[12] for instance, it is quickly apparent that these changes cannot simply be described as the transformation of the work of *art* into cultural *merchandise*. A moralizing classification like this precludes the detailed analysis of culturally significant changes in the semiotics of the object, which thenceforth falls under the threefold rule of *novelty, seriality,* and *adaptation*: new cultural products must constantly be on offer to a public that now wants (or *must*) "consume" them in order to fill ever-growing leisure time, a public constantly in search of new stimuli. Successful cultural objects are leveraged to maximize profits and appear in various media under as many guises as possible. Adaptation, from this point of view, represents the culmination of combined novelty and seriality: it is *at once* a new and serialized product, which may be thought profitable for this dual reason.

Regarding novelization, this framework proves both useful and revealing. Novelization is not something new; it actually repeats in seemingly new

---

10. Burgin, *In/different Spaces,* 22–23.
11. Storey, *Inventing Popular Culture,* 70.
12. Kalifa, *La Culture de masse en France* [*Mass Culture in France*].

ways something that existed before. In its most common forms, it perfectly illustrates the kind of mass culture that represents the cultural industry's ideal. At the same time, it also offers the chance to revisit the debate surrounding the concept of *remediation,* which in recent years has replaced the broad, indistinct concept of *adaptation* and now looms over many discussions of media dynamics. In *Remediation: Understanding the New Media,*[13] Jay David Bolter and Richard Grusin defend the idea that Western media systems aspire to a maximum of *realism,* that is, a system where signs take a back seat to things themselves. This veritable realist *drive* leads the West to seek systems where signs are more and more invisible ("Transparency") and referents more and more directly present ("Immediacy"). And if moving from one medium to another is no longer considered through McLuhan's teleological filter, media transitions are far from neutral: according to Bolter and Grusin, behind any transmedial move there is ultimately "remediation," in both senses of the term (one medium *takes over* from the other; one *improves* on the other).

Is converting a full-length film into a novel that is neither too short nor too long a good example of "remediation?" It is quite obviously nothing of the sort, and of course this blatant contradiction to the laws of "remediation" is what makes novelization (and perhaps mass culture in general) so fascinating. In a very general way, the leap from film to novel might well be considered a historical anomaly, a step backward in a context where reverse direction is generally frowned upon. As Jay David Bolter points out:

> Meanwhile, film which was often said to be the preeminent popular art form of the twentieth century, refashioned narrative forms . . . that belonged to the novel and the stage play. Because they were such vivid audiovisual experiences, films seemed to offer greater immediacy and authenticity than novels or plays.[14]

The same author has even more harsh words in store for *verbal* translations of visual or multimedia signs,[15] which he disparages as so many attempts to *recoup* the new at the expense of an outdated ideology representing a *conservative* trend in Western media history, to his way of thinking. Add to this

---

13. Bolter and Grusin, *Remediation.* The book's subtitle is a direct allusion to McLuhan's *Understanding Media.* For a critical reading of Bolter and Grusin's ideas, see Baetens, "Critique of Cyberhybrid-hype."

14. Bolter, "Critical Theory and the Challenge," 19.

15. "There is a tradition in humanistic studies of translating other media forms back into the medium of print, and this tradition continues with new media" (ibid., 24).

that novelization has no discernable wish to *improve upon* the original film nor even to *equal* the film, though the rare book may venture a timid hint that it is trying to do something different. A good example (or counterexample) would be Jean Noli's novelization of *La Banquière* [*The Lady Banker*], based on George Conchon's screenplay for the film by Francis Girod. In his foreword, the publisher himself notes:

> L'histoire était trop belle, trop riche en rebondissements, en péripéties d'amour, de haine, de mort, pour la laisser aux seuls cinéastes, pour n'en pas faire un livre. C'est pourquoi nous avons demandé à un écrivain, Jean Noli . . . et à un économiste, Éric Chanel . . . de raconter à leur manière cet exceptionnel destin de femme.

> The plot was too complex, too rich in twists and turns of love, hate, and death, to leave it in the hands of moviemakers alone, to resist making a book of it. That's why we've asked a writer, Jean Noli . . . and an economist, Éric Chanel . . . to retell this exceptional woman's life story in their own way.[16]

To understand and explain novelizations, it is crucial to abandon the traditional binary approach, always involving the concept of "remediation," and install the genre in a broader cultural context. Novelization is rooted in mass culture, which demands that it not (only) *remediate* but also *maintain constant change,* by means of the three intertwined laws of novelty, seriality, and adaptation across media. No matter what its failings may be in the area of "remediation," novelization fits perfectly into mass society, for in a society on the move, as Edgar Morin put it, the point is not to be ahead of the times, but to keep pace.[17] Novelization may appear to lag behind a variety of media revolutions, but the genre is perfectly adapted to finding its place in changing times.


## NOVELIZATION AND LACK OF VISUALITY

Is novelization a visual genre?[18] Here again, expectations may not be met. The striking feature of most novelizations, no matter their cultural standing, is

---

16. Noli, *La Banquière,* 5.

17. Morin, *L'Esprit du temps,* chapter 16: "Jeunesse [Youth]."

18. Or in more technical terms: is it an "ekphrastic" genre? Ekphrasis designates all forms of description, narrative or otherwise, in works of art, fictional, as well as nonfiction. For a historical overview of ekphrasis in Western poetry, see Heffernan, *Museum of Words.*

how astonishingly nonvisual they are: industrial novelization in no way seeks to compete with the image, but concentrates on narration, while literary adaptation emphasizes (or flat-out invents) what cinema less easily renders: an overarching narrative voice. In the first instance, that of commercial novelization, the motivation is negative: working from a screenplay, the novelizer visualizes little so as not to risk "betraying" the original through descriptions without basis or equivalent in the script. But in the second instance, that of literary novelization, the motivation is clearly positive: the novelizer wants to mine narrative possibilities that film is less equipped to handle, and literature's innovative potential is greater in the area of narrative voice than in recalling images through repeated descriptions.

The result is that far from abounding in descriptive scenes, novelization is often a rather dry narration, focusing on additions of a very different nature. As Jeanne-Marie Clerc concludes:

> Tout se passe comme si l'adaptateur du film mettait son point d'honneur à s'éloigner au maximum de sa source cinématographique en réintroduisant dans le texte du scénario, fondé sur la restitution directe et le discours immédiat, une distance narrative inconnue du récit en images. La spécificité romanesque semble donc se concentrer dans cette élaboration d'un personnage autonome, le narrateur, et de son discours propre, qui sert de médiateur absolu à l'histoire empruntée au film.

> A film's adaptor apparently makes it a point of honor to maintain the maximum distance from the cinematic source material by reintroducing into the screenplay text, which is based on direct restitution and immediate discourse, a narrative distance not found in pictorial recounting. Novelistic specificity thus seems to focus on developing an independent character, the narrator, and the narrator's discourse as the absolute intermediary of the story borrowed from film.[19]

There exists nonetheless an outright antipathy between *text* and *peritext*. In the latter, visuality is striking, especially in mass-market novelizations. The cover art often reprises the film poster; the illustrations are set photographs or stills. Within the text itself, in contrast, the visual aspects of novelization are almost systematically obscured. Only in a few "highbrow" variants of the genre[20] does the text flaunt its relationship, descriptive or otherwise, to the

---

19. Clerc, *Littérature et cinéma*, 99.

20. The difference between poetry—"highbrow" by definition?—and prose is striking here, for poets writing cinema-inspired work have no qualms about stressing the visual character of their work, cf. the analyses in the third and final part of this book.

original film. The more a volume's perigraphics exhibit its links to the cinema, the more care the text within its covers takes to hide them. Of course, this repressed visual content does find expression, even in the most popular forms of novelization, but the explicit elimination of visuality seems built into the genre.

Here again, what is truly in play regarding the genre's characteristics can only be grasped by going beyond a merely binary outlook on derivations between book and film. It would thus be erroneous to conclude that the antivisual writing in a novelized text betrays a literary "backlash" against cinema.[21] Such an interpretation disregards two important facts. First, how a novelization is seen depends less on the text itself than on its peritext, which intentionally falls into the category of a cinematic adaptation. The reader may well decide to interpret the text differently from the peritext's suggestions, but the "ordinary" reading of a novelization places little value on the work's literary or esthetic dimension. Next, the hypothesis of a book's "backlash" against its cinematic forerunner no longer fits with our overall perception of the relationship between these two media. Today cinema is at the center of our cultural system, and the very idea of "backlash" from a supposedly nobler cultural form (literature, in the present case) toward a form judged more common (here, the cinema) is at the very least outdated. The point of departure for any consideration of relations between cinema and literature should instead be that a strict separation between the two domains has worn away in our present-day media culture, and that internal forces no longer uphold the primacy of the written word. From this perspective, it is less interesting to ponder where novelization falls in relation to movies than to note how much contemporary fiction tends to be read *as if it were in fact a novelization,* even an imaginary one. Even when we know for certain that the book preceded the film, for example with works adapted for the screen, today's literary system will brand the text as a novelization. It may even be that the book is read with reference to the cinema, which confers its status and legitimacy, whether a book has *already* been adapted or whether it is *likely* to be. In the former instance, the book's marketing will be similar to a novelization, with a blatantly cinematic peritext in the classic mold (a formula such as "based on the film" or "soon on the screen" plays into the confusion with novelization wording such as "after the film by . . ." or "the book from the film"). In the latter case, the interpenetration of the respective models will go even farther, since foreknowledge of the film affects both its producers and consumers. Authors today write less with the aim of being

---

21. This interpretation surfaces occasionally in the cited works by Alain and Odette Virmaux.

read than of having their work adapted to the cinema. As a corollary, readers no longer approach a novel as if it might someday appear on the big screen, but as if that may already have happened: the impact of adaptations surrounding us is so great that as we read we can visualize the story, with the text as the record of some personal fantasy.

CHAPTER 3

# Illustrations

## *A Rhetorical Tool*

The role of an illustration in literature is never solely to illustrate the text. With other aspects of the peritextual apparatus, illustrations contribute to identifying, classifying, and highlighting the literary object they accompany, just as they help the reader to read, to understand, even more so, to evaluate the text in hand. The rhetorical dimension of illustrations is crucial. It is consequently no surprise that novelization avails itself of a well-stocked peritextual apparatus (only novelizations with decided literary ambitions can afford the classic French "white cover") and that within this, illustrations are what best hold the reader's attention.[1]

The present chapter does not propose to analyze images from a historical point of view by comparing illustrations found in books with pictures of films they set out to copy without being able to—the pictures in certain novelizations are in fact anything but clear tracings of what appears on screen—and these discrepancies can teach us a great deal about the implication of the still image in interpreting a moving picture.[2] The point here is the ambiguous status of illustrations in the realm of novelization, being both hypervisible and

---

1. A classic study of these questions is Grivel, *La Production.*

2. See Arnoldy and Le Forestier, "Cinéma, histoire, novellisation." The authors first examine how novelization iconography cancels out cinematic innovations, before concluding: "Around one of its possible centers of gravity, novelization has thus been approached as taking its own part in *making movie history.* Far from confining it to a recycling or secondhand rewrit-

inconspicuous. Illuminating this absence/presence paradox will be the essential objective of the subsequent pages.

## WEAK AND STRONG IMAGES

The rhetorical strength of an image is not a function of its ontological status.
According to context, a fictional image can possess the same ascendant as
a documentary image, if not overtake it. These differences are not theoretical. We know, for instance, that novels, read as fictional texts, have difficulty
including photographic documents, which represent a reality incompatible with works of imagination.[3] Not with the peritext of such works (novel
cover art can be photographic without infringing on the assumptions of fiction reading), but with the actual text (this is why authors like W. G. Sebald
do not use photographic images unknowingly, their intention often being to
blur the difference between document and fiction). More than its fictional or
documentary character, the strength of an image depends on a very different
factor, which might be defined as the dialectic of networking and innovation.
How much an image manages to find its place within an already existing fab-
ric—which it strives to renew—determines its real impact. In this framework,
novelization seems to be a test case.

One might have the impression that recourse to images exhibiting the
narrative's *artificial* character, with its relationship to the fictional source on
display, is a roadblock in the main pursuit of all popular literature: the illusion
of reality, identification, suspense. . . . In fact, it is nothing of the kind. Escap-
ism resists every attempt to thwart it, not only in the realm of novelization
but in all paraliterary production. This can be observed in the cinema, where
research into the home viewing market indicates that the wealth of bonus features and the new paratextual genre of "making of" documentaries in no way
interferes with the referential illusion.[4]

The image exists only in context. A material context to begin with, namely
the field of contiguity from which the image detaches itself. Next comes the
discursive context, namely the image's possible usages in the range of genres.
We are vaguely aware of what can be shown and what must be hidden as
regards book illustrations. From there, the evaluation of an image's rhetorical interest is based on an intertextual analysis, with reference to the dividing

---

ing of a cinematic narrative, our investigations have progressively led us to consider novelization as a 're-presentation' of film in writing" (146).

   3. Baetens and Van Gelder, "Petite poétique."

   4. See Gauthier, "Christopher Reeve."

point between what is *tellable* and what is *showable* and to a host of tacitly or explicitly accepted or contested proscriptions, obligations, preferences, and usages. An image's force of conviction therefore cannot be separated from its ability to respect, question, or upend the rules of its intertext. This force of conviction also appertains to an innovative strategy of retelling and networking. Two possible hindrances to such a strategy spring to mind. On the one hand, we find the *unprecedented* or the *unique occurrence*: to follow a hitherto forbidden line of thought, such images can never be completely true, lacking a network; they can obviously become true, but never in themselves. On the other hand, we find *pleonasm,* a little-examined but very frequent visual category: an apparently excessive retelling is almost never a good image; an image is better off being partially incomplete or allusive, while remaining catalyzable, and "pure" pleonasm, or the quest for it, seems to be an explosive material.[5] In other words: if the context, which determines the final effect, is a genre and an intertext, that is, an implicit or explicit form of the norms and conventions of retellings and networking, there is twice the risk that images will fail to feel true: either by staying too close or straying too far from the model of the *showable.*

With the exception of a few books that consider themselves "novels, period," novelizations systematically rely on illustration. In many respects, these illustrations are extremely convention-bound. They are never original, but reproduce or transform an already-existing image, preferably one in wide circulation: either the film poster or shots of the main actors. The rhetorical advantage of this type of illustration is also its main drawback: network and replication inevitably seem to call to each other, then destroy each other. Finding the correct balance between retelling and surprise is no easy task, and the genre must strive mightily to forge links that are ever new yet familiar.

The most sure-fire way to do this is certainly toning down illustrations. Paradoxical as it may seem, the use of images is not a given in novelized works. Despite the obvious advantages of including them, and the intense commercial pressures on novelizations, illustrations remain fairly rare, at any rate, in today's examples (1920s and 1930s film-novels were more profusely illustrated) and in the book world (not including "making of" paranovelizations and their ilk).

What does this low profile signify? Perhaps, at its own specific level, it further emphasizes novelization's curious yet undeniable hesitancy regarding *description.* The reasons behind this descriptive gap are closely tied to the genesis of these books, often written before the movie they are bound to

---

5. For a fundamental consideration of these tensions, see Burch, *Une Praxis du cinéma* [*A Praxis of Cinema*], chapter 5.

reproduce has even been filmed or edited: understandably, the commercial novelizer may be working from a shooting script, and be reluctant to include images that may not end up in the finished product. But a similar silence can be noted in novelizations written following a film's release, so that the causes of the descriptive gap, and, on another level, the spare reuse of images from the film, go even deeper. They no doubt go back to the search for an ideal balance between repetition, which would champion illustrations, and surprise, which is expressed by the exclusion of possible redundancy. Novelization's specific contribution in comparison to the film is as a *repeat* but also a *retreat*: holding back on the inclusion of images, on the level of description as well as illustration, to lay greater claim to the book's originality, namely the *text* rolling out the plot (but not the pictures!). Banishing visual elements is a direct continuation of the genre's hesitancy toward the image in general, making it a highly paradoxical instance of "remediation."

## "MANAGING" RHETORICAL EFFECTS

However, the attenuation of the image first takes place *quantitatively,* through the repression of a series of images expected to be greater in number. Yet *qualitative* aspects also come into play. Indeed, the illustrations present in novelizations are both hypervisible and inconspicuous, thanks to diversionary tactics that are sometimes isolated, sometimes grouped together, but always involve the following parameters: a) the site of insertion; b) the type of media involved; c) the temporality of the image or series of images; and d) the original or reproduced nature of the illustration. We shall give a brief description of each of these aspects before bringing them together in a consideration of image and rhetorical effects in the realm of novelization.

To clarify the first point, the site or sites of insertion, it is easy enough to make a clear separation between the text itself, generally devoid of images, and the peritext, which often debuts a typical image from the film on the cover (most often a variation on the film poster or a still or set photo showing the actors). An elegant solution, maximizing the commercial impact of the cinematic foretext (the "retelling and networking" element) without encroaching upon novelization's territory, which remains a linguistic space (the "avoiding pleonasm" element).

It may also happen, and this is a second point, that the image included or used changes media form, and photography is replaced with drawing. The novelizations of two Tati films (*Monsieur Hulot's Holiday* and *My Uncle*) and the American remake of Godard's *Breathless* show to what extent the dialectic between too much and too little, between overdoing and hollowing out, plays a role in this transformation. The use of Étaix's drawings, instead of stills, to illustrate the novelizations of Tati, is not a rejection of the film. It is also a clever marketing decision linking the novel to the film's most visible face, namely its poster, as well as a certain form of popular literature. Étaix's clean, stylized sketches, bordering on caricature, were typical of the period, for example, illustrations in the "Livre de Poche" vein and probably mail-order book clubs, very popular at the time. As for *Breathless,* adopting a strategy of "media migration" from photography to artwork[6] went along with a completely logical shift in cultural level: the illustration shows the two protagonists kissing, but registers the image in quite another category, that of romance novel covers. What is lost in terms of repetition is largely compensated in terms of restatement within a second network. In each case, images from the film are held at arm's length, but also used to advantage.

A third way to lessen the image's impact is toning down, if not flatly excluding, the temporal and narrative element of illustrations. At the level of the isolated image, the *portrait* rather than the *scene* is favored, beyond any doubt because the former is less narrative than the latter, which can easily evolve into an action scene when a more or less "decisive" moment is at hand. Thus, the portrait retains more distance from the film. Among notable exceptions is the famous *King Kong,* the 1932 version, but in this case the illustrations are not stills but rather drawings rather loosely based on stills from the film. These images owe a great deal to other forms of popular culture, like comic strips; but when the image becomes a photographic one, as in the case of the 2005 remake's novelization, the portrait mode reasserts itself, rejecting the scene. The process is even easier to spot when a novelization incorporates images into the text. Here too, series or successions of images are not true sequences: the photos or drawings alone are never enough to (re)construct some manner of narrative, unless this is in some experimental form light years away from the commercial novelizations under examination in the present study.[7] The groups of images in traditional novelizations often fail to connect with the text, thus conserving their peritextual status as "illustration inserts."

A fourth point is that illustrations eventually prove to be less and less original, since they tend to reuse iconographic matter from a film's publicity campaign (most often with the film poster pressed into service, once again).

---

6. At least, this is the case in the French edition ("J'ai Lu" paperback collection). In a subsequent chapter we shall return to this novelization, so typical of the genre.

7. For one example, we will later come back to a book by Olivier Smolders. In fact, the narratives inferred from the iconographic content of these works are not necessarily the same as in "novelized" films.

At first glance, this strategy appears contradictory to the quest for a minimum difference as observed above. A mistaken impression, since the often literal recasting of the film's poster is a most efficient way to deal with the problem that utilizing an unfamiliar and original photographic image would pose, contradicting the novelization's cinematic foretext.

Each of these strategies tends toward the same effect: toning down a novelization's images. At first glance, this is paradoxical, since the genre has need of illustrations, at least when it is aimed at the general public. Yet it is also understandable, since an overabundance of images would necessarily detract from the text (which might be reduced to "caption" status), and, again paradoxically, even from the image itself (a result of strong competition from moving pictures awkwardly translated into series of photographs). With the image simultaneously highlighted and toned down, publishers optimize a novelization's shelf life as a product.

## THE IMAGE'S TRAJECTORY

Nevertheless, the particular treatment of the image in novelizations offers yet another lesson, stretching well beyond the realm of mere illustration.

As we have seen, the rhetorical impact of these illustrations depends on the image's ability, through retelling and networking, to strengthen the bonds between a text (in this instance, a hybrid text, made up of words and images) and an intertext (a discursive universe with its own governing norms). The complex interplay of these diverse elements allows us to take a further step in analysis and to tie the question of images more directly to novelization's dual identity, mixing the act of reading with the act of *seeing*. However, reading and seeing are two quite distinct entities. They diverge first of all in how they operate: verbal reading falls under the heading of *semiotics*, meaning a type of reading that must "recognize" signs on various levels within a code, while visual reading essentially has to do with *semantics*, meaning a type of reading that must "comprehend" the totality of a work whose composition is intuited from perception.[8] But reading and seeing are also opposites in the relationship they maintain with the foretext. Insofar as the novelization's images are presented as "already known,"[9] the act of reading is on the order of "recognition" (and based on semiotics). Insofar as the novelization's text is presented

---

8. See Benvéniste, "Sémiologie de la langue."

9. At least in commercial novelization, since it goes without saying that a novelization project with "original" illustrations, making use of images without reference to the original film, is not unthinkable, at least theoretically.

as something "to discover," the act of reading is of the semantic and "comprehending" order. To put it another way: the text *is read* for the first time (for even if the film is already familiar, the text itself is new), the image is *reseen* (for even without seeing a film, it is hard to escape being exposed to the cinema's advertising juggernaut).

In both cases, that of the image and that of the text, novelization therefore poses the question of relations between *reading* and *rereading,* which are known to be at the heart of any rhetorical process: the power of conviction necessarily relies on a mixture of recognition and surprise, and the combination of the (previously unpublished) text and the (familiar) image seems to head in the right direction for expected rhetorical effects. However, just as there is no very strict separation between "reading" and "rereading" in the verbal system,[10] the antipathy between "reseeing" and "seeing" in the visual domain is also less decided than one might think, even in a genre as replete with repetition and replication as novelization, where the margin for innovation would appear to be stuck at zero. Concretely, one might wonder whether novelization's strategies for illustration seek less to "show" than to "show again" (for instance, a familiar movie poster or images already overexposed in the press). If such is the case, assessing the role of the image becomes more complex. From this perspective, the image would function both as an intertextual anchor and as a tool for revealing surprises.

Literally, the hypothesis that images in novelization serve less to "show again" than to "show" is absurd. But if only we let go of strictly formal analysis, new avenues open up. Perhaps that is what happens from the moment we observe the cultural convergence between integration of images into a novelization and new techniques available for distributing cinematic images. Ever since theatrical release has stopped being the major distribution mode for cinematic works, a film's viewing has been spread out over time, as if it were subject to a progressive unveiling. This trajectory transforms what was once the screening experience into an unending striptease: the film's plot is circulated, then the trailer, next the film, and finally the DVD, which often serves up an "encore" version of the film and does not pretend to be anything other than a temporary version of a work in perpetual evolution; pirated versions, remixes and samplings, alternative versions, and so on, add to the explosion of forms at the heart of today's film industry. Novelization is one example among others of this media-wide diversification of the film product, which is multiplied in a synchronic manner (as video games, T-shirts, Internet sites that come out along with the film) as well as a diachronic one (if the film "catches

---

10. See Matei Calinescu's seminal study, *Rereading.*

on," it is brought back in ever-changing forms). In such a context, it is never the image that is shown but something more complex that *at the same time* includes the image and the promise of a new image, still to come, never totally revealed. The suggestion is that the viewer has never seen all there is to see, even when the same image is repeated. The insinuation is that every image will have a sequel, whether or not it is substantially different from what we already know. Even if novelization deals with images that are nothing new, this does not impede the process and does not prevent the images from "showing" rather than "reshowing." These images need only add to something (the novelized book) that in principle could do without any images at all: in this way, the illustrations ensure that the process continues and structurally pave the way for a sequel. The fact that these images are often mere repetitions is a real asset, insofar as such a reprise proves that the system is capable of infinite transformation while remaining invariably the same. Thus, the rhetorical status of novelization's images once again metamorphoses: initially the images create an impact that could be called "elementary" (their recognizable nature anchoring the novel in a precise intertext and their presence serving as a foil to the text and stressing its newness); subsequently, the toning down of these images insinuates a more indirect effect, which endeavors not to upset the always precarious balance between repetition and novelty; finally, novelization's images suggest that the film product is an object in permanent metamorphosis and that the "view" of the film that they offer is only an ephemeral and temporary stage, programmed for replacement by the specific cultural practice, half-cultural and half-industrial, of the cinema itself.

The subtler pragmatic effect of novelization's images is found in the way they are processed, allowing the eye to run quickly over them, directing attention toward a context that goes beyond genre or intertext to encompass the cultural forms or practices from which they ultimately derive.

# PART II

# A Sample of Case Studies

~

# CHAPTER 4

# Transcription of a Silent Film

## The Passion and Death of Joan of Arc
## *by Pierre Bost*

### BIRTH OF A SERIES

As we have seen in the historical overview of the genre, novelization does not derive from the field of the popular press alone, but also deals with highly regarded authors and major publishing houses. Contacts between cinema and literature were a characteristic trait of all twentieth-century writing. The involvement of Gallimard, under its *Nouvelle Revue française* banner, the most prestigious imprint of the interwar period, should not be uniquely understood as a clever way for "great literature" and high-end publishing to profit from the commercial potential of the "film raconté." This publisher's interest in novelization revealed a more basic intertwining of practices and media, with the present chapter analyzing a forgotten yet revealing example.

Gallimard's role in the exchanges between literature and cinema was to be intense and daring during the transition years from silent to talking pictures. But it would not remain the same once the shift was complete. During the silent era, the publisher fostered adaptations, opened its doors to "original" cinematic writing, and directly or indirectly encouraged its stable of authors toward filmmaking (the *NRF* would even publish screenplays starting in 1925). But above all, it would launch real collections open to exploring possible exchanges between cinema and fiction writing. First came the

"Cinario" collection of 1925–26, or five volumes containing scripts for proposed movies (with forthcoming titles from better-known house authors:
Duhamel, Mac Orlan, Kessel, Arnoux, Achard . . . ).[1] Then in 1928, after the
failure of "Cinario," came a collection inspired by competing series from Tal-
lendier and Fayard but under Gallimard's *NRF* logo, underwriting the quality
of the text as well as their paratextual presentation (prefaces, introductions,
forewords, etc.): "Le Cinéma Romanesque" ("The Fictional Cinema"). This
collection would produce twenty-two volumes in 1928–29. It included several reprints and the relatively small number of volumes was a distinguishing
characteristic: unlike Tallandier, churning out novelizations on a near-weekly
basis, Gallimard was more sparing and supposedly more distinguished, even
though in physical appearance the Tallandier and Gallimard collections were
hard to tell apart.

"Le Cinéma Romanesque" was swept away by the influx of talking pictures, which radically changed the order of things at Gallimard. Its authors
then offered their services directly to the film industry, for instance, as adaptors, screenwriters, or dialogue advisors (even filling various on-set roles, like
Antonin Artaud), and organized into a group called the "Film Parlant Français" ("French Talking Film"):

> Certains participent enfin à l'entreprise du Film Parlant Français, créée par
> Gide fin 1929, dont l'ambition est de rénover le cinéma français contre l'ex-
> pansion de l'industrie américaine en Europe. Initiative qu'il faut rapprocher
> de la création en 1913 d'un Théâtre de la *NRF* au Vieux Colombier, sous
> l'égide de Jacques Copeau "pour réagir contre toutes les lâchetés du théâtre
> mercantile, et pour défendre les plus libres, les plus sincères manifestations
> d'un art dramatique nouveau, (et) entretenir la culture des chefs-d'œuvre
> classiques, français et étrangers."[2]

> Some writers took part in the Film Parlant Français project, created by Gide
> in late 1929 with the aim of bolstering French cinema against the expansion
> of the American film industry in Europe. This initiative was similar to the
> 1913 founding of a *NRF* Theater at the Vieux Colombier under the direction
> of Jacques Copeau "to react against everything wrong with for-profit theater,
> and to defend the freer, more sincere offerings of a new dramatic art (and)
> safeguard the survival of classic masterpieces, both French and foreign."[3]

---

1. See the complete list of these volumes in the Appendix.
2. Assouline, *Gaston Gallimard,* 69.
3. Ibid.

The Film Parlant Français, which has its own studio, production, and distribution network, is a real *NRF* cinema.[4] Here, too, as was the case a few years earlier for Surrealist cinema, increased production costs after the silent era, along with other factors, doomed this "Made in France" initiative.

## A LANDMARK BOOK FOR A CULT FILM

Before the Film Parlant Français initiative, the concern for *"NRF* quality" had been displayed in the selection of films included in Gallimard's novelization catalogue. Carl Theodor Dreyer's silent film, *The Passion of Joan of Arc* (1928), was a perfect candidate.[5] The director's previous Danish silent film, *The Master of the House,* had its Paris premiere in March 1926 and was critically acclaimed. Dreyer was consequently signed by the Société Générale des Films and given a choice of three historical subjects for his next film: Marie-Antoinette, Catherine de Médicis, or Joan of Arc. According to contemporary accounts, he decided on Joan of Arc somewhat by chance. The historic and cinematic context may well have been a deciding factor. After Joan of Arc's 1920 canonization by Pope Benedict XV, and in the nationalistic postwar climate, Saint Joan inspired any number of artistic creations. Among these, Dreyer's work stands out in several respects: his unfaltering directorial choices, refusal to sensationalize, insistence on historical accuracy, and ability to distance the character of Joan from any nationalistic fervor (the film drew protests from the Archdiocese of Paris as well as from English censors, for obviously conflicting reasons . . . ).[6]

The novelization by Pierre Bost (1901–75) made Dreyer's work a typical entry in the *NRF* collection, although we should call it an order rather than an entry, as it was inarguably a work for hire. This was common in both the "Cinéma Romanesque" series and its more commercial avatar, the "Cinario" collection.[7] Comparing this book with other volumes in the collection[8] (with certain titles, according to the genre's skillfully maintained lack of clarity, representing adaptations disguised as novelizations, rather than novelizations in

4. Brangé, "Le cinéma chez Jean Prévost," 44.

5. I owe the information that follows to Prof. Livio Belloï of the University of Liège, with many thanks.

6. On all these points, the difference is clear between Dreyer's work and Marco de Gastyne's contemporary film *La Merveilleuse Vie de Jeanne d'Arc* [*The Wondrous Life of Joan of Arc*] (1929).

7. Brangé, "Le cinéma chez Jean Prévost," 45.

8. See the complete list of these volumes in Appendix 1.

the strictest sense[9]), it is easy to see that Bost's is an exceptional work. Not that he departs from the series' format (a uniform one, rarely seen in a literary product: the same cover, illustrated in black and white with a single accent color; same number of pages; same layout with two columns of text), but of all the published volumes, this is clearly the standout. There are several reasons for this. First in the book's eventful origins: the first draft of Dreyer's film was cowritten by Joseph Delteil, based on his *Jeanne d'Arc,* a prizewinning 1925 novel. Delteil then had a falling-out with Dreyer—on the heels of Delteil's falling-out with the Surrealists—only one of the many difficulties in a troubled production (Delteil would always refuse to see the finished film). Next was, of course, the reworked film itself: the popular and critical success of Dreyer's *Joan of Arc* was limited, but its reception by the intelligentsia was overwhelmingly positive. A third distinguishing factor was the choice of novelizer; though he was only twenty-seven years old when the book was published, Pierre Bost was no novice writer, already well known in literary and cultural circles. Finally, the book came with some singular credentials. No fewer than four "big names" endorsed the film (and its star, Mlle. Falconetti of the Comédie Française, in her one and only film role) in a series of short prefaces (all four taking up only three pages) unlike any in the history of movie-related publishing: Valentine Hugo, the costume designer, talked about the film's direction, filming, and editing, singling out both the director and lead actress; Jean Cocteau, who added Silvain's and Artaud's names to those of Falconetti and Dreyer, said he found the film as moving as Eisenstein's *The Battleship Potemkin*; Jacques de Lacretelle analyzed and justified Dreyer's spare style; Paul Morand, finally, decreed that with this film French cinema was born. These testimonials, based on the film, were followed by a foreword from the novelization's author, Pierre Bost, putting him in very distinguished company. The author, as if to flaunt the truly literary status of his work, adds a dedication at the beginning of the text, quite an unusual move in the often-industrial world of novelization: "À Jean-Loup Falbet, amicalement, P. B." [To Jean-Loup Falbet, in friendship, P. B.]

It comes as no surprise that none of the preface writers has much to say about the novelization itself, which was probably not ready for publication when the "blurbs" were commissioned, but this explanation is purely anecdotal. In a more general manner, it shows that what counts is not the novelization, but the film, with the fictional version passing for an unproblematic complement, meaning one that cannot stand alone. Of course, this

---

9. Hence Joseph Kessel's *L'Équipage* [*The Crew*] in a second edition, or Anita Loos's *Gentlemen Prefer Blondes,* best known in Howard Hawks's 1953 version, but written in 1925 and adapted to the silent screen in 1928.

lack of autonomy is not absolute, and in this regard, the author gives precious information about his own approach and his notions about the novelization process. Given how interesting this piece is, and the rarity of any such documentation, we include it here in its entirety.

Pour toucher à l'histoire de Jeanne d'Arc, il faut une grande érudition, un sens historique très sûr, beaucoup de temps et encore plus d'audace. Je ne me réclame, malheureusement, que cette dernière qualité.

Ma seule excuse, je crois, est dans la beauté même de cette histoire; et si, en écrivant, trop vite ce court récit, je ne me suis pas senti plus coupable, c'est qu'en vérité le sujet est trop grand pour qu'on puisse le diminuer beaucoup si seulement on le respect et l'aime.

Avant d'écrire, je me suis instruit dans des livres, et surtout dans le texte même du "procès de Condamnation de Jeanne d'Arc." M. Pierre Champion, qui en est l'éditeur, aura donc été le "conseil historique" du film de Carl Dreyer, et celui aussi de ce petit livre. J'ai eu également toujours sous les yeux le scénario même de Carl Dreyer et Joseph Delteil, et je l'ai suivi page par page. comme le film tiré de ce scénario est sans doute le plus beau et le plus purement émouvant qu'on ait vu sur un écran, j'écris ces lignes pour avertir que ma part est très faible, dans le texte qui va suivre.

Quelques passages ne sont pas en accord absolu avec la stricte vérité historique; c'est que, justement, j'ai suivi de très près le film, qui avait le droit de s'écarter parfois de la lettre même, puisqu'il gardait si bien l'esprit. Et d'abord il fallait bien rassembler en une seule journée les vingt-huit séances du procès. Carl Dreyer l'a fait avec beaucoup d'adresse et de tact, et ce n'était pas facile.

J'ai un peu étendu les interrogatoires de Jeanne, en y introduisant quelques incidents que le film ne pouvait conserver sous peine de s'alourdir.

Le film présente les Juges de Jeanne, Cauchon en tête, comme des hommes acharnés à la perdre, et conduits par des sentiments violents et cruels. Je les ai présentés aussi sous ce jour. Je sais bien qu'on peut trouver à leur conduite de très acceptables explications, même des excuses, et Bernard Shaw y a presque réussi; pourtant, il est au moins aussi vraisemblable de croire, avec l'opinion commune, que les juges de Rouen ont été odieux et ont réellement agi envers Jeanne comme des bourreaux. Cela admis, on peut bien dire que les circonstances, l'époque et leurs propres caractères interdisaient d'agir autrement, mais c'est tout.

Quant à Jeanne, il est impossible, dès qu'on s'approche d'elle, de n'être pas saisi d'une admiration et d'une émotion sans limites. Je ne sais si l'on trouverait personne pour résister à ces sentiments-là. Tout est emporté. Il me semble que ce grand film fera beaucoup pour la mémoire de Jeanne d'Arc, qu'il amènera à méditer sur elle beaucoup d'entre nous qui ne l'avaient jamais fait assez bien, et qu'il nous rappellera qu'il y a là une des plus belles histoires de l'humanité. Il n'aurait donc pas besoin d'être, en outre, une réussite technique admirable pour qu'on en parle avec enthousiasme.

P. B.

*Les treize premières pages du texte qui suit sont une sorte de prologue historique à la carrière même de Jeanne d'Arc. On pourra donc ne pas les lire si vraiment on ne cherche ici que le récit du film.*

To work on the story of Joan of Arc requires much study, a sure sense of history, a great deal of time and even more daring. Unfortunately, I can lay claim only to the latter qualification.

My only excuse, I believe, lies in this story's real beauty; and if, while writing this short narrative too quickly, I have not felt as guilty as I should, it is because in truth nothing much can spoil this subject as long as it is treated with respect and love.

Before starting to write, I did research, especially into the "Proceedings of the Trial of Joan of Arc." Pierre Champion, who edited that text, will have been the "historical consultant" on Carl Dreyer's film and also this little book. I also had at hand the screenplay by Carl Dreyer and Joseph Delteil, which I followed page by page. This screenplay gave rise to what is no doubt the best and most moving film ever to appear on screen, so let me confess that my share in the text that follows is slim indeed.

A few passages are not in absolute agreement with strict historical truth; that is because I did in fact base my writing very closely on the film, which was allowed to stray from some particulars of the story, while preserving the essence. And if the twenty-eight trial sessions had to be condensed into one day, Carl Dreyer performed this difficult task with a great deal of skill and tact.

I extended Joan's interrogation, including a few incidents that were cut from the film to trim its length.

~

The film presents Joan's judges, headed by Cauchon, as men determined to condemn her, full of cruel and violent feelings. I have also portrayed them in that light. I know that perfectly acceptable reasons, even excuses, can be found for their behavior, and Bernard Shaw almost succeeded in this regard; however, it is just as plausible to believe, as it is commonly held, that the Rouen judges were hateful and truly acted like henchmen toward Joan. This being understood, one may certainly say that the circumstances, the times, and their own character prevented them from doing otherwise, but that is all.

As for Joan, as soon as she comes into focus it is impossible not to be overwhelmed with admiration and emotion. I don't know how anyone could resist being swept away by these feelings. It seems to me that this great film will enhance Joan of Arc's memory, that it will lead many to think of her as never before, and will remind us of one of humanity's finest stories. Even without its technical brilliance, the film would be a success.

P. B.

*The next thirteen pages represent a sort of historical prologue to Joan of Arc's career. They can be skipped if the reader only wishes to follow the plot of the film.*

Of note, Bost clearly indicates that he worked from the screenplay (more exactly the shooting script, the most complete version of the screenplay before actual filming) and limits himself to dealing with the difference between "story" and "film." At a given moment, he suggests that his double concern for faithfulness (to the screenplay as well as the film) caused a few problems: "The film presents Joan's judges, headed by Cauchon, as men determined to condemn her, full of cruel and violent feelings. I have also portrayed them in that light." These sentences may appear enigmatic, neutral, or insignificant when read in the author's preface. After study of the text and especially comparison with the film, it becomes clear that Pierre Bost has still tried to distance himself from the images to some extent, explicitly emphasizing certain doubts in Cauchon (the main accuser) or remorse in Loyseleur (the betrayer in the story).

Cependant Cauchon n'oublie pas qu'avant d'être juge, il est prêtre. Cette femme qu'il envoie au bûcher, il entend qu'elle ait reçu d'abord les derniers secours de la religion, et il fait venir à lui deux des prêtres du procès.

Par quel dernier scrupule, par quel retour d'humanité fait-il alors appel à ces deux qui, durant les cérémonies cruelles, ont montré pour Jeanne le plus de bienveillance et de respect? Espère-t-il encore que ce geste lui sera compté dans l'Éternité? . . . Ou si seulement le hasard a guidé son choix?

Still Cauchon could not forget that before being a judge, he was a priest. This woman he was sending to the stake he first made sure to give the final rites of the church, sending her two priests from the trial.

What final scruple, what glimmer of humanity led him to those two clerics, who showed Joan the most benevolence and respect during the cruel spectacle of her trial? Did he still hope that this gesture would be reckoned in Eternity? . . . Or did mere chance guide his selection?[10]

It might be interesting to tie these writerly interventions to Pierre Bost's later career. He was a friend of the Surrealists and the inventor, with Jean Aurenche, of the "cinema of quality" screenplay later attacked by François Truffaut, particularly for ideological reasons.[11] What counts more is the general acceptance of film, text, and equivalents, with the screenplay as intermediary. Bost's preface mentions faithfulness several times, both that of his text to Dreyer's film and the film's faithful rendering of history, taking great care to explain any infractions in light of utter respect for the story's spirit (a virtual stereotype of this sort of reasoning, which Bost has no intention of questioning).

The film, however, is anything but missing from the book, richly illustrated with twenty-five plates (three photos taken during the filming process, a sort of primitive version of a "making of" feature, then twenty-two set photographs, not actual stills from the film), enough for anyone in the least familiar with Joan of Arc to grasp the plot outline. But do these photos look like the film? Are they to the film's images what Bost's text is to Dreyer's narrative? Apparently, the answer, at least from those in charge of producing the book, was in the affirmative. Just as Bost followed the screenplay, the succession

---

10. Bost, *Jeanne d'Arc*, 81–82.

11. Truffaut goes after the "Aurenchebost" system's anticatholicism in his famous article "Certain Tendency," which we will examine in detail in the chapter on novelizing Jacques Tati. As it turns out, the changes made to Dreyer's film do not go in the highly irreligious direction that Truffaut later denounced in the Bost-influenced screenplay of Georges Bernanos's novel *Diary of a Country Priest,* for example.

of illustrations would allow the reader to reconstruct, in a fragmentary yet almost continuous way, the story shown on the screen.

Nevertheless, how the reader imagines the relationship between the text, on one hand, screenplay and film, on the other, is not quite the same. Indeed, if the reader is "missing" the screenplay and film, this absence is of a different nature in each case. Regarding the script, the lack of it is relative, since it is easy to imagine a novelization having little trouble following in a screenplay's footsteps. Regarding the film, this lack is harder to evaluate, insofar as there is a real gap between a grouping of still images and a 73-minute cinematic work.

## JOAN OF ARC IN THE TEXT, BUT IN PLURAL FORM

Further complicating the study is the fact that Dreyer's project not only had difficult origins but the film existed in a great number of versions that were very different, one from the next. *The Passion of Joan of Arc* was first mutilated by censorship, then by a series of tragic accidents. After a prescreening in Paris and the premiere in April 1928 at Copenhagen's "Palads Teatret," the film's release in Paris on October 25 was already a different offering, a nationalistic campaign having demanded and obtained an initial reworking. Next, two fires destroyed the master negative of the film: after a first fire in 1928, Dreyer had been able to reestablish a working print with the help of unused footage, but a second blaze in 1929 had an even more devastating effect. The film was considered "lost" until the historian Lo Duca's 1951 rediscovery of the 1929 self-remake. Unfortunately, the work was heavily and clumsily "restored," to the point that for several decades a barely authentic version was shown, without Dreyer's approval, in theaters. In Lo Duca's revision, *The Passion of Joan of Arc* was less altered by cutting and censorship than disfigured by a set of additions and pseudo-embellishments. These included a blaring, nonstop sound track, as well as a series of interposed images, with repeated shots of stained glass windows and medieval-looking architecture (the towers and rooftops of Rouen), or images with a charged symbolic value (flames). These served in part as a background for the translation of intertitles (with none appearing on a black background, as in the original film), but not exclusively: the translated intertitles often overpower the images, while certain pictures remain clear of any inscriptions. Only by the purest chance did the original film resurface, unearthed in 1981 in a Norwegian psychiatric asylum.[12]

---

12. In 1985, the French Cinémathèque produced an authentic restoration, which remains regrettably difficult for the European public to access, since only a so-called "Zone 1" version is

Unremittingly catastrophic as they were, Lo Duca's changes were highly indicative of a certain material approach to cinema, all carelessness and ignorance, that it is too easy to reject as a question of detail. The history of Dreyer's film (and perhaps the entire history of cinema at the time) is full of such details, meaning that several (competing) versions were in circulation, that the public was never sure which version it would find (supposing they were lucky enough to see the film at all), and that the director had only relative control over the result (which was in a permanent state of transformation, as it were). To which one might add that some of Bost's reading public would only have known the film by hearsay. After all, for every film-crazy Surrealist there was at least one Georges Duhamel railing against this philistine entertainment.

For the evaluation of the "cinematic novel," this observation is not unimportant. Here some autonomy is restored to the literary work, autonomy lost to its status as a "secondary" text, adapted from a screenplay and derived from another work, the film, which has every priority over it. Analogously, the unstable balance between film and novelization only goes to show that the public still needed a written tracing of the cinematic work, without which only memories and secondhand accounts might survive. The genre's very survival, in our times when more and more screenplays are published and many films have an infinitely longer life cycle, is proof positive that for the viewer a film is less an object than an experience. Hence film necessarily falls within a multimedia network.

In the case of Dreyer's *Joan of Arc*, this media interconnection was pronounced from the outset. Even a rapid overview would include the following elements:

- Historical documentation, which the film claimed to have used (and even scrupulously followed);
- The "legend" of Joan of Arc, which in some form or other was known to every French viewer at the time (and still is, even if the 2018 iteration will be different from the 1928 one);
- The multiple intermediary representations, some visual, others literary; even if one can imagine that during the film's production it was difficult to discount Péguy's intertext: though Bost never breathes a word of them, his reading public might well have kept Peguy's words in mind;
- The film's "source," *Joan of Arc*,[13] Joseph Delteil's biographical novel, which inspired the film: Delteil began writing a completely original screenplay,

---

available (Dreyer's work is featured in the prestigious Criterion collection, but not in the "Zone 2" format viewable in France).

13. Delteil, *Jeanne d'Arc*.

which he quickly turned his back on, and it is no doubt the division between Delteil's "Vitalist" novel and Dreyer's "Jansenist" film, and the men's quarrel, that prompted the decision to novelize the cinematic work;

- The screenplay, meaning several scripts . . .

This kind of multimedia profusion, as one might suspect, made any discrete reading of the novelization almost impossible.

## READING BOST

This media stockpile has a double effect on interpreting the novelization. On one hand, an isolated reading is not only unsuitable but strictly unthinkable and unrealistic. Behind every line of Bost's lurks an intertext that begs consideration. From this point of view, the following study, while oriented toward a comparison with the film, can only serve as the outline for an overall interpretation. On the other hand, the work's dissemination also makes reading the novelization absolutely crucial. In the media complex surrounding Dreyer's film, it is impossible to favor one supposedly more valuable element over another judged less important. The physical aspect of Bost's novelization shows the limits of such speculation: it was published in a collection aimed at a broad readership, but everything about it makes the book suitable for a respectable home library.

But what kind of book does the moviegoer encounter? Given how the four separate introductions and the preface stress the experience of Dreyer's film, we can reasonably posit that the intended reader is one who had seen, or at least heard of, *The Passion of Joan of Arc,* recently shown in Parisian movie theaters. The text was completed in "August 1928," as the copyright notice indicates, and Valentine Hugo's introduction is dated September 7. Everything points to the novel's publication shortly after the film's French release, several months after the world premiere in Copenhagen on April 21, 1928. We know that the "official" version shown in Paris theaters no longer matched the Danish release, which was comparable to the preview seen in . . . Paris. Some of the preface writers must have known about or even seen the preview, while others were only familiar with the edited version of the film that finally made it into wide release.

Caution is warranted when approaching Bost's work in the light of Dreyer's, or vice versa. Still, even while bearing in mind the problems stemming from the film's troubled history, the contrast is glaring. If nothing is probably closer to factual events as set out in *The Passion of Joan of Arc*'s final screenplay, nor can anything be farther from the film that Dreyer made from that final draft: Bost wrote a novel that at the same time *pared back* its visual and cinematic specificity and *added on* a certain number of elements that he (or his higher-ups in the publishing house) must have deemed indispensable in a "film raconté."

These twin transformations, one reinforcing the other, are not unknown in the genre of novelization. But the fact that the genre's rules unabashedly apply to the verbal representation of a work of startling formal and visual innovation makes Bost's novelizing efforts even more significant. Apparently, the idea of writing something "other than" a standard novelization did not occur to him. His work, interesting as it may be in many regards, does not rise above the level of a boilerplate product.

The most visible transformation concerns the various additions, divided into three categories:

*Diegetic*: throughout the text, "expansions" occur. Bost first precedes the story of the trial with a historical sketch, either to refresh certain readers' memory (as he specifies at the end of the preface, this chapter can be passed over). Next come certain details that, as the preface again suggests, would have slowed down the film but are fine in the book. Finally, left unstated in the preface, is a scene added at the novel's end: not just the description of the body burned at the stake, but of the heart torn out and thrown in the Seine (this quasi-epilogue, corresponding structurally to the explanatory introduction, stresses the comparison to the Passion of Christ, whose side was pierced after his death).

*Narratological*: The narrator becomes omniscient (alternating between "showing" and "telling" mode) but is never given personal expression. Some characters may be addressed at high points in the story ("Maître Nicolas Loyseleur, c'est vous. C'est vous, chanoine de Rouen, maître-ès-arts, homme plein de passion et de fourberie, vous qui avez tant fait souffrir la Pucelle, et par tant de mensonges odieux." [Master Nicolas Loyseleur, it is you. You, Canon of Rouen, Master of Arts, a man full of passion and deceit, you who have brought the Maid of Orleans so much suffering, through so many hateful lies])[14] yet the narrative voice is an almost transpersonal, somewhat collective one. The narrator does not use "I" but "we," and this pronoun visibly includes the book's supposed reader, who also seems to be the film spectator: "Le drame le plus cruel peut se dérouler près de nous, qu'à peine nous y prenions garde. Les spectateurs de la scène au cimetière, qui pleuraient tout à l'heure aux souffrances de Jeanne, les voici maintenant, aussitôt franchie la grille, qui tombent

---

14. Bost, *Jeanne d'Arc*, 84.

au milieu de la grande fête de mai." [The cruelest drama can be played out as we stand by, without even noticing. The onlookers at the cemetery scene, who earlier cried over Joan's suffering, now crowd through the gate, right into the Mayday feast.][15] The narrator becomes the spokesperson for the public discovering the story, and this public is in turn imagined through every stereotype of the *vox populi*.

*Psychological*: The omniscient narrator penetrates his characters' minds to probe their most intimate thoughts and motivations, which he does not hesitate to reproduce textually. In short, he explains what Dreyer only shows or insinuates. In certain cases, the transformation is complete. Thus Bost several times sets forth the famous "voices" Joan heard and even quotes them, while nothing in the film would lead us to hypothesize that Joan continued to hear such voices during her trial:

> Et voici que, par la fenêtre grillée du cachot, ses saintes, soudain, descendent vers elle, dans la lumière, et les Voix parlent, douces mais graves, disant: "Jeanne, Dieu a compris quelle grande détresse de ton cœur t'a induite à le renoncer pour ton maître et ton conseil, et Dieu t'aime encore. Mais sache, Jeanne, qu'en reniant ton Dieu et en nous reniant, nous, tes saintes, nous, tes Voix, tu n'as point agi selon le gré de ton Dieu . . . Car tu es, Jeanne la Pucelle, fille de Dieu, envoyée de par Lui . . . " Jeanne pleure, en écoutant ces tendres reproches.

> And here, through the barred dungeon window, her saints suddenly descended upon her, through the light, and the Voices spoke, soft but grave, saying "Joan, God has understood what great distress of your heart has led you to denounce Him as your master and counsel, and God loves you still. But know, Joan, that in denying God and denying us, your saints, us, your Voices, you have not acted in accordance with the will of your God . . . for you, Joan the Maiden, are the daughter of God, sent by Him . . ." Joan wept, hearing these gentle rebukes.[16]

Certainly, Bost's narration is not absurd, per se; it could even be said that he remains almost faithful to the letter of history, but what he does is the opposite of what the film does in trying to *show* the voices, show *Joan* hearing the voices, instead of having *us* hear them. The use of this device is not limited only to Joan's character: Cauchon's doubts or Loyseleur's remorse, backed

---

15. Ibid., 79.
16. Ibid., 76.

up by historic documents but not implicit in Dreyer's film, are boldly stated in Bost's text.

Inversely, Bost's novel also undercuts many aspects of Dreyer's film, especially visual ones. The reader would be hard pressed to find any equivalent, however freely interpreted, for processes such as:

- Systematic recourse to close-ups (there are only a few places in the text where the author gives details about Joan's face);
- Establishing the relationship between the parameters of distance versus point of view (to give a basic example, the suffering Joan is at first filmed almost exclusively from a bird's-eye view, the visionary Joan is regularly shown in a frontal shot, and the "triumphant" Joan at the stake is filmed in a low-angle shot);
- The spare and ultimately artificial, meaning symbolic, quality of the set design, both interior and exterior;
- The sometimes slow, sometimes accelerated rhythm of the editing and the combination of speed effects with the actors' movement or lack thereof (the torture chamber scene, with its high-speed edits, is one good example);
- The alternation of images and intertitles.

The term "undercutting" is ambiguous, though, as it suggests the possibility of an evenhanded transition between film and text. For diegesis, such a transition may still be within the realm of possibility, but for the visual aspects of cinema, the idea of "gain" and "loss," of additions and cuts, must be handled with care. Nevertheless, a reading of Bost's text clearly shows that at no time did the author ever ask himself such questions. Having started from the screenplay text, he novelized the story found within it, never dealing with the visual language Dreyer developed.

On this subject, we should make note of the only true element of analysis found in critical reaction to the book, however little such criticism may exist. According to Jeanne-Marie Clerc, *The Passion and Death of Joan of Arc* is indeed revelatory, though in its mishandling of the problems involved with the insertion of intertitles:

Une caractéristique des adaptations romancées de l'époque du muet est l'importance conférée aux mimiques et jeux de scènes, aux dépens du dialogue par ailleurs souvent très gauche. L'adaptateur du film muet, dans la majorité des cas, ne tente guère de pallier l'incapacité du cinéma d'alors à faire parler les personnages. Preuve supplémentaire que le prestige du 7ᵉ Art était bien

lié aux possibilités expressives que lui conférait son indépendance à l'égard
du langage. Signe aussi de la situation paradoxale où se trouvait le romancier tentant de transposer avec les mots un art du récit qui, précisément, se
définissait contre eux.

A feature of fictionalized adaptations in the silent era is the importance conferred on miming and playacting, at the expense of often very awkward dialogue. The silent film adaptor, in the majority of cases, made little attempt
to compensate for contemporary films' inability to make characters talk. An
additional proof that moving pictures' prestige arose from the expressive
possibilities conferred by its independence from language. A sign as well of
the novelist's paradoxical situation, trying to transpose into words a narrative art that essentially defined itself in opposition to words.[17]

Clerc continues by giving an awkward attempt on Bost's part:

Elle l'a dit déjà:
   "Pour ce qui est des révélations que je tiens de Dieu, je le ne les révélerai
pas. . . ."
   Et elle a dit encore:
   "J'ai beaucoup plus de crainte de faillir en disant quelque chose qui
déplairait à mes voix."

She said it before:
   "As for revelations God has granted me, I will not reveal them. . . ."
   And she said again:
   "I have a much greater fear of failing if I say something to displease my
voices."[18]

Clerc's interpretation, criticizing the abrupt and mechanical repetition
of "attributive" phrases (such as "she says," "he said," "again he said," etc.) in
Bost's text, may be overly harsh. On one hand, the dryness of the dialogue
represents the novelizer's obligation to stick to the screenplay, with exchanges
that are anything but clumsy, and the supporting historical documentation.
On the other hand, the attributive elements are not systematically spare and
terse. In contrast to the above example, here is a passage detailing the remorse
felt by Loyseleur, one of Joan's accusers:

---

17. Clerc, *Littérature et cinéma,* 97–98.
18. Ibid., 98. Clerc does not give page numbers of the fragment cited, which is taken from
page 29 of the novelization.

Et dans les rues étroites et inégales, on le voit marcher vite et chanceler, tré-
buchant parfois, comme s'il était ivre. Sa bouche serrée est tordue par l'an-
goisse, et il entend résonner à ses oreilles une voix implacable qui le poursuit:
   "Prêtre, qu'as-tu fait? Songe maintenant au salut de ton âme!"
   Et Loyseleur ne peut calmer le remords qui le ronge, ne peut oublier
l'image de Jeanne recevant, avec les larmes d'une ferveur sans exemple, le
corps de son Dieu, de ce Dieu martyr qui mourut sur la croix, comme elle
va mourir sur le bûcher.

And down the narrow, uneven streets we see him scurry, stumbling at times
as if drunk. His mouth is clamped and twisted, and in his ears rings a voice
relentlessly pursuing him:
   "Man of God, what have you done? Think now on your soul's salvation!"
   And Loyseleur cannot stifle the remorse that torments him, cannot forget the image of Joan receiving, with the tears of an exemplary fervor, the
body of her Christ, this martyred Christ who died on the cross, as she was
to die at the stake.[19]

Finally, the intrusiveness that Jeanne-Marie Clerc points out was no doubt
much less jolting for the reading public at the time, which was able to adjust
gradually to the style and was further quite aware that Joan of Arc's story was
partly concerned with the gap between what is said and what cannot be said.
The "bareness" of the dialogue would thus be less readily attributed to some
clumsiness on the novelizer's part than his wish to stay true to the story.

Bost's overall strategy (and the aim of the Gallimard collection that commissioned his work) has the advantage of clarity. It would be absurd to subject
it to Guiding Principles, the semiotic break between a literary text and a cinematic work being such that at any rate no attempt at a "correct" translation
or transposition would be desirable. The important thing is to understand
why Bost did what he did, and consequently, why the public reacted as it did:
coolly, with no outrage at Bost's "destruction" of Dreyer's film, nor any great
appreciation for the author's efforts to produce a well-told tale, worthy of both
the historical sources and their representation on film (Bost's novelization was
quickly forgotten, and the rare nods from scholars—Clerc, Odette and Alain
Virmaux, or Bangé, for instance—are only in passing, as if there were nothing
especially striking, either good or bad, in this "novel").

Without documentation on *The Passion and Death of Joan of Arc* and its
critical reception at the time, we can formulate a certain number of hypoth-

---

19. Bost, *Jeanne d'Arc*, 85.

eses on the why and how of Bost's undertaking. Two elements are of crucial importance here. First is the novelization's inclusion in a singular collection, "Le Cinéma Romanesque," aimed at winning market share from less elite publishers like Tallandier and Fayard. Bost was no doubt given a format to follow strictly, in terms of both quantity and quality: the story's slight outline had to be "inflated" to ninety-four pages (fairly large pages at that, with two columns of type), the text had to follow the plot, and nothing should get in the way of immediately identifying the cast of characters, with easily flowing prose. As a seasoned professional, Bost worked around these constraints. Still, commercial demands cannot be the only determining factor in the author's work. After all, Gallimard might have offered its readers something slightly different, and the paratextual presence of a few major references to the zeitgeist of 1928 points clearly in this direction. Yet this did not happen, and the reluctance to break the mold of novelization based on the clichés of popular fiction probably, if paradoxically, owes a great deal to the fact that "Le Cinéma Romanesque" was a Gallimard collection. Plainly, the publisher did not care to relive the "Cinario" fiasco. And the way collections work within a broad-based publishing house left little or no room for new forms of literary and cinematic writing if other collections already claimed this sphere of operations. Thus "Le Cinéma Romanesque" was unfortunate in that it shared an imprint with the *NRF*, where Jean Paulhan fostered writing—often, but not always, Surrealist texts—that might have been part of the "Cinario" collection a few years earlier.

The times seemed ripe. And yet they were not. The talking picture revolution put an end to many experiments, at Gallimard and elsewhere, just as it did away with serials and their variants, at least until television brought them back. Novelization, however, would remain, sometimes building on its best-known forms, sometimes venturing into new territory.

~

# CHAPTER 5

# Jean-Claude Carrière, Tati's Novelizer

Jean-Claude Carrière's *Monsieur Hulot's Holiday* ("Novel after the film by Jacques Tati, illustrations by Pierre Étaix," the cover proclaims in large type) is a relatively neglected landmark in the history of relations between literature and cinema.[1] This "novel-like adaptation," in Jeanne-Marie Clerc's terminology, indeed provides a chance to qualify a number of platitudes regarding the genre of novelization. This book by Jean-Claude Carrière, at the time a young screenwriter who had just published a debut novel, allows for a detailed examination of what happens when a novelization loses its traditional supporting structure: the film's narrative outline and dialogue. In *Monsieur Hulot's Holiday*, plot in the usual sense is kept to a strict minimum, while dialogue is almost entirely eliminated. We shall thus see that the eponymous novel, in its own modest yet precise way, as intelligent as the film, shows the place a writer's work can take in a wealth of practices whose complexity goes well beyond the mere transformation of text into pictures, or vice versa.

---

1. Carrière, *Monsieur Hulot*, 1958. The same author would also produce a novelization of *Mon Oncle* [*My Uncle*], also in 1958. To the best of our knowledge, there have been no other novelizations of Jacques Tati's films. In 2006, Laffont republished these two books, long out of print.

# JEAN-CLAUDE CARRIÈRE IN THE
# HISTORY OF NOVELIZATION

In the ever-changing tableau of novelization, and in light of the few examples already considered, what are we to make of a novelization like *Monsieur Hulot's Holiday*? We should clarify from the outset that this book is partially a joint effort, the work of an outside writer who took no part in the 1953 filming, but visibly benefited from contributions by Tati's working group—notably via Pierre Étaix's illustrations. Étaix designed the film poster and went on to collaborate with Tati; his stylized drawings determined Hulot's characteristic "look."

Before approaching the book itself, one can only wonder why it is so little known, despite Carrrière's active presence in the field of novelization.[2] Jeanne-Marie Clerc's definitive work, *Littérature et cinéma,* barely gives it half a line ("texte comique de Jean-Claude Carrière, alors au début de sa carrière de scénariste" [comic text by Jean-Claude Carrière, early in his screenwriting career]).[3] The work is never cited in studies of novelization (still rather rare, truth be told). The probable reason for this neglect is that *Monsieur Hulot's Holiday* belongs to a type of novelization now out of date: neither blatantly commercial, nor more or less avant-garde, this novelization is serious, personal, ambitious, but at the service of the film as well as the public; in short, novelization that was overshadowed by the rise of experimental film-novels of the 1960s or by today's literary novelizations, then by the explosion of Hollywood or para-Hollywood tie-ins, "Made in France" or otherwise.

*Monsieur Hulot's Holiday,* the film, then the novel, belonged to a key period in French cinema. The year the film came out was the same one that saw the publication of François Truffaut's famous article, "A Certain Tendency in French Cinema," which launched a critique of the "cinema of quality." This was a system based (among other things) on a conception of the cinema as literary adaptation and of adaptation as a process mainly involving the creation of a dialogue-based screenplay (with Aurenche and Bost as its main practicing partners). Criticism by the future New Wave showed that the system was nearing a breakdown, just as it heralded the arrival of a quite different cinema (that Truffaut and his friends would define in terms of directorial "staging," the most typical aspect of filming when the "shooting script" is the only guide). Moreover, there was a very different conception of adaptation (the New Wave

---

2. Jean-Claude Carrière is the author of several novelizations, the latest being *Les Fantômes de Goya* [*Goya's Ghosts*] in 2007. Most often these works are self-adaptations, with the author as screenwriter or cowriter on the novelized film.

3. Clerc, *Littérature et cinéma,* 97.

certainly did not reject literary adaptation outright, but conceived this process in terms of a literary text's appropriation by a cinematic "author").[4] In the same way, *Monsieur Hulot's Holiday* is also a decisive step in Tati's stylistic development.[5] After *Jour de Fête* [*The Big Day*], it was a more stylized and less anecdotal attempt at "non-speaking" cinema, that is, a cinema seeking to reestablish the richness and complexity of silent film imagery within the world of talking pictures (Tati was far removed from Rudolph Arnheim's nostalgia pieces trying to reclaim the mythical and mythologized presound era), making maximum use of the sensual impressions resulting from the contact of image and sound. The repurposing of physical comedy and invention of a cinema rich in sound, distinct from films with dubbed-in dialogue and background music, came together in the world of *Monsieur Hulot's Holiday,* paving the way for Tati's even bolder experiments in *My Uncle* and *Play Time.*

The particular situation of the film in these years of ferment in French cinema, along with Tati's experimentation, posed very intriguing problems for the novelizer, which could only have fascinated a young writer like Jean-Claude Carrière, still exploring various types of writing. Directorial independence from the script's demands and constraints would obviously be problematic for the practice of novelization, "naturally" close as it was to dialogue as well as narrative portions of the screenplay. If certain New Wave films were novelized, the very existence of these texts was not evident. Serious novelizations produced at the time were meant to be different, to stand out not only from the usual assembly-line production of commercial novelizations but also from the film, with the return to "shooting script" format to be avoided at all costs. In short, the author of an "acceptable" novelization had to adopt the same position toward the film as the New Wave directors did toward material they adapted: that of an author appropriating another's work, and trying to equal it, in his or her own way and choice of medium. Dealing with a Tati film could only make the technical and intellectual stakes higher in the novelizing arena. Few directors were so highly visual, so critical of the role of traditional dialogue, or had such a reckless disregard for plot. Only a real writer could handle the novelization of *Monsieur Hulot's Holiday.*

## A MISLEADING SURFACE

What do we find upon opening Carrière's book? First, perhaps to the surprise of the modern reader, the real film. With minor exceptions, the author follows

4. For more details, see De Baecque, *La Cinéphilie.*

5. For more details on Tati's career in general, see Bellos, *Jacques Tati.*

the outline of *Monsieur Hulot's Holiday,* scene by scene, without many cuts or additions, as if able to include almost the whole cast of characters, both man and beast. Generally speaking, Jean-Claude Carrière's writing did not stray far from contemporary conventions of novelization. If the work is successful and original, it is not, in a negative way, breaking the usual mold. From the very first pages, we realize that the book's main traits form a strong analogy to the "universal" characteristics[6] of fictionalized adaptation:

> Tout se passe comme si l'adaptateur du film mettait son point d'honneur à s'éloigner au maximum de sa source cinématographique en réintroduisant dans le texte du scénario, fondé sur la restitution directe et le discours immédiat, une distance narrative inconnue du récit en images. La spécificité romanesque semble donc se concentrer dans cette élaboration d'un personnage autonome, le narrateur, et de son discours propre, qui sert de médiateur absolu à l'histoire empruntée au film. . . . Le récit romanesque tire sa valeur, non de ce qu'il montre ou raconte mais de la "communication" qu'il établit avec son lecteur grâce à un discours qui affiche "sa présence": celle-ci agit comme un filtre permanent à l'égard de l'image qu'il est censé restituer.

> Everything happens as if the film adaptor made it a point of honor to stay as far away from the cinematic source as possible by inserting into the screenplay, founded on direct reproduction and direct speech, a narrative distance not found on film. Fictional specificity thus seems to rely on the creation of an independent character, the narrator, and his own discourse, which serves [as] an absolute mediator with the story borrowed from the film. . . . The fictional narrative derives its value, not from what it shows or tells but from the "communication" it establishes with the reader thanks to a discourse that stays "up front," acting as a permanent filter in regard to the images it is supposed to replace.[7]

---

6. That is, in Jeanne-Marie Clerc's view, valid during the period from the 1920s, when traditional novelization takes off, until the end of the 1950s, when the first cinema-novelisitic works by Duras and Robbe-Grillet come along: "Il est curieux de constater que, malgré les bouleversements qui, durant cette période, ont affecté le cinéma comme le roman, l'évolution subie par l'adaptation romancée reste minime, ne portant souvent que sur des points de détail comme la disposition typographique, ou des caractères inhérents au film muet et que l'apparition du parlant rend caducs, ne modifiant rien en profondeur à la structure romanesque de l'adaptation." [It is curious to note that, despite the upheavals affecting the cinema as well as the novel during this period, fictionalized adaptation evolved only minimally, sometimes only in parsing details such as typography, or inherent characteristics of silent film that talking pictures rendered obsolete, making no basic changes in the novelistic structure of adaptation] (*Littérature et cinéma,* 97).

7. Ibid., 99–101.

Carrière really does nothing different. In his work, too, the center of gravity moves from the (iconic) utterance to the (verbal) enunciation and the objectivity of action changes into the subjectivity of narration. Something is added: the narrator's point of view and language. Something is withdrawn: the narrative material's excess visuality. In *Monsieur Hulot's Holiday,* the emphasis is placed on how the narrator tells the tale and especially how he interprets events. This narrator, moreover, is by no means a modern one (recalling that 1958 was the height of the "École du Regard" controversy): he has an identity, even quite a strong one; he indulges in introspection and behaves like an omniscient narrator, able to read his characters' minds; finally, he dominates the text to the point of including several interlocked stories, each told by a separate narrator, each having its own language and narrative tags, according to another long-established tradition.

Superficially speaking, Carrière does not stray far from the beaten path. However, the way he involves himself in the role of narrator is anything but common. Instead of producing a narrative voice likely to act as a go-between for the film viewer's questions, the author picks one of the film's most insignificant, perhaps blandest, characters as his narrator: the character dubbed "The Walker" in the film credits, named "Arthur" in the film (in the book he remains anonymous). In the film, we see this character accompany, or more precisely lag behind, his taller and stouter spouse ("Ma femme continue, et je vais son chemin, qui est aussi le mien." [My wife walks on, and I go on her way, which is also mine.]).[8] His exceptional inaction obviously makes him a peerless observer, at least in the book.[9]

Promoting a character to the role of *homodiegetic* narrator (meaning a narrator belonging to the fictional world he conjures, without being at the center of things), rather than inventing an *extradiegetic* narrator (meaning one completely outside the world he's describing), radically transforms the direction of the work. The filmgoer taking up the book stops looking at the characters; he can hear them, even slip into their skin. This is far removed from traditional fictional adaptations that stress the difference between what is seen and what is understood. At the same time, this change is not unrelated to what happens in the film, for it recalls the multiple roles played by Jacques Tati, at once the film's director (extradiegetic) and protagonist (diegetic). Jean-Claude Carrière's novelization, transforming a character into the narrator, also

8. Carrière, *Monsieur Hulot,* 76.

9. Another character could have served the same function: the waiter in the hotel dining room, also an inveterate observer, but perhaps handicapped, structurally speaking, by the fact that he plays too active a part in too many scenes.

exhibits the plural logic of Tati's cinematic and, more broadly, artistic outlook: to avoid being pigeonholed.

But let us take a closer look at this character that Carrière chose as the narrator of *Monsieur Hulot's Holiday*. The fact that this "Arthur" was part of the collective "de-Germanizing" of the hotel guests[10] is not without significance: Carrière's satire targeted the French, not foreigners (and since the signing of the Treaty of Rome in 1957, which firmed up 1951 trade agreements on steel and coal, some of these foreigners had become respectable European partners).[11] The France represented by the narrator, however, may be more complex than he himself thinks. To be sure, the narrator bears a heavy load. He is a civil servant, disposed toward calm, rest, inaction; he is married to a matron who inspires unbelievably misogynist rants; a Parisian, he feels out of place in this provincial setting; and so on, and so on. But within this placid beachgoer lurks a troublemaker who gradually surfaces. Unlike the film, less subtle on this point, in the novel we experience a real story of emancipation. Coming in contact with Hulot, who first both amuses and confuses him, the narrator progressively comes to identify with this unique character's subversive spirit, finally indulging in an act of (symbolic) insubordination: he refuses to follow his wife on one of their walks, and if this rebellion remains passive and understated (his wife will not even notice), it is obviously of great importance (and this touch is one of the rare scenes added to the book!).

The essential point, though, is found in the exchanges among the diegetic layers fanning out from the narrator. Taking over the privileges of the traditional extradiegetic narrator, since the character tells his own story instead of the story told by an outside narrator as in traditional fictionalized adaptations, he also establishes a very strong connection to the book's reader, by definition, extradiegetic. "I am like you," he keeps on saying. Now, this "you" is simple to pinpoint sociologically (the France of fed-up "Frenchies,") yet at once a "you" with multiple personalities. It is the novel reader, but also, at least in theory, the filmgoer, and this filmgoer may have seen Jacques Tati's latest film, *Monsieur Hulot's Holiday* "for real," while being the "virtual" viewer of Tati's next production, already announced on the book's back cover: *My Uncle*, a prizewinner at Cannes in 1958, just a few weeks after Carrière's novelization appeared in bookstores.

Resembling this "you," the one who may have seen *Monsieur Hulot's Holiday*, the one who should go see *My Uncle*, Carrière's narrator loses a great deal

---

10. If a few German-speaking vacationers remained, some of the key characters changed nationality, if not language: "The Intellectual" became visibly French, while "Smutte" turned into a French-speaking Belgian.

11. The English suffer a strikingly different fate, maintained in the book.

of his innocence. Insofar as he represents Tati's "real" audience, the narrator Carrière creates can only rely on the author's observations once the film has been screened: Carrière knows what worked and what didn't, and he could take note of that, either to corroborate the audience's attitudes or to adjust the film's aim. And insofar as the narrator also represents the "virtual" audience for Tati's new film, Carrière could also indirectly suggest what this audience could expect from the follow-up to *Monsieur Hulot's Holiday.*

## GENUINE WRITING

The narrator of *Monsieur Hulot's Holiday* is not someone who talks, but who *writes.* He keeps a journal where stylistic flourishes abound; his writing choices show unerring insight into the risks and rewards of novelization.

As we have seen, traditional novelization can be roughly divided into two types of sequences: those coming directly from the film, more particularly from the screenplay and dialogue; and those added by the narrator that tend to feature the questions and reactions of an anonymous, unspecified viewer (though in this sort of novelization, it is never someone in the real film's audience, but rather someone witnessing the action that the film is meant to show).

Each of these tactics raises very specific problems for the writer. We have already analyzed how Jean-Claude Carrière handled the question of the narrator. What he managed to do with the screenplay is no less ingenious. The absence of an actual narrative screenplay in a film full of visual sketches like *Monsieur Hulot's Holiday* meant that Carrière had to invent things in an area where the novelizer can usually rely on sorting and rearranging. In concrete terms, he did not try to fill the film's "gaps" with stage direction or dialogue after the fact; instead, he opted for specifically verbal humorous touches that gave him another way of recreating Tati's visual adventures. In themselves, the stylistic devices used by the narrator are nothing spectacular, but their judicious use, and above all the deft pacing, keep the reader amply entertained. Among these devices, let us point out:

- The parody of ready-made phrases (endlessly parroted by the narrator's wife: "Que de vert" [Nice view], "Il fait chaud" [Hot out today], "Le fond de l'air est frais" [There's a nip in the air], etc.);
- Recourse to a wide variety of metaphors to qualify the same referent (for instance, the backfire of Hulot's car, then Hulot himself: "coups de feu" [cannon fire], "cyclone" [cyclone], "coup de vent" [downdraft], etc.);

- The choice of a tone, a lexicon, a syntax for each speaking part (the written equivalent of each character's verbal tics);
- Soundplay (when Smutte gets a phone call, which happens every few pages, a staccato repetition of "B'" sounds denote the character);
- The placement of highly dense paragrammatical networks (very striking as regards Hulot, whose name is scattered through the story in an almost systematic way: the paired U/O vowels and L/T consonants are often echoed whenever his name is mentioned, as in this quotation: "Butor . . . Malotru . . . bougonnait l'officier. Ce malotru qui s'appelait Hulot" [Oaf . . . lout . . . groused the policeman. That lout called Hulot];[12]
- And most of all, the combination of these various techniques, playing off one another, as in the passage below (where Carrière adds the bonus of an oblique reference to Flaubert's three-part cadence);

> Mais déjà jaillissait au loin, dans la direction de l'hôtel, un cri qui se répétait:
> "Monsieur Smutte! Té . . . Téléphone!"
> Le garçon, la voix du garçon!
> La chaise longue craque. Le Belge bondit, court. Ah! Business, business. . . .
> Notre train-train quotidien. Une mer grise, quelques embarcations craintives. Des pêcheurs de crevettes, là-bas, près des rochers.

> But already hailing from the direction of the hotel came the cry:
> "Mr. Smutte! Phone . . . a phone call!"
> The waiter, the waiter's voice!
> The beach chair creaks. The Belgian bounces up. Ah! Business, business. . . .
> Our daily grind. A gray sea, some bumbling boat launches. Shrimpers, down below, by the rocks.[13]

In addition, and this is a second component of Jean-Claude Carrière's stylistic efforts, the novelization also takes a very coherent position regarding time, or as Jean Ricardou so poetically put it, "the chronic problem"[14] of a text priding itself on "representing" the world: the impossibility of faithfully transposing visual simultaneity into the written word's linearity. Yet simultaneity

---

12. Carrière, *Monsieur Hulot,* 30.
13. Ibid., 43.
14. Ricardou, *Une Maladie chronique,* 1989.

is one of the keys to Tati's directorial style: in his films, and *Monsieur Hulot's Holiday* is already a full participant in this esthetic, the plot mainly consists of echoes and connections that weave together a wealth of onscreen elements. To translate this simultaneity, Jean-Claude Carrière must adopt certain techniques likely to lessen the conflict between the referent's simultaneity and the linearity of his means of representation. First, the choice of illustration, not only plentiful but quite varied in terms of insertion points, making it a true partner to the text and very close to the film's iconography,[15] going as far as literal or near-literal quotation of film material (thus on page 141, the poster for the costume ball is reproduced exactly). Then there is the very marked preference for an alternating montage, each time concordant sound must be accounted for: overlapping conversations or conversations intercut with radio broadcasts are always rendered in such a way that the voices interrupt one another, with the reader losing a bit of information in the process (since these voices are delivering platitudes, it is easy enough to reconstruct what they are saying and become aware of how the process works). Finally, there is the use of an "impressionistic" or "artistic" style on the sonic level. Through this style, which seeks to change what the painter *saw* while painting into what the reader should *see* while reading,[16] "la qualité est mise en avant, au détriment de la réalité qui sert de support; l'emploi du pluriel renforce la notation de l'impression, donne la vision du concret (alors que l'article défini singulier pousse vers la généralisation); il décompose la surface de l'objet en touches multiples—produisant des effets comparables à ceux qui sont créés dans la peinture de la même époque." [quality is moved forward, undermining reality; the use of the plural reinforces the notation of impressions, gives a vision of the concrete (while the singular definite article encourages generalization); it breaks down the object's surface into multiple strokes—producing effects comparable to those created in paintings from the same era.][17] Favoring the nominal sentence typical of literary impressionism (very rare in novelization, governed as it is by the narrative impulse), Carrière transfers the same style to the representation of sonic objects so important to Tati's poetic concept; then he plays with steeping his text in phonic effects, as is evident from the novel's opening page, highly revelatory of this technique:

---

15. Keeping in mind that Pierre Étaix, who signed the illustrations, also designed the poster and especially the famous stylized drawing of Monsieur Hulot, imprinting this character's visual representation on our collective memory.

16. For a methodological and philosophical discussion of the problems related to this stylistic movement, see Vouilloux, "L' 'Impressionisme littéraire.'"

17. Pagès, "L'Écriture artiste" (l'École des lettres, No. 8, March 1992, 17), cited in Vouilloux, "L' 'Impressionnisme littéraire,'" 64.

Sacs tyroliens et cannes à pêche, contrôleurs ahuris qu'on houspille et dont on secoue, dont on arrache les boutons dorés, coups de sifflet, piétinements, appels, enfants giflés, chuintements des machines.

Rucksacks and fishing tackle, harried conductors to jostle, pinching their shiny buttons; whistles, stomping, shouts, spankings, hissing machinery.[18]

Finally, Carrière's fourth tactic for rendering simultaneity goes even farther. This is the introduction of a strong component of simultaneity in enumerations through syntactically symmetrical structures. Faced with the dilemma of conveying something that happens all at once to a number of people in the same place, the traditional novelist often resorts to an enumeration, whose linearity upsets the visual flow. To compensate for this loss, Carrière proffers a variety of syntactic symmetries in the enumeration sections, thus diminishing their linear effect: once we understand that the structure of an initial unit will be reprised and reworked, this operates as a "transphrastic" fusion, so much so that the reader no longer goes from one sentence to the next but rather relates each of these sentences to an implicit model that transcends a simple linear declension, through a summary effect that is not unlike that of a title. Examples of this tactic are legion:

"Silence!" demanda monsieur Smutte.
Le commandant baissa la voix. Ceux qui lisaient ne levèrent pas les yeux de leurs livres. La dame qui brodait resta tout entière à sa passementerie, l'intellectuel à son journal, monsieur Fred à son apéritif. Le garçon jeta un regard à l'extérieur, en écartant le rideau d'une fenêtre.

"Silence!" demanded Mr. Smutte.
The Major lowered his voice. Those who were reading kept their eyes glued to their books. The lady doing needlework concentrated on her embroidery, the intellectual on his newspaper, Mr. Fred on his mixed drink. The waiter tugged at a curtain and glanced outside the window.[19]

Le commandant au garde-à-vous près de sa chaise. Monsieur Smutte qui consulte une dernière facture. Une dame assez jeune et assez jolie, mais piquée d'élégance, se repoudre les joues.

---

18. Carrière, *Monsieur Hulot*, 7.
19. Ibid., 25.

The Major at attention by his chair. Mr. Smutte studying one last invoice. A fairly young and fairly pretty lady gave a knowing glance at her compact mirror.[20]

*Monsieur Hulot's Holiday,* a novelization like so many others? Only a cursory reading could lead to such a conclusion. Jean-Claude Carrière's novel stands out through the quality of writing that makes it a true novel, a worthy equivalent of Tati's film. It also renews the poetics of novelization insofar as it moves the two poles of (filmic) utterance and (verbal) enunciation much closer together, resolving a problem in traditional novelization. Modest as it may seem, this book is a very ambitious example, at a decisive moment in the genre's history, of how much can be done to make a novel out of a film.

---

20. Ibid., 51.

CHAPTER 6

~

# Scandalous Novels, Shocker Collection

## *Vian's Seghers Saga*

## A CASE OF TWISTS AND TURNS

As Noël Arnaud pieces it together in his "case file,"[1] there is no story more comical, tragic, nonsensical, simple, enigmatic, infuriating, and stupid than the story of Boris Vian and *I Spit on Your Graves*. Arnaud even calls the novelization a rewrite of the script, with its subtitle "Based on the Cinematic Work by Boris Vian and Jacques Dopagne."[2] This story begins in 1959, somewhat by accident as we shall see, and ends in 1963 with the verdict in a new trial, the sad conclusion of the endlessly tangled legal history of this title, this text, this theme. It had begun a decade earlier, in 1947, with the publication of Vernon Sullivan's novel.

Thanks to Noël Arnaud's documentation, it is now possible to form a better idea of the editorial, social, and human implications of one of the most publicized literary and cultural "affairs" in Postwar France.[3] *I Spit on Your Graves,* a novel by an unknown author, Vernon Sullivan, seemed from the start a scandal-ridden but also mysterious book.

1. Arnaud, *Dossier de l'affaire.*
2. D'Eaubonne, *J'irai cracher,* 1959. For this study, we used a paperback edition published in 1972 by les éditions de l'inter.
3. The historical overview in the first part of this chapter is broadly based on Arnaud, *Dossier de l'affaire.*

The scandal came from its subject, touching both politics and morals: it dealt with racial discrimination in the United States, and the means it used to convey its message were drawn from the dual traditions of American crime fiction (with reference to Chandler, Cain, etc.) and pornography (this was also the period when France was discovering Henry Miller). Exactly why the novel was banned in the United States, as the book trailer claims ("L'œuvre que l'Amérique n'a pas osé publier" ["The Book America Didn't Dare Publish"]), is unclear: did the political message infringe on a societal taboo, or did the crude, sadistic sex scenes rouse the censors' ire? Reading Sullivan's text, one must credit the impression that the sex must have been more disturbing than the author's political stance, even if reviews of the book tend to put more emphasis on segregation and discrimination. The novel does indeed tell a story of revenge, caused by a racially motivated crime. The book's narrator, a "white Negro," meaning someone with only one-eighth Negro blood and therefore able to pass as white, rebels against white society after his brother is lynched for falling in love with a white girl and, worse, being loved in return. However, his revenge is quite particular, since he decides to seduce, abuse, then murder two young white sisters, not neglecting the ultimate revelation to each that they had unknowingly slept with a black man. What such a summary conceals is no doubt more important than what it reveals: the narrator's style does the "hard-boiled" novel one better and abounds in orgies and sex scenes, occasionally to the point of overwhelming the political message.

This persistent uncertainty about the novel's thematic dominant, nimbly navigating between politics and pornography, is heightened by an even more nagging question, one regarding the author's identity. Sullivan's work, which remained completely anonymous, was in fact "translated from the American" by Boris Vian, who also authored a highly ironic preface. A star of St. Germain-des-Prés jazz clubs (playing trumpet in Claude Abadie's band at a prime Existentialist haunt, Le Tabou), contributor to Sartre's Les Temps Modernes (where he wrote "The Liar's Chronicle"), a young novelist already with one book behind him (Vercoquin et le plancton [Vercoquin and the Plankton]), and special protégé of Raymond Queneau, young Boris Vian wasn't yet famous, but he had enough of a reputation to make rumors fly: that there was no such author as Sullivan, or rather, the writer was none other than Vian. The success of Gallimard's "Série noire" crime fiction imprint (launched in 1945), led some publishers to copy the concept with pseudo "Made in France" hard-boiled crime series (as with Les Éditions du Scorpion, I Spit on Your Graves's original publisher, which also brought out the first two volumes of Léo Malet's Trilogie noire [Black Trilogy]). Added to this, the many books published under pseudonyms in the postwar period (especially given the "blacklist" of writers who collaborated with the Occupation) meant that questions about the real identity of authors was part and parcel of the literary landscape at the time.[4]

The conflict over the novel's meaning and the speculation surrounding the author's identity combined to make Sullivan's book a best seller (at more than a hundred thousand copies, *I Spit on Your Graves* sold better than many literary prizewinners) and a social phenomenon (debates about the book were a sounding board for a number of postwar obsessions, from the never-ending rationing after the Liberation to America's growing influence on the French way of life, for instance). And since reality always copies fiction, a true-crime story ended up fanning the flames. A few months after *I Spit on Your Graves* came out, a traveling salesman murdered his girlfriend, supposedly after reading Sullivan's novel and using it at his modus operandi. The book's detractors tried hard to have it banned, but despite determined efforts by their leader, Daniel Parker, president of the "Cartel d'action sociale et morale" [League of social and moral action], the campaign came to nothing.

Just as the public and the press turned their attention elsewhere, Vian came up with a theatrical adaptation of the book, produced in 1948 at the Théâtre Verlaine in Paris. It ran for about three months, but disappointed scandalmongers. The play was substantially different from the novel, in that the political message was emphasized over the sexual or pornographic elements. If the essence of the story—revenging a brother's murder—remained the same, in the play there was much more talk than action (there was sex, there were rapes, there was nasty business, but all offstage). As a result, the antiracist message became clearer, but failed to compensate for the racier content the audience had been led to expect. The play was compared unfavorably to Sartre's *The Respectful Prostitute* or, even less kindly, *Uncle Tom's Cabin.*

Unexpectedly, especially in light of a 1947 amnesty that should have obviated any legal proceedings, the controversy finally resulted in a trial. After the scathing portrayal of a certain "Dan Park" in Vernon Sullivan's second novel, *The Dead All Have the Same Skin,* and above all after Boris Vian's 1948 admission that he was indeed the author of *I Spit on Your Graves,* Daniel Parker managed to have Vian and his publisher tried and convicted on morals charges. After a long legal battle, the initial 1950 verdict was overturned on appeal in 1953. Another amnesty ensued. The book, however, remained banned until the 1960s. As Noël Arnaud stresses, this ban was no great loss for Boris Vian, who wanted to leave Sullivan behind to become Vian, turning toward new pursuits, particularly songwriting.

---

4. For more on Malet, see Lacassin, *Sur les chemins qui marchent,* 233–58.

So it would seem that revisiting the theme and title of *I Spit on Your Graves* was not an idea that came from Vian himself, now occupied elsewhere, but from one of the book's admirers, Jacques Dopagne. Involved in the movie world, Dopagne approached Vian in 1953 with the newly written first draft of a screenplay. This adaptation, which Vian curiously ended up endorsing, was a departure from the book, much as the earlier stage version had been. Dopagne, with a blind eye toward any salacious material, viewed the book in a humanist, almost mystical sense. To quote Noël Arnaud, a reliable judge on the subject:

> Pas le moins du monde libidineux Jacques Dopagne, la pornographie le laisse de glace. On oserait dire qu'il y a chez lui un double inversé de Daniel Parker: insensible à la pornographie, il ne la voit pas, serait-il entouré de toutes les filles de Camaret, mais il voit le reste—y compris les bons sentiments—qui l'enchante. . . . Ainsi constitué, Jacques Dopagne retient du roman non le thème de la vengeance, mais celui de l'amour, et non l'amour bestial, le déchaînement des instincts, mais l'amour qui transporte au-delà de soi-même, l'amour qui transcende.

> Jacques Dopagne was not the least bit prurient; pornography left him cold. One might almost say that he was an inside-out version of Daniel Parker: indifferent to pornography, he never noticed it, even if it stared him in the face. But he saw the rest, including the book's good intentions, which appealed to him. . . . With a mind like his, what Dopagne got out of the novel was not the theme of revenge, but the theme of love, and not carnal love, not savage release, but the love that leads beyond the self, transcendent love.[5]

In Dopagne's reinterpretation, the protagonist is saved from his dubious inclinations by the love of a white woman (one of the two victims in the original text), who like him will lose her life to an intolerant, narrow-minded society the two cannot escape. So great is the gap between the two works that a new title was needed: Dopagne came up with "La Passion de Joe Grant [The Passion of Joe Grant]," which Vian accepted, just as he agreed to the revamped theme. Even better, he seemed to find merit in Dopagne's idea and soon got down to writing what would become the basis for a contract with the producers: a hundred-page "treatment." Vian's turnaround cannot be explained solely by the author's friendly feelings toward Dopagne and his longtime fas-

---

5. Arnaud, *Dossier de l'affaire*, 296–97; original punctuation followed throughout.

cination with cinema (as early as 1947, he had considered a film treatment of his own, but never completed one). Noël Arnaud also cites Vian's pressing financial needs following his divorce from his first wife, Michelle, while stressing the author's relative indifference to a work he had put behind him (by the time Dopagne approached Vian, *I Spit on Your Graves* was out of print and also banned). However, Vian slowly warmed to his story once more, and the new controversy surrounding his song "Le Déserteur" ["The Deserter"] (1954) seems to have been a catalyst. Not only did Vian regain interest in *I Spit on Your Graves* and its theme, he also set to work seriously on the screenplay, following Dopagne's outline fairly closely but restoring some of the original novel's spirit of rebellion.

A contract was signed, first with Pathé, then with a number of others, and from setback to deadline, dispute to obstruction, forfeiting options to renegotiating rights, the filming was repeatedly postponed. But the accumulated delays were nothing compared to the final producers' trickery, manipulating the contracts to gain control first of Vian's work and finally his title. Claiming there had been noncompliance with certain contractual provisions, they declared Vian's screenplay unworkable, in the process granting themselves the right to make changes, which they hastened to do. Vian could only look on helplessly as his screenplay was discarded (his "reject screenplay," as he remarked with bitter irony) by the new regime: the director and new scriptwriter, Michel Gast; dialogue writer Louis Sapin; and cowriter Luska Eliroff. Since the author and publisher still held the rights to the title, Vian was able to win a couple of concessions: in exchange for his title and a promise not to make claims against Gast's screenplay, he was given a sizeable financial settlement and the removal of the new writers' names from the credits (the audience would only see the words "after the cinematic work of Boris Vian and Jacques Dopagne"). Only once these questions were finally settled did the filming start, in March and April 1959, and the first screening—a private one, on June 23, 1959—proved literally the death of Vian. Already seriously ill, he collapsed and died barely ten minutes into the film.

The novelization seems far removed from this wretched drama, and yet it is at the very heart, at least of the next plot twist. The novelization is what confirmed postmortem that when Boris Vian ceded the rights to his title, he had really given up the copyright to the work. But let us give Noël Arnaud the floor once again:

Tandis que s'achève le tournage, le "scénario-bidon" remonte à la surface. Pierre Seghers publie une collection de scénarios de films. Jacques Dopagne, son voisin de Montparnasse, le rencontre un jour sur le trottoir. Ils bavardent. Dopagne lui parle de *J'irai cracher sur vos tombes*. "Ça m'intéresse," conclut Seghers. On décide que le scénario du film paraîtra dans la collection. Forts de leur nouveau contrat avec la C.T.I. Boris Vian et Jacques Dopagne sont sûrs de leurs droits, droits sur le titre pour ce qui est de son exploitation littéraire, droits sur le scénario, celui qui se tourne et ne les satisfait pas comme sur leur scénario original ou tout autre qu'il leur prendrait fantaisie d'écrire. Mais quoi faire? Assurément, le "script" de Gast et Sapin n'est pas, tel quel, acceptable; on peut en conserver le thème, la ligne générale, tracée dans le premier scénario. Ils tergiversent. Au fond, ils sont las de *J'irai cracher sur vos tombes,* de toutes ces embûches qu'on leur tend. Simultanément, ils songent que le livre pourra, un tant soit peu, contrebalancer le film, montrer ce que le film eût été si on les avait suivis. Seghers les tire de leur embarras: "Pourquoi vous tracasser? Vous me confiez tous les éléments: vos scénarios, celui du film, j'ai des rewriters-maison, j'en propose un qui connaît son métier: Françoise d'Eaubonne; avec tous vos papiers elle vous refabrique un scénario à votre goût." D'accord, répondent Boris et Dopagne, et Boris remet à Seghers, parmi les autres documents du film, le scénario-bidon, en exprimant le désir qu'on en tienne compte. Le contrat avec Seghers, Boris le renvoie signé le 23 juin, jour de sa mort. Les survivants oublient ce contrat, ne se préoccupent plus de Seghers et du rewriting, jusqu'au jour d'août 1959 où paraît le livre de Françoise d'Eaubonne, *J'irai cracher sur vos tombes*, "d'après les travaux cinématographiques de Boris Vian et Jacques Dopagne." Abandonnée à elle-même, allant au plus pressé, Françoise d'Eaubonne a pris le scénario du film, tel que malaxé par Michel Gast, Louis Sapin et une de leurs collaboratrices (car on n'est jamais trop nombreux au cinéma) Luska Eliroff; elle en a fait une quasi-copie conforme, relevée par-ci par-là de quelques grains de poivre de son épicerie personnelle.

As the filming drew to a close, the "reject screenplay" resurfaced. Pierre Seghers was publishing a collection of screenplays. He ran into Jacques Dopagne, a Montparnasse neighbor, on the street one day. They chatted. Dopagne told him about *I Spit on Your Graves*. "I'm interested," Seghers said. The screenplay was slated for publication. With their new C.T.I. contract in hand, Boris Vian and Jacques Dopagne were sure of their rights, the right to the title and its literary development, rights to the screenplay, the one in production that they found less satisfactory than their original work, or any other screenplay they might dream up. But what to do next? To be sure, Gast and Sapin's script could not be used as is; the theme, the general direction found in the first screenplay could instead be salvaged. They wavered. Deep down, they were tired of *I Spit on Your Graves* and the endless pitfalls. They both decided that the book might somehow serve as a counterweight to the film, show what the film might have been if they had prevailed. Seghers proposed a way out: "Not to worry. Give me everything you have, your screenplays, the film script; I have house writers, and I'll give you a professional: Françoise d'Eaubonne. She'll take all your drafts and turn them into a book that will work for you." Fine, replied Boris and Dopagne, and Boris brought Seghers, among other documents related to the film, his "reject screenplay," asking that it be looked at. Boris returned the contract to Seghers, signed and dated June 23, the day of his death. His survivors forgot about the contract, with no further thought for Seghers and the screenplay rewrite, until the day in August 1959 that Françoise d'Eaubonne's book came out, *I Spit on Your Graves* "after the cinematic work by Boris Vian and Jacques Dopagne." Left to her own devices, with a tight deadline, Françoise d'Eaubonne took the screenplay, worked over by Michel Gast, Louis Sapin, and a female script doctor, Luska Eliroff (since there are never too many cooks in the movie world); the result was a near-exact copy, with an occasional sprinkling of Eaubonne's personal style.[6]

A new trial ensued, pitting the screenwriters and the director—who wanted Françoise d'Eaubonne's book taken off the shelves—against the publishing house and Vian's literary executors. At the end of this legal battle, which dragged on until 1963, the conclusion was that, on one hand, Françoise d'Eaubonne's book was not an adaptation of Vian's screenplay but in fact of Gast's and, on the other, that the latter script was a freestanding work used to produce the film, unlike Vian's "reject screenplay," declared without artistic merit by legal experts. The book was ultimately neither recalled, nor banned, but the royalties were to be divided up, according to one more legal oddity, among Gast, Sapin, and Eliroff on one side and Vian's widow, Ulrika, plus Jacques Dopagne on the other.

## REWRITING, CREATION, DISPLACEMENT

In many regards, Françoise d'Eaubonne's novelization is exceptional in the history of the genre. The legal imbroglio surrounding its appearance is one reason; the unavailability of the original—lost in a legal bind—is another; but the essence is of course a combination of all these factors. However detailed

---

6. Ibid., 327–28.

and well documented as Noël Arnaud's study may be, his work leaves certain aspects in the dark. To begin with, he exaggerates the novelizer's work as slapdash, no matter how much Boris Vian's admirers love to hate it. Next, he has little to say about the author, whom he introduces only through a passing remark of Pierre Seghers. Yet Françoise d'Eaubonne was not unknown in the milieu of "rewriters," as he terms it. Finally, Noël Arnaud also remains quite evasive on the status and role of the "screenplay collection" in Seghers's catalogue, even though in this case it was the famous "Romans-choc" or "Shocker Novel" series, so vital in the history of the genre, as we have seen.[7]

The collection's principal characteristic remains the selection of films and the way their design, as well as their rewriting, builds on a singular common theme, the theme of youth, or more precisely, what was known at the time as "the youth problem," which one always takes to single out "a certain kind of youth." The sociologist Edgar Morin pointed to the combined phenomena he calls the "degerontocratization" and "pedocratization" of modern societies,[8] the maladjustment of young people associated with the emergence of a new social category, adolescence, and the difficulties of finding fulfillment in life:

> Les groupes de zazous, houligans, blousons noirs, affirment le nihilisme rageur, la révolte, le mépris, l'asocialité de l'adolescence. . . . L'adolescence actuelle est profondément démoralisée par l'ennui bureaucratique qui suinte de la société adulte: et plus encore peut-être par l'inconsistance et l'hypocrisie des valeurs établies; elle ressent de façon extrêmement vive la grande question du sens de l'existence humaine; elle est peut-être très profondément marquée par ce sentiment d'anéantissement-suicide possible de l'humanité qu'a fait naître la bombe atomique. Elle trouve toutefois dans la culture de masse un style esthético-ludique qui s'adapte à son nihilisme, et l'aventure imaginaire qui entretient sans l'assouvir son besoin d'aventure. C'est ce qui peut expliquera que l'adolescence ait pu opérer une trouée dans la culture de masse: James Dean a été le premier et le suprême héros de l'adolescence, incarnant fureur de vivre et rébellion sans cause, frénésie et lassitude, aspiration à la plénitude et fascination du risque.

> The groups of hipsters, hooligans, rockers, affirm the raging nihilism, the rebellion of adolescence, with its anti-social scorn. . . . Today's teenager is profoundly demoralized by the bureaucratic boredom oozing from adult society: and even more, perhaps, by the hypocrisy of established values. Teenagers keenly sense the great question of the meaning of human life: they

---

7. See Appendix 3 for further details.

8. Morin, *L'Esprit du temps,* 174.

may be profoundly impacted by humanity's possible annihilation-suicide in the atomic age. Yet in mass culture they find a play-esthetic style that adapts to their nihilism, and imaginary adventures that feed their need for escape without satisfying it. This is what may explain how adolescence has made a breakthrough in mass culture: James Dean was the first and supreme teen hero, embodying a lust for life and rebellion without a cause, frenzy and lassitude, the striving for completion and the fascination of risk.[9]

A glance at the volumes published in the collection is all it takes to realize that the "Romans-choc" novels obviously exist in direct symbiosis with youth-oriented cinema. The collection opens with *Rebel Without a Cause,* includes several novelizations of French "New Wave" films, meaning films promoting what Morin calls "juvenility," and further features books based on films by more traditional directors, but who had box office hits focusing on modern youth (*Les Tricheurs,* a 1958 Marcel Carné film with the American title *Young Sinners,* was novelized by Jehanne Jean-Charles, a pseudonym of . . . Françoise d'Eaubonne's sister, who had already penned another novelization in the same collection, of Claude Chabrol's *Cousins,* in 1959).

This insistence on the theme of youth, trite and understandable as it is (after all, why blame a publisher for wanting to be in sync with the spirit of the times?), is nonetheless fundamentally important to the consideration of relations between cinema and literature. The "Romans-choc" collection in fact does much to illustrate the complex impact of the practice of novelizing. Seghers's publications did more than reproduce films or move them into the realm of (para)literature; they actively mediated how the contemporary movie going public thought about cinema, ultimately influencing directors who could not help responding to their audience's interests and preferences. The emphasis on "problem youth" ramped up the scandal (and sales) potential of these novels. It also led to the consideration of the films from a sociological perspective, that is, the placement of works of fiction within a documentary frame of reference. The "Romans-choc" novelizations not only added to the New Wave's growing success, they also shepherded these films toward the documentary leanings of Neo-Realism, where the border between fact and fiction was fluid by definition. The strong point of the Seghers collection's publishing initiative was its grounding in the realm of operations. A nonfiction text is not the meeting point between a fictional work and the theme of real life; emphasis on the *referential* instead operates through a *fictional* rewriting all the more

---

9. Ibid., 183.

effective for not being thought likely to substitute documentary reality for creative invention.

More comprehensively, this initiative highlights an aspect of novelization that is too little understood. Rather than being a more or less immediate, more or less faithful, more or less freestanding reflection of the life of a film, the novelizing genre changes how we look at cinema.

## NOVELIZATION IN THE TEXT

But let us return to Françoise d'Eaubonne, whose work was far less slipshod than Noël Arnaud's commentary would imply. What first strikes the reader, and what no doubt angered Boris Vian's friends and fans, was the near-total neglect of the "reject screenplay." D'Eaubonne followed the final film, not the Vian-Dopagne screenplay. Thus nothing remains of the Vian version's highly ironic tone, as described in Noël Arnaud's account of the proceedings. We know that this screenplay, or more specifically this "shooting script" the producers ordered, alternated between two types of writing: first the dialogue, which Vian claimed to have written with the utmost care; next the plot outline, which the author turned into pure provocation, as if trying to sabotage any chance for his work to be produced. This pseudo-screenplay narrative is ironic on three levels. First, Boris Vian was refusing to share any elements necessary to previsualize the film with an eventual director, less by means of cutting descriptions than by stuffing the screenplay with "useless" information. The script's prolix opening sets the tone:

> La caméra découvre un plan de forêt tranquille dans le Sud des Etats-Unis pendant une nuit d'été, plus précisément le 17 juillet à 21 heures 45. Au premier plan à droite, un arbre planté en 1874 par un fonctionnaire des Chemins de Fer retraité, orme dont la hauteur atteint au bas mot 97 pieds et qui, à 18 pieds du sol, se ramifie en deux branches de grosseur inégale.

> The establishing shot is a quiet forest scene in the American South on a summer night, more specifically July 17 at 9:45 p.m. In the right foreground, a tree planted in 1874 by a retired railroad supervisor, an elm at the very least 97 feet tall, branching at 18 feet above the ground into two unequal trunks.[10]

Next, Vian also attacks all the conventions of screenwriting. For instance, he mistakes or makes fun of cinematic techniques:

---

10. "*J'irai cracher sur vos tombes*, Film, 1958," in Arnaud, *Dossier de l'affaire*, 419.

Les visages des filles et des garçons s'éclairent en voyant Joe (il est bien entendu que ceci est une métaphore et qu'il n'est pas question de mettre en marche un projecteur supplémentaire de 5 kilowatts, ce qui ferait perdre du naturel à la scène).

The faces of the boys and girls light up when they see Joe (understanding that this is a metaphor and that there is no need to shine an additional 5 kilowatt spotlight, which would make the scene feel less natural).[11]

(Cette note technique destinée au preneur de son doit être déduite de la continuité en ce qui concerne la durée de celle-ci).

(This technical note intended for the sound engineer should not be counted in the continuity in terms of its duration.)[12]

All this while denying the importance of dialogue, in the name of an esthetic of "pure" image that was hardly the norm in "official" French cinema in the 1950s:

(L'auteur s'excuse, mais se voit dans l'impossibilité d'introduire un dialogue à cet endroit du film, purement visuel, et dont tout le charme doit résider dans la perfection plastique.)

(The author apologizes, but finds it impossible to introduce dialogue at this point in the film, purely visual, and better left to the charm of its formal perfection.)[13]

At a time when writing for the cinema mainly consisted of producing a "shooting script," and when playwrights were more highly regarded than screenwriters,[14] this was a blatant provocation. However, as the "reject screenplay" moved along, the tone became more serious, edgier, and Vian obviously became attached to his story. To the point where one finally wonders whether the author quite intentionally turned out this unacceptable script as an insult, a taunt to the screenwriter's profession, to disassociate himself from a rehash of *I Spit on Your Graves,* even if it only survived as the early draft of an unfilmed screenplay. Pure speculation, of course, but not unfounded, considering what a mess the film industry eventually made of Vian's original text . . .

---

11. Ibid., 478.

12. Ibid., 434.

13. Ibid., 430

14. Just as, in the so-called "cinema of quality," the filmmaker saw his role as that of theatrical stager, directing lead actors in front of the cameras.

Françoise d'Eaubonne, who categorically rejected Vian's version, sticking as close as possible to Gast's film, did allow herself one (small) departure indicative of her literary ambition. She brought back one of the "reject screenplay's" peculiarities, slightly modifying the order of the film's opening sequences to "set aside" the dialogue that Vian wanted to exclude but Michel Gast clumsily included through flashbacks. But this was an unusual case of "resistance" for her. Most of the time, Françoise d'Eaubonne's rewriting followed "team Gast-Sapin-Eliroff." A few of the modifications to the final screenplay had to do with the rules of the genre: novelization always adds certain elements, gives details about the characters' psychological state (as novelization is in the realm of telling rather than showing) and inserts or includes bits that may have been in the screenplay but were omitted from the screen version (especially toward the end, the novelized version is definitely longer and more explicit than the film). Other changes were no doubt due to the wish or need to make the book just a little spicier than the film. Since the book, without illustrations, cannot show the (partially) nude scenes, the writer "steps it up" with references to full nudity in certain scenes. In the same way, when the final party scene is described in the book, it includes a game of strip poker that the eager reader would never find in the film.

Still, the choice of Gast's film over Vian's "reject screenplay" is no passive choice. Rather than simply copying the screenplay found on film, Françoise d'Eaubonne tailors it to the "Romans-choc" collection. This transformation can be seen in two ways.

To begin with, the novelization clearly "de-Americanizes" the plot, or, put another way, anchors it in the host country's reality. Where Vernon Sullivan's book could fool readers into thinking it truly was "translated from the American," Gast's film, though still set in the American South, shows characters farther from their American originals (when the novel came out, there was a lot of buzz about its portrayal of "bobby-soxers")[15] and closer to some of their French counterparts ("blousons noirs" or rockers; Vian, on viewing the film, is said to have hooted, "Those kids are American as my ass!").[16] Very much in the vein of the "Romans-choc" collection's mock-sociological reinterpretations, Françoise d'Eaubonne stepped up this "Frenchifying," clearly evident in the descriptions of rock songs on the jukebox:

---

15. Noël Arnaud includes long extracts of a France-Dimanche report on this group of teenagers, shown as the successors to the "hep cats" ("zazous" in French), cf. *Dossier de l'affaire*, 50–51.

16. Ibid., 36.

Son rire éclata, en même temps qu'une musique démente: comme un choc de casseroles, ou le grésillement du lard sur le feu, mêlé de miaulements et de hurlements. Janet venait de mettre en marche le disque de son choix.

Her laughter rang out at the same time the music blared: like pots and pans rattling, or bacon sizzling in the pan, mixed with shouts and screeching. Janet had just put on her favorite record.[17]

This is a departure from Gast's film, less strident on this subject and even farther removed from Vian and his proverbial love of jazz. Françoise d'Eaubonne's prose reveals minimally reworded echoes of letters to the editor in the popular press. The same remark could be applied to the partying, orgies, and drinking sprees, clearly inspired by the way the Parisian general public imagined American-style "wingdings" at the time (and that Françoise d'Eaubonne's younger sister, writing under the pen name Jehanne Jean-Charles, had previously described in other novels). Similarly, all of the characters in the book seem to be big readers of novels, French novels, no less: Gide, Giradoux, Mauriac (his *Viper's Nest* is mentioned), something of a clash with what little "local color" remains in the text.

Second, and more daringly, Françoise d'Eaubonne's novelization makes specific reference to a certain number of current events, which contemporary cinema censorship would not have let pass. Note this mention of the "American" war in Korea:

"Je vous le disais!" chuchota le patron en se prenant la tête à deux mains. "Un asile, des fous, des dingues! ils y arriveront bien, à flanquer le feu à ma baraque!"

"J'espère que ces jeux ne vous paraissent pas trop violents?" susurra Chandley en se courbant vers Joë, plein de prévenance.

"Ce sont des enfants," répondit Joë. "De cruels enfants . . . On en fera de drôles de soldats!"

"Il y avait," répliqua sentencieusement Chandley, "un philosophe français qui disait en parlant des enfants: 'Ce sont déjà des hommes.'"

"I told you so," the owner said, holding his head in both hands. "A madhouse, a bunch of kooks! They'll end up setting the place on fire."

"I hope you don't think things are getting out of hand," said Chandley, considerate, leaning toward Joe.

---

17. D'Eaubonne, *J'irai cracher*, 48.

"They're kids," answered Joe. "Mean little kids. They'll make some pretty strange soldiers."

"A French philosopher once said," Chandley intoned, "that children are men already."[18]

"Je te rappelle la règle du jeu," dit Sonny. "Si tu flanches, Janet est à eux deux. C'est la règle, et ce n'est pas pour rire. Tu ne sais pas qui est Reno; pas un dégonflé comme toi; il a fait la Corée."

"Let me remind you of the rules," said Sonny. "If you give in, those two get Janet. That's the rule and it's for real. You don't know who you're dealing with. This Reno isn't a punk like you; he's been to Korea."[19]

But one may suppose that these remarks, not found in the film, underline what was left unsaid in Gast's work, namely the Algerian War and the question of torture. The ultimate taboo subject, according to the director, who spoke about it in an interview accompanying the film's DVD release,[20] but a subject all the more present, that is to say *deliberate,* on-screen for being entirely absent from Vian's "reject screenplay." The film does contain a torture scene that seems to be all about American gang violence; but the French filmgoer, and even more so, the novelization reader, "helped along" by the repeated mention of the Korean War, was likely to make the connection to the situation in North Africa.

This contemporary take alone would make the novelization worthy of closer attention, yet Françoise d'Eaubonne adds a second element, and this one is actually literary. The author chose a very particular tone, indicative both of her writerly aims (the *stylemes* used consistently connote "belles lettres" and are the antithesis of "writing degree zero") and of her attempt to strengthen the filmmakers' stance. The style in question is what film historians have called the "surface beauty" of attempts to legitimize novelization during the 1920s, an overall style setting it apart from clumsy, lowbrow, serial-type novels as well as from avant-garde scenario experiments of the same time period. According to Andrea Meneghelli, this "surface beauty," an almost textbook example of "midcult," would define itself by the conflict between the desire to "write well" for an audience that is neither uneducated nor particularly cultured, on one hand, and, on the other, an excessive solemnity, a certain sentimental cast,

18. Ibid., 59.

19. Ibid., 162.

20. "Sexe, jazz, et violence," Interview with Michel Gast and Alain Riou," supplement to the DVD released in 2005.

an overuse of paraphrase and a reliance on pithy quotations.[21] The relation between these two sides of such writing is obvious: from this point of view, the only way to go about writing *well* is to rely on what we now see as second-rate literature, and the inverse.

The same holds true for Françoise d'Eaubonne, who seeks to modernize "surface beauty" without steering clear of its silly or outdated tenets. Thus the author makes excessive use of comparison, the ultimate hackneyed technique for those with "literary" pretentions. The results are catastrophic. It is common to find phrases like "le visage rouge comme une sombre rose" [blushing like a deep red rose].[22] As a more complete example, consider the book's opening paragraph:

> La nuit tombait sur les collines accroupies comme des chiens qui tremblent de fièvre, dans la lueur vacillante du ciel.
>
> La voiture de Joë trouait l'obscurité; ses phares imitaient devant elle les ailes du Moulin, la brasse d'un fantôme lumineux. Les graviers giclaient sous ses pneus; derrière le plus bas des mornes éclatèrent des aboiements. Les pentes escarpées surplombaient cette course, le papillonnement de la clarté jaune et le crissement des roues.

> Night was falling on the hills huddled together like feverish dogs, in the wavering gleam of the sky.
>
> Joe's car pierced the darkness: its headlights acted like windmill blades, the breaststroke of a luminous ghost. Gravel crunched beneath the tires: behind the lowest rise barking exploded. Rough slopes loomed above the speeding car, the flitting yellow light and the squealing tires.[23]

Yet Françoise d'Eaubonne sticks faithfully to this system, drawing again and again from the same lexical reservoir of comparisons. The characters' behavior (especially that of the "bad guys") is compared to animals (the city of Trenton where the story is set becomes a barnyard, menagerie, or zoo depending on the action), while the "good guys" and victims are regularly described in religious terms. No doubt a vestige of the fundamental refashioning that began with Jacques Dopagne's initial screenplay "concept," transforming the story of racial revenge at the heart of Boris Vian's novel into a tale of the

---

21. Meneghelli, "La bellezza facile," 225.

22. D'Eaubonne, *J'irai cracher*, 118.

23. Ibid., 11. To put this prose style in context, it is fitting to recall that it appeared at the same time Alain Robbe-Grillet was attacking anthropomorphic metaphors. See Robbe-Grillet *For A New Novel*.

protagonist's redemption through love and suffering—a "passion play." Gast's film would only weakly reflect this transformation, torn as it was between a humanist message and the desire for shock value.

There is great coherence in the way the imaginary is maintained throughout the book's major themes, brimming with this type of comparisons and metaphors. And how can a reader not be astonished by certain departures of d'Eaubonne's when she occasionally dips into Vian's "reject screenplay" for nuggets of writing that allow her to reinterpret the work by Michel Gast and his collaborators? Indeed, notwithstanding its extreme violence and devastating humor, the "reject screenplay" contains traces of Jacques Dopagne's original contribution, converting the revenge story into one of redemption through love. Consider this outstanding example, curiously one of the rare fragments of the "reject screenplay" that Françoise d'Eaubonne recycles in a relatively straightforward (but not necessarily faithful) fashion: the river swimming scene, where Joe plays a cruel game with one of his Trenton girlfriends. To begin with, here is Vian's description:

> Elle se détache du groupe en courant et plonge dans la rivière. L'eau est douce et limpide. Judy est maintenant assez éloignée de la rive où se trouve la bande. Elle nage, heureuse, sous l'ombre des frondaisons qui frôlent la surface de l'eau.
>
> À ce moment, l'appareil cadre Joë, un peu plus loin, qui nage en silence, avec une souplesse extraordinaire, pareille à celle d'une anguille. Il s'approche de Judy qui ne l'a pas encore aperçu. Il plonge sous elle, la regarde un instant et, brusquement, avec la rapidité d'un éclair, la saisit par un pied et la tire vers le fond. Il remonte à la surface, maintenant la tête de la fille sous l'eau. Judy se débat. Joe, dont personne ne soupçonne la présence, paraît décidé à en finir avec elle. Mais les mouvements que cette dernière fait sont tels que les yeux de Joë sont comme fascinés. Une lueur soudaine allume alors son regard, et il se décide à lâcher sa proie. La tête de Judy émerge. Au moment où la fille, le visage tordu par l'angoisse, va se mettre à hurler, Joe lui ferme la bouche d'un baiser brutal. Peu à peu, la fille plie sous la caresse, cependant que Joe l'enlace au milieu de la rivière.

She breaks away from the group and dives into the river. The water is pure and clear. Judy swims fairly far from the group on the riverbank. She splashes happily in the shade of branches overhanging the water.

The camera now pans to Joe, a slight distance away, swimming silently and smoothly as an eel. He closes in on Judy, who doesn't see him coming. He dives beneath her, looks at her for a moment, and suddenly, quick as lightning, grabs one of her feet and pulls her under. He pops back to the surface, keeping the girl's head underwater. Judy struggles. Joe, with nobody watching, seems determined to end things with her. But the girl's movements grab his attention and Joe's eyes seem fascinated. A sudden gleam lights up his expression, and he decides to release his catch. Judy's head surfaces. At the moment the girl is about to scream, her face twisted in anguish, Joe seals her mouth with a brutal kiss. The girl slowly melts in his arms as they embrace midstream.[24]

This scene, with little evidence of the irony or cynicism shown in much of the "reject screenplay," dances around the key metaphor of hate turning into love, which Gast's film transposition would maximize. In d'Eaubonne's rewrite, the same sequence, apparently preserved more or less intact, changes radically in tone.

Cette danse allongée à la surface de l'eau avait quelque chose de fascinant, en accord total avec les éléments, et ce mouvement, cette liberté, ce corps intégralement nu qui apparaissait et disparaissait sous la surface de l'eau évoquaient irrésistiblement l'amour.

Joë longea le rivage en commençaient à ôter sa chemise. Puis il déboucla sa ceinture et le slip tomba. À son tour, il piqua une tête dans l'eau.

À dix pas derrière lui, la silhouette de Chandley, fusil de chasse en bandoulière, se profila. Les yeux du vieux libraire clignotaient derrière ses lorgnons comme ceux de miss Wake devant "le Pendu Souriant."

"Parfait! parfait!" marmonna-t-il, un peu congestionné, au moment où Joë plongeait, tandis que Janet se retournait avec surprise à ce bruit.

Joë eut tôt fait de la rejoindre.

Il la saisit par les pieds et l'entraîna vers le fond. Elle s'y attendait et avait pris le temps de gonfler d'air sa poitrine. Nus comme des pierres, les deux jeunes gens coulèrent à pic.

Au bout d'un instant, Janet se débattit. Elle commençait à suffoquer. Son corps glissa entre les mains de Joë comme une anguille et remonta à la surface où le garçon la suivit. Il était derrière elle au moment où elle émergeait; elle ouvrit la bouche, l'air se rua dans ses poumons; Joë l'enlaça et il se laissa couler à nouveau de tout son poids.

Chandley, debout sur la berge, regardait Joë noyer la fille.

Sous l'eau, Janet se débattit plus fort, et Joë enlaça ses cuisses. Elle se tordait comme la blanche chevelure d'une torche. Ses membres minces ondu-

---

24. Arnaud, *Dossier de l'affaire,* 472.

laient et se détendaient furieusement, frappaient à la façon de fléaux ou de fouets; de ses pieds, Joë heurta sa taille creusée comme une volte de sirène. Dans ce mouvement, elle se renversa complètement sur l'épaule de Joë et son visage fut placé sous le sien. À deux bras, elle lui enserra le cou à son tour; ses ongles étaient des griffes qui le lacéraient, il la lâcha.

Ils remontèrent, Janet d'abord, Joë ensuite.

This horizontal dance on the water's surface held something fascinating, in complete agreement with the elements, and this movement, this freedom, this bare body that dipped in and out of the water spoke irresistibly of love.

Joe walked down the riverbank, peeling off his shirt. He unbuckled his belt and shed his underwear. Then he, too, jackknifed into the water.

Ten feet behind him came Chandley, hunting rifle slung over his shoulder. The old bookseller's eyes blinked behind his spectacles like Miss Wake beholding the "Smiling Hanged Man."

"Perfect, perfect," he snuffled, as Joe dove in, while Janet reversed in surprise at the splash.

Joe soon caught up with her.

He grabbed her feet and pulled her under the water. She knew what was coming and had filled her lungs. Stark naked, the young couple sank like a stone.

Soon after, Janet began to struggle. She needed air. Her body slipped between Joe's hands like an eel and shot up to the surface, where the boy followed. He was there behind her when she emerged; she opened her mouth and gasped. Joe put his arms around her and dragged her underwater once again.

Chandley, standing on the bank, watched as Joe tried to drown her.

Under the surface, Janet fought harder, and Joe held tight to her thighs. She was twisting like bright strands of torchlight. Her slender limbs waved and floated in a wild tangle; Joe's feet knocked against the mermaid whiplash of her hips. She flipped onto his shoulder, her face beneath his. She worked both hands tight around his neck; as her nails dug in, he let go.

They surfaced again, Janet first, then Joe.[25]

At first glance, the modifications can be explained simply by the need to follow the movie plot closely; it adds certain details to the "reject screenplay." Thus the scene is focused through an observer not found in Vian's text: the old bookseller, representing the "voyeur" perspective, which is also the mov-

---

25. D'Eaubonne, J'irai cracher, 117–18.

iegoer's (the scene in question is also the most erotic one in the film). Other discrepancies no doubt arise from Françoise d'Eaubonne's literary superego, which lengthens the text and does not skimp on "surface beauty" elements. Yet it is easy to point out how much farther the transformations go. In the novelization, all motivation and psychological complexity are lost. Instead of recreating a scene where Joe, as in Vian's text, "seems determined to end things" with Judy but finally "releases" his "catch," the girl who fascinates and subdues him, the rewrite flatly states at the outset that Chandley is watching Joe "drown [Judy]" (the modal verb "seem," essential in Vian's text, is lost here), then makes the outcome of the struggle a simply physical matter: if the girl escapes drowning, it is not because of a sudden change of heart on Joe's part, but because of the pain she inflicts (she claws his neck and he lets go). The dialectic of love and hate, sadism and seduction, is thus stripped away in the novelization. Françoise d'Eaubonne's text is diametrically opposed to the "reject screenplay," which may seem normal. It also departs from the film, which is obviously less so. No doubt the author thought her allegiance to the Gast version meant she needed to return to its plot points rather than following the "reject screenplay" story. As it happens, in the scene in question, staying faithful to the plot led to less psychological intensity and ambivalence.

Yet we cannot conclude that Françoise d'Eaubonne delivers a "faulty" novel. It hardly matters how her text relates to the series of works preceding it, from the Sullivan novel all the way to Gast's screenplay. What really counts is the book's placement in the "Romans-choc" collection, whose specifications it follows to a T. The style, which we might call a "New Look" version of "surface beauty;" the "hook," a racy film; and finally, the youth problem theme with America standing in for contemporary France, obvious on every page; all these elements ensure that the final link in the *I Spit on Your Graves* saga was a prime example of what novelizations were, what they could only be, at this point in the genre's history. More generally, Françoise d'Eaubonne's *J'irai cracher sur vos tombes* affords proof that novelization is definitely not a genre like any other and that its study requires a constant back-and-forth between the reading of text and context, between corporations and creation, between art and society. In this sense, novelization may be the most "complete" literary genre there is.

# CHAPTER 7

~

# Out of Breath

## *A Novelized Remake*
## *Translated Back into French*

Better to come right out and say it: Jim McBride's 1983 film *Breathless* was a flop. This American remake of *À bout de souffle,* produced and released at a time when Jean-Luc Godard's iconic film was not widely available through the fledgling video market, strives to mimic the French original in a laudable but ultimately painful way. The broad outline of the plot remains: young thug kills cop by accident; love interest turns him in just as they're planning their getaway. The setting moves to America, a mishmash Godard might have seen in his dreams. In Godard's film, Patricia Franchini (played by Jean Seberg), an American college student in Paris, hawks the *Herald Tribune* on the Champs-Élysées and falls for Michel Poicard (Jean-Paul Belmondo). The American remake instead has Monique Poicard, a French student enrolled in a Masters in Architecture program at UCLA, drop out to pursue Jesse Lujack (played by Richard Gere) instead of a degree. This change in setting with identical characters also comments on the clash of civilizations. The balance of power is obviously reversed, since in 1983's *Breathless,* French culture (Monique Poicard—played by Valérie Kaprisky—is an upper-class young lady), yields to the force of New World energy. Richard Gere embodies American youth, vigor, and, above all, erotic prowess (the novelizer even clocks his sexual performance: up to an hour at one point!). In short, from a technical standpoint, nothing is missing from this remake. Except for what really matters, in this case, the "auteur." Jim McBride is no Jean-Luc Godard, and consequently everything falls flat. The film is slow and meandering, further weighed down by the star's gesticulations. Gere seems like Douglas Fairbanks in *The Thief of Bagdad,* to put it mildly. A loud pop soundtrack makes the overacting even harder to stomach.

McBride's *Breathless* is nevertheless a key film for our purposes because its written adaptation uncovers the workings of the globalized market for novelization. The remake was first novelized when the film came out in the United States; the book was then translated into French for the movie's European release, looping back on itself. Nurtured by a fascination with American popular fiction, Godard's film, with a 1960 novelization that scarcely registered, inspired an American variant. This film in turn produced a trite, flat, professional novelization that was retranslated for the French audience when McBride's *Breathless* premiered in France. The feedback loop is complicated: there's no going back to the beginning after a pleasant trip through movieland. This is more like a Mobius strip, or rather a spiral, turning back on itself but always on different levels.

## *BREATHLESS*, A NOVEL BY LEONORE FLEISCHER

How can we even approach Leonore Fleischer's work? The novel's front cover specifies, "Based on the screenplay by Jim McBride and L. M. Kit Carson."[1] The first point is that the book makes every effort to hide its sources.[2] Worse than the American film version, which gives only a nod to *À bout de souffle,* the novelization makes no reference whatsoever to Godard's film.[3] The highly developed peritext of the American *Breathless,* as usual with Hollywood-style novelizations, piles on every possible endorsement and tie-in without so much as a mention of Godard or *À bout de souffle* (a marked difference from the film, with both Godard and Truffaut credited as original screenwriters). The next ingredient in this French intertext mashup is Jerry Lee Lewis and his 1958 cover of Otis Blackwell's "Breathless," the film's theme song, which it appears to show on film. . . . Not only is the song title an inexact translation of the French expression *à bout de souffle* ("breathless" in English means "out of breath," not exactly the same meaning conveyed in the original film narrative,

---

1. Fleischer, *Breathless,* cover.

2. Note that the inverse is more unusual, since Hollywood studios are highly protective of intellectual property rights.

3. The DVD version is equally dismissive of the film's origins; like the novelization, it fails to mention that McBride's *Breathless* is a remake.

with the protagonist at the end of his rope). But within the filmic narrative, the song takes on an importance that has no equivalent in Godard's *À bout de souffle*. The aim of this theme music is clearly to ground McBride's film in an American context. However, this strategy is all the more intriguing in that the film is still a virtual remake, even if it follows the original more in plotline than in inspiration. Clearly, Fleischer's paperback publisher must have concluded that mentioning the movie's origins might hurt sales, even the mere suggestion that the novelization was a "remake" of some French precursor. Further, the publisher thought that novelization readers might follow movie news, but for the most part, their audience would be Richard Gere fans with no idea of who Godard was.

The basic marketing techniques for McBride's *Breathless* were almost the same for both movie and novelization. Each featured Hollywood stars front and center. The same was true for melding film and literature: an experienced novelizer, Leonore Fleischer, was tapped to write the book. Her output was considerable without being distinguished.[4] Fleischer could be characterized as a serious writer, but only as a hired gun, never as a personal quest. Her solid reputation was probably why the front cover of her book qualified it as a "novel," where one would expect to find the less positively connoted term "novelization." At the same time, moving from novelization to novel mimics the rebranding of *À bout de souffle*: just as Jim McBride's adaptation of Jean-Luc Godard shows off its originality, the novelization has a self-important peritext. The way the novelization was written confirms this. Fleischer was allowed to do more than flesh out the screenplay; she was to give the text some cultural credibility.

This leeway is at once the hallmark of the experienced, trustworthy novelizer and also a tribute to the film, with a well-crafted novelization making it more "Oscar-worthy." (Fleischer novelized an average of two films a year from 1970 to 2000, many of them award winners.) Any departures from screenplay and film remain closely monitored. There are, to be sure, a few plot variations, but these can be explained by the unknowns of postproduction, always complex in Hollywood where even a final screenplay rarely makes it unscathed through the successive phases of filmmaking. In this instance, the main modifications are twofold, relating to both plot and style. To begin with,

---

4. Examples: *Agnes of God, The Fisher King, Rain Man, Scorpio,* etc. The novelization of *Annie* is a standout, not surprising from an author who admits being uncomfortable describing overly violent scenes: "I loathe violence, and I find it hard to write. . . . *Betrayed* was hard because of it, and because I couldn't understand a bright young FBI agent like Deborah Winger falling for a redneck Nazi like Berenger. I like writing comedy, because I'm naturally droll, and most of all I like writing about developing relationships, such as the one Charlie developed with Raymond in *Rain Man*" (Larson, *Films into Books,* 139).

the book narrative is slightly more complex (in plot twists, not in meaning), which goes with the novel's "superior" profile and further distinguishes it from rote retelling. Likewise, it comes as no surprise that Fleischer is sometimes heavy-handed in the two areas where early novelization writers excelled: the characters' psychological motivation, very detailed here; and filling in their biographies with extensive backstory. Second, the novel occasionally strives to be more "adult" than the film. One may still wonder if the book's some-what daring descriptions are enough to satisfy the film audience, since the movie featured Richard Gere in several relatively explicit nude scenes. As if by chance, the sexualizing of the written material is more concerned with the heroine's sensations rather than the male protagonist's (Fleischer has her say she's "getting wet," while the hero simply takes action). This would seem to suggest that the novelization's target audience is more male than female—unlike the film, aimed as much at women as men after the worldwide success of *American Gigolo* (1980). In short, here again, the novelization reader is in familiar territory. Compared to the film, the disorientation is minimal.

## À BOUT DE SOUFFLE MADE IN USA

Unlike Leonore Fleischer's approach, staying as close as possible to the direct source (McBride's film), the French translation of *Breathless* shows divided loyalties, both regarding the novelization and the carefully crafted cinematic intertext, both French and American.[5]

The most striking feature of the peritext is the skillful reframing of the cover art. On one hand, no doubt for contractual reasons, top billing is again given to the two American screenwriters, while the director's name is rele-gated to the overleaf, and then only in small type. On the other hand, the back cover displays the original director's name. The lead sentence introducing the cover blurb reads as follows: "In Homage to Jean-Luc Godard: A Gripping and Passionate Love Story." Such a vague statement assumes that the reader will understand its meaning. Relying on research that showed about forty percent of all French people would have seen À bout de souffle, in a theater or on tele-vision, this was an easy assumption. The American novelization is glaringly different, with a bold sidebar just above and to the left of the cover image: "Cheat the devil! / Grab the moment / Make it happen / Make it hot!" And the DVD cover makes it even clearer, labeled "Sexy Entertainment." In the realm of commercial novelization, these transformations are normal and usual. One

---

5. Fleischer, *À bout de souffle*, 161 (French translation by Michel Darroux and Bernadette Emerich).

may theorize that while the American audience—at least the intended audience for the film and book—might be put off to learn that *Breathless* was based on a French work, the French audience (more informed on this point) would be just as disappointed if Godard failed to appear in the peritextual apparatus.

Peritextual reworking is pursued elsewhere, but in this case, the adaptation of the novelized book bends to more ambiguous motivations. Everything seems to work toward making it more attractive to the French reader. Hence the use of the term "unpublished" (a practice relatively rare in the paperback industry in the early 1980s) or "for the discerning reader" (a detail probably intended to convince the French readership that McBride's film had evaded the moral censure and prudery affecting so many Hollywood remakes). Thus the distinctly more suggestive nature of the French version's cover art, based on the movie poster just as for Fleischer's book, but otherwise with more of an "ooh la la" factor, with some of the typography moved around. Gere and Kaprisky no longer seem to be in a close-up shot, but an (almost) medium shot, and one of Gere's arms has gone missing, providing a more enticing view of Kaprisky's breast. Furthermore, the French version's cover art discards the soft focus (while the *Breathless* cover still shows the dreamy David Hamilton influence then in vogue) to become a drawing. This conversion allows for a more contrasted chromatic representation of the protagonists' skin tones, so that the added contrast in the French cover illustration suggests something completely absent from the U.S. version: a moist atmosphere; saliva, sweat, and, metaphorically, semen. However, despite this adaptation of Fleischer's book to French tastes, *À bout de souffle Made in USA* goes not one step farther and fits neatly into the Hollywood star system. While claiming to acknowledge Godard, the information in the peritext fades out, not to call attention to the film but to the *actors,* Gere and Kaprisky, both famous enough in France[6] to be instantly recognizable, unlike the American novelization where their names rank above the author's in type size and color—and also to the book's *subject,* namely passion (read sex). A quick glance at the reworked cover art, which might see it as an effort to "Frenchify" the book and stress its importance to French film culture, ends up as a more mixed result. All things considered, the main point communicated to the reader is not the link to Godard, but the couple's kiss, Gere's face and Kaprisky's partial nudity.

Michel Darroux and Bernadette Emerich offer a translation fairly faithful to the original version. Anyone comparing the two books side by side will note only a small number of omissions, of liberties taken with Fleischer's text, and, relatively speaking, of translation errors—always bearing in mind that

---

6. Even Kaprisky was easily identifiable, though she was only at the start of her brief but meteoric career (after a few years and a few racy films, she would mainly work in television).

this type of project is done on deadline and regrettably underpaid. By way of examples, there are typical mistranslations, such as "basse ville" for downtown, which should be "centre ville"; "collège" (middle school) for college, which should be "fac"; "lieutenant" (army rank only in French) for police lieutenant, which should be "inspecteur"; and so on. The interest here lies in the fact that they show that the translation was done without reference to what is shown onscreen. In *À bout de souffle Made in USA*, the translators at one point confuse "copy" (of a book) with "photocopy" throughout a fairly long passage. An unusual error, if frequent in this type of translation, and it would have been totally impossible if the translators had enjoyed access to the film images as they worked. In the film, we see clearly that the object is a book, and the action is all the more notable since it leads up to the film's first big nude scene.

Overall, the translation respects the reading contract between Fleischer and her audience. Yet there is at least one trouble spot where the translators must have done something other than trying to reconstitute the original's style and tone as correctly as possible. This is the eternal question of a text's "local color," risky whether it is preserved intact or transposed to another cultural context. How to translate *freeway* into French? *Autoroute*? That's not quite it. *Autoroute sans péage*? Awkward. Leave it as "freeway" in the French text? This is how it ends up, skirting the problems of translation while rewarding the lesser effort of nontranslation with a "real feel." In one way or another, all translations have to take a stand in regard to this sort of hesitation and vacillation, but in the case of *Breathless*, the difficulty is compounded. One of the story's themes is in fact the meeting of two cultures, French and American, which is also the meeting of two languages. It would therefore be apt to make use of a problem inherent in any translation, highlighting this dimension of the work. However, we find none of the linguistic interplay, the mutual misunderstanding, the flirtatiousness that might be expected in *À bout de souffle Made in USA*, (even if only as a passing "homage to Jean-Luc Godard," who worked the language difference to great effect). Instead the language aspect ends up as a bit of a mess. A fine example is how Jerry Lee Lewis quotations are treated, either left in English in the French text (when the title song, "Breathless," comes up), or translated (as for "Great Balls of Fire"). By way of comparison.

Leonore Fleischer's original text:

That luck of his, had he given it away?

Hell, no! The next tape his hand closed around was the very one he'd given up hope of finding. Jerry Lee himself, king of the piano, jumpin', rockin' Mr. Jerry Lee Lewis. He slammed it into the tape deck and the four speakers sent the sound caroming around his ears. Oh, yeah! Music at last. "The killer rocks on," chortled Jesse.

"If you love me, please don't tease," sang Jerry Lee in that harsh dark voice, rough and intoxicating like moonshine whiskey. "If I can hold you, just let me squeeze . . ."

This is what living was all about—money in your pocket, a honey in your bed, and Jerry Lee Lewis on the stereo. "My heart goes round and round," he sang along with Jerry Lee. "My love comes tumblin' down . . . You leave me, ahhhhh, breathless!"[7]

The French translation:

Pourvu que sa chance ne l'abandonne pas.

Mais non! La preuve: la cassette qu'il venait de tirer du sac n'était ni plus ni moins qu'une de celles de Jerry Lee en personne. Le roi du piano. M. Jerry Lee Lewis. Il enclencha le magnéto et les quatre haut-parleurs déversèrent un flot de *vraie* musique dans la Porsche. *The Killer rocks on!* gloussa Jesse.

*If you love me, please don't tease,* chantait Jerry Lee de sa voix rauque, profonde, aussi chaude et raide que du whisky. *If I can't hold you, just let me squeeze. . . .*

Ça, c'était vivre! Du blé dans la poche, une gonzesse dans le plumard et Jerry Lee en stéréo dans la charrette. *My heart goes round and round,* chantait-il avec Jerry Lee. *My love comes tumbling down . . . You leave me, ahhhhhh, breathless!*[8]

Again, Fleischer's original:

"Look!" said Monica suddenly, pointing.

Jesse's eyes followed her finger. At the top of a mountain, a palm tree was burning. One of those sixty-foot Krazy Kat trees set aflame by the Santa Ana winds, standing alone with its upper leaves burning. It was a macabre, eerie sight, the crown of fire against the night sky. For a long moment they stared at it, Monica and Jesse, each caught up in the tree's silent, solitary immolation.

Then, "Great balls of fire!" laughed Jesse, and he stepped hard on the gas.[9]

---

7. Fleischer, *Breathless*, 15–16.
8. Fleischer, *À bout de souffle*, 15. Author's italics.
9. Idem, *Breathless*, 75.

The French translation by Darroux and Emerich:

> "Regarde!" s'écria Monique en pointant un doigt.
>
> Au sommet de la montagne, un palmier brûlait. Un gigantesque Krasy [sic] Kat dont le Santa Ana avait embrasé les hautes branches. Cette couronne écarlate qui se détachait contre le ciel de velours offrait un spectacle macabre, étrange. Un long moment durant, Monique et Jesse le regardèrent, captivés par cette immolation solitaire et silencieuse.
>
> "De grandes couilles brûlantes!" fit Jesse en éclatant de rire, et il redémarra en trombe.[10]

In the second passage, also a car scene where Monica and Jessie are listening to Jerry Lee Lewis, Fleischer plays on the double meaning of the song title. In the French version, though the English double-entendre is translated literally, it is doubtful that the reference, perfectly clear to an American reader, would be understood by his or her French counterpart.

Yet it would be unfair to blame the translators, who were only following their American blueprint here. It would be equally unfair to criticize Fleischer on the same point. The novelizer was confronted with a film that strangely toned down this aspect, fundamental as it was in Godard's work. In Jim McBride's remake, the hero and heroine speak different languages, of course, but the differences have more to do with levels of language in English than with switching languages. Monique Poicard sometimes has trouble expressing herself, but not overly (and she's a very quick learner: the theme of verbal misunderstandings appears at the beginning of the film, but then vanishes). She uses French interjections and exclamations from time to time, but again not overly, and most important, the film does not keep the Frenchwoman from understanding her lover's language at the most dramatic turning points. In this regard, the comparison between the famous final lines of Godard's *À bout de souffle* and what *Breathless* does to them, though it *visually* replicates certain elements of the final scene, is puzzling to say the least. McBride's film simply cuts Godard's ending, stopping with a sketchy gesture whose (predictable) consequence is never shown: the screen goes black when Jesse gets hold of the fallen gun and points it at the police squad. Fleischer's novelization spells out the rest, in line with the genre's tendency to expand, a technique in place since the first "film stories" were given a minimum of free rein. Exactly as in the novelization of *La Règle du Jeu* by Raymond Varinot, Leonore Fleischer

---

10. Idem, *À bout de souffle*, 85.

takes particular care with the beginning and end of her book, constituting an explicit "prologue" and "epilogue" to a narrative that is partially incomplete in the film. However, the way in which this expansion proceeds does not stray from the remake, thus departing from Godard's work.

First let us revisit the famous final lines of *À bout de souffle*:

"Faut téléphoner," dit un policier.

"Regarde," dit l'autre, "On croirait qu'il veut parler."

"Ils font tous ça," dit le premier.

"Celui-ci, ils ne l'acquitteront pas," dit l'autre.

"Je vais téléphoner . . ."

. . . Les ombres se mirent à bouger . . . À nouveau, il entrevit le ciel, strié de bandes noires et blanches . . . "Patricia! . . ." Il y avait ces cochonneries qui l'empêchaient d'ouvrir la bouche . . . "Oh! Patricia! . . . Regarde un peu le ciel d'Italie!"

Impossible . . . Une boue de plus en plus épaisse . . . Il se raidit:

"C'est vraiment dégueulasse!"

Patricia sursauta.

"Qu'est-ce qu'il dit?"

Le policier la regarda rapidement, puis détourna la tête:

"Il dit que vous êtes vraiment dégueulasse!"

La petite Américaine fronça les sourcils. Le corps du jeune homme eut une brève secousse et s'immobilisa.

Elle se tourna vers le policier:

"Qu'est-ce que c'est 'dégueulasse?'"[11]

"Call it in," one of the cops said.

"Look," said the other, "he's trying to say something."

"They all do that."

"This one won't get away with anything."

. . . The clouds started to move . . . once again, he glimpsed the sky, streaked with bands of black and white . . . "Patricia!" . . . but something was choking him. "Oh, Patricia, look, the sky is like Italy!"

Impossible . . . such thick mud . . . a contortion:

"C'est vraiment dégueulasse!" [It's really disgusting!]

Patricia recoiled.

"What did he say?"

"He said you're really disgusting."

---

11. These lines at the conclusion of the book are quoted from the novelization by Claude Francolin, *À bout de souffle*, 234–35.

The American girl frowned down as the young man's body briefly convulsed, then went still.

She turned toward the policeman:

"What's 'dégueulasse?'"

Now let us look at what *Breathless / À bout de souffle Made in USA* does with them. The book improvises freely here on McBride's film, which cuts off *before* Jesse's shootout with the police:

He was trying to say something to her and she bent close to his mouth.

"All or nothing, I warned you," he whispered.

*Between affliction and nothing, I choose affliction.*

She took his hands in hers. Overcome with pain, his fists closed, and she covered them with kisses, held them against her breast, her belly.

"No, Jesse, this isn't nothing."

She wished so hard that he could understand. His eyes were starting to go blank, he *had to* understand before it was too late.

He patted her belly, then his hand fell. Once again, he tried to smile at her and almost managed it.

"Yeah, the *muchacho*," he mouthed.

His labored breathing grew much too slow. He eyes opened wider and wider, as if in amazement. *When I woke up this morning, I never imagined it was the day I'd die.*

"Say . . . it . . . Monica," he begged her one final time.

Monica's heart was breaking into little pieces, shards of pain, seeing only Jesse, wanting only Jesse.

"Je t'aime, Jesse," *I love you,* she whispered in his ear (why had she waited so long to admit it?). *Yes? It's true, you are my love, my only one.*

Just as he wished, these were the last words Jesse heard.

One last breath broke through his lips in a swirl of bloody bubbles. Time started once more.

The police were on them. Hands gripped Monica, pulling her backward, a kick sent the gun flying, weapons prodded Jesse's neck and ribs as if he were still alive.

Monica flailed at Enright to get loose. He let her go.[12] (A few more paragraphs elaborate Monica's feelings.)

In her novelization, Fleischer tries to salvage something, but without much room to maneuver (it would have been unthinkable to change McBride's

---

12. Fleischer, *Breathless*, 189–90.

film, which neutralizes the unhappy ending with a testament to love and especially the unending love between the couple). The author puts a few words of
Spanish in Gere's mouth (in the passage quoted, "muchacho" refers to the baby
Monica is carrying) and sometimes uses phonetic English to transcribe the
male protagonist's less educated speech. For instance, in the "prequel" scene
when the pair meets in a Las Vegas casino, there are spellings like "whaddya,"
obviously contrasting with the non-native speaker's usages such as "I do not"
instead of the contraction:

> "*Mais c'est merveilleux, ça. Tu es formidable!*" Jesse couldn't understand the
> words, but there was no mistaking the tone of approval in her voice. With
> the last quarter safely stowed away, Monica asked,
>
> "What do we play next?"
>
> "Doctor," grinned Jesse.
>
> "I do not understand."
>
> "Never mind. I'm starving. Whaddya say we drop a few of these quarters
> on a bowl of chili?"
>
> "But I wish to gamble!" Monica protested, beginning to pout. "I came
> here all the way from Los Angeles to gamble."[13]

The French version:

> *Mais c'est merveilleux ça, vous êtes formidable!* (1) Il ne l'avait pas comprise,
> mais son ton admiratif n'était guère trompeur. Une fois la dernière pièce soi-
> gneusement ramassée, elle lui avait demandé:
>
> "A quoi jouons-nous à présent?"
>
> "Au docteur," avait-il répondu, en riant.
>
> "Je ne comprends pas."
>
> "Aucune importance. Je meurs de faim. Qu'est-ce que vous diriez d'un
> chili?"
>
> "Mais je veux jouer! avait-elle protesté avec une moue fâchée. J'ai fait
> toute cette route depuis Los Angeles pour jouer."
>
> (1) En français dans le texte.[14]

The jumble of comprehension and communication problems makes the
translation slightly baffling. Discounting the standardized pronouns (the formal "vous" is used, unlike what Monica says in the original and incompatible
with Jesse's coarser speech), one can see how improbable Monica's reaction

13. Ibid., 18.

14. Idem, *À bout de souffle*, 18.

to Jesse's sexual allusion is (she could hardly be that naïve, but in the American text it seems possible that she has trouble understanding because of her unfamiliarity with the language). By the same token, it is striking to note that the two characters' contrasting speech registers have disappeared (both Jesse's somewhat vulgar English and Monica's overcorrect usage blend into similar grammar, vocabulary, and spelling in *À bout de souffle Made in USA*).

These gaps between the American and French version do not, however, particularly get in the way of the reading experience. Not because the French reader would obviously not have Fleischer's original text in hand, but because Darroux and Emerich use translation strategies in line with how the remake steamrolled the original film—a simplification that Fleischer's novel had done nothing in the least to counteract. From Godard's film to McBride's, then from Fleischer's novelization to the French translation, a long process of cultural and linguistic normalization was under way, following the logic of all adaptations and transformations: while pretending to follow their original model, they exclude anything that departs from their own code.

This example—which would benefit from the addition of a thorough reading of McBride's film dialogues and the movie's French subtitles—allows us to reach a few general conclusions about the way intermedia "chains" are built over the lifetime of a work, be it film or book. First, the very idea of a "chain" is a dangerous metaphor. The various mutations in a work are not strung together like pearls, for the common-sense reason that no such chain exists: there are instead connections that tighten or loosen, but the homogenous and unique whole is only viewed in the mind's eye, not as readers or viewers might experience it. In the second place, the succession of elements cannot be conceived in terms of sedimentation, where each addition informs and transforms the previous layers. Each entity may not be autonomous, but they tend to proceed in a line rather than forming a feedback loop. However, this process must not be analyzed only as a loss—for instance, of cultural memory—but also as what makes new creations possible, freed from the weight or reputation of the original. A third and final point is that connections between different versions of a work are liable to skip around, as in nature: a new link may not communicate with the one just before it; this interaction can also occur at a distance. Thus the translation of Fleischer's book, where the relationship to the original version plays no role whatsoever, would probably find a French reader projecting memories of Godard's film onto it, however distant that film might be from McBride's remake or Fleischer's novelization thereof.

CHAPTER 8

～

# Cinephilia and Screenplays

## A FRENCH EXCEPTION?

Unlike film adaptations, which may stray so far from their literary original as to make it unrecognizable, novelization supposedly only parrots a film plot. A novelization, some say, is nothing but a product derived from a screenplay, they say, something both stripped bare (the novelization retains none of the screenplay's technical details) and dressed up (novelization adds a bit of diegetic sauce to make everything read more smoothly).[1]

The connection between novelization and screenplay is undeniable. The history of the genre reveals numerous contact points, even though the two have never been truly united. In the French tradition, the connection between novelization and screenplay is even less clear due to the wealth of intermediary forms, on one hand, and, on the other, because of the screenplay's own highly complex status. The film-novel, apparently closer to the screenplay form, seems more prestigious than novelization. Film novelizations look more like Harlequin romances, except for one detail: in the genesis of French cinephile culture, the published screenplay, which appeared as a genre during the 1950s, is considered a literary model in its own right, and even, within the

1. Part of this chapter first appeared, in a slightly different version, in *Fabula LHT (Littérature, histoire, théorie)*, 2 (December 2006) (www.fabula.org/lht/2/baetens.html).

film-novel universe, as one of the most highly rated. Further, it is understandable that French authors, inclined toward the more ambitious forms of novelization, would be attracted by the screenplay model. The French approach to the genre characteristically has more porous borders between published screenplays and novelization (in the English-speaking world, it seems that novelization's attraction to the screenplay model is less intense). In this context, it is vital to take a closer look at the interchanges between novelization and screenplay, since novelization's classic approach tends to suppress the scenario form.

In the French tradition, the "author's" greater presence should also be noted, in both the literary and cinematic sense of the word. Here again, French-style cinephile tradition seems to play a determining role. As Antoine de Baecque points out, this love of film is both a passion and a discourse: a way of being, of living for the cinema, but also a way of talking about and critiquing films, surrounding the image with a framework of discourse that gives it real meaning. From this perspective, the "caméra-stylo" or "camera-pen" concept quickly became no mere *fusion* of literature and film but rather a *reciprocal stimulus,* the true "author" being one who composes in both cinematic and literary terms. Rather than abandoning literature in favor of cinema, literary "authors" were urged to move toward filmmaking, while cinematic "auteurs" were encouraged to become writers (the arc of Truffaut's career is a prime example, moving from film criticism to directing, then from filmmaking to novelization, among other outlets). In so doing, it is hardly surprising that novelization, often dipping into the screenplay and vice versa, plays a major role: Carrière (who novelized Tati before embarking on a brilliant career as screenwriter and novelizer), Duras and Robbe-Grillet (who collaborated with Resnais but also self-novelized and self-adapted their work, often indiscriminately), but also Godard (one day the four volumes of his *Histoire(s) du cinema* [*History/Histories of Cinema*] should be reconsidered as an example of novelization) and Jean Cayrol (who wrote both the screenplay and novel of Resnais's *Muriel*) are so many examples of notable film novelizers who lay claim to the status of author, whether in cinema or literature. Here novelization's enhanced prestige is present on every level, not only when great directors turn to writing: witness fewer mass-market publications (Stock published several early New Wave film novelizations in paperback, but in higher-end trade paperback format); the involvement of major publishers (Gallimard, after its 1920s venture into movie tie-ins, would now publish white-cover novelizations of Truffaut, Louis Malle, or Fellini); and above all, the strict separation between film novelizations and books based on televised series (either French or foreign).

In trying to analyze the deep connections between film-novel, published screenplay, and novelization, as well as the author perspective, it is readily apparent that in both cases this is culturally based, deriving as much from the notion of film "auteurs" as (even more meaningfully) the articulation of a work and its screenplay. In the French tradition, screenwriting seems to be a legitimate form of writing (and publication), and the screenwriter's work is not walled off from the filmmaker's. This outlook has a considerable effect on the genre of novelization. Just as filmmaker "auteurs" are not recognized as "real-life" authors until they have also written books, this cultural pressure will push them to publish something between novelization and book-form screenplay, each of these considered as valid forms of writing. Inversely, when cinema and literature are bedfellows, nonfilmmaking authors also venture into writing inspired by movies, including novelization. If we agree that a screenplay is a legitimate form of writing, not frozen in time, ending when the script starts shooting, then we must also accept that novelizers, arriving "after" the film just as screenwriters came "before," seem to approach their work with a greater degree of latitude.

## A FEW CONTEMPORARY TRENDS

In contemporary novelization, two major trends emerge. The first features novelists who turn toward the cinema to produce a work sui generis. Such texts stand apart from traditional novelization even as they follow in its footsteps: *Cinéma* [*Cinema*] by Tanguy Viel,[2] *La Tentation des armes à feu* [*The Temptation of Firearms*] by Patrick Deville,[3] and *Le Goût amer de l'Amérique* [*The Bitter Taste of America*] by Alain Berenboom[4] are a few examples. The second trend involves filmmakers publishing new forms of screenplays that do not flatly reject the shooting script model (which also lives on, perhaps even thrives), but rather invent a new mixed genre, fed by many influences (novel, film-novel, screenplay, novelization) but informed by a deep connection to novelization as practiced by contemporary fiction writers. Some representatives of this trend are works such as *La Vie de Jésus* [*The Life of Jesus*] by Bruno Dumont[5] or *Nuit noire* [*Dark Night*] by Olivier Smolders.[6]

Let us begin with the fictional component of this new output. Just as in the past, authors—in this instance Alain Berenboom, Patrick Deville, and Tan-

---

2. Viel, *Cinéma*.

3. Deville, *La Tentation*.

4. Berenboom, *Le Goût*.

5. Dumont, *La Vie*.

6. Smolders's *Nuit noire* will be analyzed in detail in the following chapter.

guy Viel, three writers quite different one from the other—are no beginners, nor would they come to novelization as a moneymaking venture. These are well-known authors having already produced one or several books with major publishers. But their work has two things in common.

First of all, the basis of novelization is never a film's simple diegesis, carried over as a "film raconté," for example Lubitsch's *The Shop around the Corner* or Capra's *It's a Wonderful Life* for Berenboom; Hitchcock's *Topaz* for Deville; or Mankiewicz's *Sleuth* for Viel. The original film instead appears as a fragment, aspect, or theme *within* a new diegesis. The film is thus named within the text, the opposite of standard procedure for novelization.

Next, the filmic material that inspires the novelist goes back and forth between the film story as diegetic continuity and a series of images, visual impressions, and snippets of script—in short, *parts* of the film, but parts likely to engender a new whole, with the help of fiction.

These two defining features—recourse to novelization identified as such; the back-and-forth between continuous sequence and discontinuous image—explain more generally that novelization by fiction writers above all follows a pattern both tightly woven and porous: the film becomes the backstory or a narrative serving as counterpoint to a different one. The novelization is never the sole fictional material but is mixed in with another narrative. This structure gives rise to three variants, which are of course far from mutually incompatible:[7] First comes synecdoche, the *mise en abyme, pars pro toto,* or part for the whole: in *La Tentation des armes à feu,* the novelization based in part on *Topaz,* this works like a magnifying glass allowing for a deeper understanding of the complex, shifting love story in the book. Next is *commentary*: in Viel's *Cinéma,* which follows the plot of *Sleuth* shot by shot, so that what slow emerges is not (only) Mankiewicz's movie as it runs on the tape the book's narrator is watching, at home and turned up loud, but even more an image of the narrator himself, defined by his unusual attachment to the film. Finally, there is *transposition*: in *Le Goût amer de l'Amérique,* projecting onto a context (today's multicultural Brussels) and onto local characters (including one who thinks he's no less than James Stewart, the man as well as the actor) a series of Stewart's most famous films.

A counterclaim might be that these changes in level, which upend, which hijack the originals, arise merely from a need to skirt copyright problems, never a concern for traditional novelizations ("authorized" if not commissioned outright by a film's producers). This may be undeniable, but it ignores

---

7. A fine example of these three intertwined functions can be found in a novel by jazz great and writer André Hodeir, *Play-Back* (Paris: Minuit, 1983), which starts from a film scene with Harry Langdon.

the positive aspects of this second-wave novelization, which allows for the opening of a dialogue between the retold film and the novel relating it, on the one hand, and for increasing the breadth of fictional material on the other. Unlike traditional novelizations, a reworked film undergoes one or two transformations. First, the narrative framework of this work no longer appears as the mold of novelistic hypotext, but instead acts like a *springboard*: the original film no longer need be exactly replicated; it invites the author to rework and reimagine, not repressing the cinematic hypertext, of course, but recasting it (from an ekphrastic, visual point of view). Second, the film-object also opens to the much more extensive world of cinephile culture encompassing it.

On this subject, it is worth noting that narrators in contemporary novelizations often enjoy concealing, or at least waiting to reveal, the title of the film that inspired them: this withholding of information establishes complicity with the reader, at least the "savvy" reader liable to spot the book's cinematic intertext and appreciate the interplay of sampling, commentary, analysis, speculation, and modifications offered by the narrator. The importance of cinephile culture is also obvious in the choice of films to be novelized, rarely recent ones: just as cinephile culture places a great deal of emphasis on situating a film within a time frame, endowing the cinema with a history as rich as literature's, so Berenboom, Deville, and Viel select films they must have found unforgettable that coincided with the moment they first became film lovers (Berenboom even makes *forgetting* James Stewart one of his narrative's guiding threads). Finally, the relevance of the cinephile outlook is demonstrated in the passion tying the narrators to the films they watch, retell, and interpret. Cinema is never a mere pastime; it is a gateway to certain secrets that are rightly deemed existential. The narrators of the novels in question feel manipulated by movies, which seem to overpower them, yet they do not resist the temptation to manipulate movies in turn, in the hope of unlocking hitherto unknown secrets. Novelization thus becomes a true linguistic act, but of a singular nature: in Berenboom, Deville, and Viel, cinema "must" be talked about (the narrators cannot do otherwise, discussing movies is an imperative), but always with a twist (and this remove gives them a margin of freedom).

This distance from classic novelization translates to every level that denotes the genre: traditional novelization sees itself as the film's double, not as separate from it. In all the examples cited above, however, adaptation is the dominant mode: Berenboom, Deville, and Viel make use of the cinema for their own ends, even when they seem to stick obsessively to their subject. In the same way, the narrators feel free to describe and to give visual details that in traditional novelization often remain stereotypes, literal clichés lifted from a ready-made supply of descriptors. An example of this new opening to visual possibilities might be Deville's experiments with illustrations, weaving a very subtle network of connections between an image from *Topaz* and other outside images, exactly as his prose blurs the border between various fragments of his book's narrative and thematic mosaic. Finally, they obviously aim to achieve at least as much, in terms of impact, textual density, and imparting emotion, as the films they mirror. This is very clearly what Berenboom is trying to do, bringing a now-neglected actor, Jimmy Stewart, back to life as a character.

## NEW SCREENWRITING APPROACHES

On to filmmaker-authors, meaning "auteurs" in the cinematic sense who also become writers. Here we find, provided we discount the technical differences separating an "offbeat" novelization from new forms of screenwriting, the same underlying trends. Just as fiction writers' novelization takes shape as a second-wave form of writing, including various reworked parts of a film, Olivier Smolders's "written" synopsis of *Nuit noire* in *La Part de l'Ombre* [*The Shadow's Share*],[8] or Bruno Dumont's written version of *La Vie de Jésus*, appearing a few years after the film release,[9] also represent a double or split form of novelization. In each case, Smolders's a shorter form and Dumont's longer, we are dealing with the description of a film to come, its production no sure thing: Smolders produced his highly literary text in search of underwriting (which was very slow to come, to the point where *Nuit Noire* might only have existed on paper); Dumont does not call his work a screenplay but rather "text of the screenplay for the film *La Vie de Jésus*," (and the differences between this "text" and an actual screenplay are such that we may and should consider Dumont's book a quasi-independent work). Yet, also in each case, the as-yet-unmade film (and both authors may well have believed their film was never to be, at least as they envisioned it) is described with such precision, at once visual, narrative, psychological, and emotional, that the works in ques-

---

8. "Oscar et Marie Neige" was the original title of what would later become *Nuit noire*. This text is found in pages 125–40 of Smolders, *La Part de l'ombre*.

9. An analogous yet different case is *L'Humanité* [*Humanity*] by the same author, in theatrical release in 1999, then published as a novel in 2001 (Paris, Éditions Florent Massot). Insofar as the novel follows the film, at least in institutional terms, it can only be read as a novelization. But this time the book came first, so that the film appears retrospectively as a self-adaptation. Dumont's case is plainly close to what other writer-directors (Pasolini, Antonioni, probably Robbe-Grillet and Duras, as well) have done when they worked in both fields simultaneously. For practical reasons, we will deal only with the Dumont text that seems to stay closest to the extant shooting script.

tion strike the reader as out-and-out novelizations, or else as novelizations of the new type being explored in the realm of prose fiction. More than simply revisiting a film plot (in this case virtual, but quite vivid in our imagination) the director-author also adds a second dimension by including commentary and analysis, even though this return to the film takes different forms in the case of a self-adaptation (Dumont and Smolders) versus adaption of another's work (Berenboom, Deville, and Viel). Just as fictional novelizations do more than relive a story, directors' self-novelizations are not simply screenplays rewritten more or less in novel form, but in fact are works that are truly written, even reinvented in the act of writing (and not conceived under the rule governing screenplays, to be turned into something else, namely a film).

Analogies to fictional novelizations do not end here. Thus in Dumont and Smolders we find the same rejection of the genre's theoretical platitudes (anti-adaptation, lack of visuality, non-"remediation") as in Berenboom, Deville, or Viel. This creative and independent concept of their screenplay-related novelization is easily observed in the highly original use of illustration. In Smolders, the layout, then a sequence of a few stills from the film, allow for the creation of a third state of the work, in between the film imagined in the first screenplay draft and the film that was shot (but not yet edited): a variation on the narrative thread, evoking a story neither readable in the text or visible in the film. In Dumont, who does not use stills but rather set photographs, the gap between the "text for the screenplay," which is not the screenplay, and the illustrations, which are not images from the film itself, is stressed no less strongly. This difference is evident in the area of content, with images that do not always correspond to something going on in the text. It also concerns chronology. Written earlier than the screenplay, the text is illustrated with set photos not found in the film, since here film equipment and crew members are in plain sight.

A brief analysis of the enunciative and modal structures in *La Vie de Jésus* shows the sometimes dizzying complexity of this type of writing, which is impossible to categorize simply as a shooting script. From the text's very first words, we are struck by the pervasive presence of the narrative voice, which breaks sharply with the cliché of "objective" film writing: *narration* and *monstration* (to borrow André Gaudreault's terminology[10]) prove indissolubly joined. Except, identifying the narrative voice is immediately problematic. Is this the screenwriter speaking? Certain hints point in this direction, such as the use of technical vocabulary (like "traveling shot"), or more strongly, the use of the simple past tense (which assumes an "omniscient" point of view).

---

10. Gaudreault, *Du littéraire au filmique*.

But the technical terms are used only sparingly, and verb tenses vary wildly. Even more than the screenwriter (or the director, since in the French film "auteur" tradition these roles sometimes overlap), the narrative voice might be thought to represent that of the film audience, experiencing the action and images as they occur. Yet far from filling an anonymous narrative role, these characters appear as witnesses to the scenes represented, almost as actors about to step into the diegesis in which they are clearly participating. The narrative voice in the text sometimes employs a collective "we," but unlike the "we" in *Madame Bovary*, the collective actor designated by this pronoun does not exit after the first few paragraphs. Finally, there is the intermittent inclusion of two very surprising stylistic devices in a text that first seems a sort of screenplay: first, Flemish patois, all the more striking in the text since the narrator uses it intrusively, unpredictably, almost spasmodically; and second, extensive use of indirect free style. Both of these tie the narrator's voice to the characters' as they tell their own story.

By way of example, the opening passage of *La Vie de Jésus*:

Novembre

C'est un jeune qui bourre en mob à fond de régime, en Flandres. Casque intégral, peinturluré, sans visière aucune, qu'on voit s'in regard bleu et tout son corps derrière aplati. Recherche de vitesse probable pour être ainsi à l'extrême, penché sur le guidon, immobile, et attendre que ça vienne. Drôle, sur son casque, l'autocollant: le Cœur Sacré! Mais c'est Freddy! il a la vingtaine et souvent qu'il oscille dans ses plus grands virages avec la force centrifuge. Ça dure pas mal: c'est la vitesse jointe à l'inactivité de Freddy qui se traîne autant que sa bécane fait du boucan dans s'paysage. C'est un jogging de lumière qu'il porte sous son blouson, c'est un Décathlon. Alors nous, on accélère et on laisse notre Freddy devenir petit, l'abandonne et fonce sur sa route prochaine, mais on s'élève aussi, s'essore donc.

Hideux novembre dans le Houtland, une ville donc blottie d'où qu'c'est la mobylette ichi qui parvient à s'insurger. La tranquillité de la nature avec son ciel et si bas et mon Freddy alors qui s'annonce à bourrer encore, à emmerder le monde si reclus là.

À tous ceux qui attendent décembre, voici venir Freddy!

November

A kid going flat out through Flanders on his motorbike. Full helmet, all decals, no visor whatsoever, just beneath that let's check out his blue eyes, his body to the wind. Finding the fastest gear, bent over the handlebars, holding on hard and leaning into it. Funny touch, huh, the sticker that says "Sacred Heart!" You betcha, it's Freddy! Barely twenty and peeling through the curves with centrifugal force. This goes on a while: the speed and Freddy's stillness as his bike whizzes through the countryside. A sparkling jersey under his jacket, Decathlon brand. Then we step on the gas and watch our Freddy get little in the rearview, we head up the next road, twisting higher, too.

Hideous November here in Houtland, the Flemish boondocks this crotch rocket buzzes through. The calm of the country with its sky and so low and my Freddy who's on the move again, getting on everyone's last nerve.

For all of you out there awaiting December, here comes Freddy![11]

Along with jarring shifts in narrative voice, accentuated by abrupt and repeated changes, sometimes within a single sentence, there is an even more intriguing instability, alternating "omniscient" and "restricted" narration. The narrator is generally omniscient, experiencing images from the film and elements of the story (not as plot points, but conjuring images from the film) at the same time as we, the book's readers, do. This feigned ignorance, since the narrator knows the characters but does not seem to understand what they are going through, is not maintained in any absolute or systematic way. At times, and no doubt because of the unpredictable, fluctuating nature of its focus, the narrative voice offers a broad view of the action, eventually assuming the role of chorus in Greek tragedy. Thus the "chorus" announces, toward the middle of the book, that events are about to take an inevitably tragic turn that transforms a series of misadventures into a tale of fate, of crime and punishment, and finally of "grace" (the narrator uses this term several times, with a pronounced and inescapable effect on the text's ideological interpretation). The very fact that the narrative voice admits to limited knowledge of the events described strengthens the interpretations it suggests. The narration's strength is not the kind that imposes a single meaning on the work (at the end of the book, it is unclear who "Jesus" may be: Freddy, both kind-hearted and violent, a Christ-like figure and a murderer; or perhaps Kadder, Freddy's Arab victim, who pays with his life for flirting with Freddy's girlfriend). But it clearly illustrates that moving from shooting script to novelization enhances film writing: including images from a "vision" of a film in the written version may enrich and restart a dialogue with the reader.

---

11. Dumont, *La Vie*, 15.

~

# CHAPTER 9

# Olivier Smolders and the Self-Novelization of *Nuit noire*

## *The Possible and the Preferable*

It is often posited that the only "good" novelization is a clever, slanted, tongue-in-cheek one.[1] To novelize in a more stimulating way, the thought goes, authors need a way around the restrictive legal parameters plaguing the genre. Plagiarism is one, quite popular online (only consider *Star Trek* fan fiction). Skirting copyright law is another: take the case of a film novelized through the use of a completely fictional narrator, mediating between the reader and the original concept (Tanguy Viel's tactic in *Cinéma*), or else rewriting films through characters who imagine they are starring in a film (in Tierno Monénembo's *Cinéma* [*Cinema*],[2] the protagonists reenact *The Oklahoma Kid*, among other roles). But the simplest solution, as long as the screenplay copyright is secure, is to write your own book, to "self-novelize." Graham Greene did it, Jean-Claude Carrière did it, even Steven Spielberg did it (with the help of a ghost writer, true). However, as Alain Berenboom emphasizes, these novelizations—he refers to Greene's—sometimes fail to maintain enough distance from the screenplay *avant-texte*:

---

1. An earlier version of this text appeared in *Image (&) narrative*, No. 16, 2008 (www.imageandnarrative.be/house_text_museum_baetens_smolders.htm).

2. Paris, Seuil, 1995.

Revenons aux trois novellisations de Graham Greene (*Le Troisième Homme, Le Dixième Homme, Qui perd gagne*, J. B.). On peut en effet s'interroger sur leur échec littéraire. Y avait-il écrivain mieux placé que lui pour réussir l'opération? Romancier d'exception, manifestement influencé lui-même dans son style et dans ses sujets par le cinéma, souvent adapté et par les meilleurs, écrivant lui-même directement pour le cinéma qu'il connaissait bien, écrivain de théâtre aussi donc de dialogues, pourquoi de toutes ces multiples facettes de sa personnalité littéraire, celle de novellisateur est-elle la plus faible et la moins intéressante? . . . Pourquoi un roman est-il si différent d'un scénario? Cela tient peut-être à ceci: un roman est un univers à lui tout seul. Alors qu'un scénario n'est qu'une des pièces du puzzle que formera le film terminé. . . . Or, dans ses novellisations, Graham Greene ne parvient pas à donner un équivalent littéraire aux autres pièces du puzzle. Il fait un roman d'un seul des éléments, le scénario ou l'histoire et, à la lecture, il manque le reste.

Let us return to Graham Greene's three novelizations (author's note: *The Third Man, The Tenth Man, Loser Takes All*). We may indeed wonder why they were literary failures. What writer could have been better equipped for the task? An acclaimed novelist, clearly influenced by cinema in both style and subject, often seeing his films adapted by the best directors, writing directly for the cinema himself and familiar with its ways, playwright as well and thus experienced in dialogue writing: why, of all the multiple facets of his literary personality, was novelization the weakest and least interesting? . . . Why is a novel so different from a screenplay? Perhaps this is what is at work: a novel is a universe unto itself. While a screenplay is only one piece of the puzzle that will be the final film. . . . Yet, in his novelizations, Graham Greene does not manage to come up with a literary equivalent for the other pieces of the puzzle. He makes a novel out of just one element, the screenplay or plot, meaning everything else is missing from the reading experience.[3]

Even as regards Carrière, despite his clear and correct notions about the screenplay's impermanent, transitory status, his self-novelizations are less convincing than his Tati novelizations, *Monsieur Hulot's Holiday* and *My Uncle*. As for Spielberg, novelizations put out under his name are not far removed from novelization's industrial format, which leaves little room for an author's literary superego.[4] This makes it hardly surprising that directors and screenwriters who are would-be novelists often opt either for a variant of the script, whether

---

3. Berenboom, "Les pratiques virtuelles," 166–68.
4. Tsala Effa, "La novellisation du film."

or not they wish to innovate within the genre (Duras and Robbe-Grillet being the most noteworthy recent examples) or opt for a "derivative" book with a film setting rather than a novelization, per se (Ingmar Bergman penned several books of this type[5]).

Belgian director Olivier Smolders and his work on *La Part de l'ombre*[6] should be approached in this context. Smolders produced a very complex novelization proving that this writing strategy was far from bankrupt. Knowing that Olivier Smolders's film work skirts traditional narration, it may seem contradictory that he chooses a literary form that, while experimental, seems likely to compromise the author's project by assigning it a traditional novel framework. The danger here is not producing a bad novelization, as most often happens, but novelizing at all.

## ADAPTIVE AND LITERARY CINEMA

Reactions from certain parties—funders, media professionals, friends, or simple filmgoers—allow Olivier Smolders to cast his directorial work as "literary." Here are two instances cited in *La Part de l'ombre*:

> Ce jour-là, je me présentai dans un atelier de production afin d'obtenir un financement pour un film dont le scénario, inspiré d'un fait divers, tenait en une phrase: en 1983, à Paris, un étudiant japonais invite une jeune femme dans son appartement et la mange. On me répondit d'emblée que ce projet avait bien peu de chances d'aboutir, d'une part *parce qu'il était trop littéraire*, d'autre part parce que le traitement que j'envisageais n'était pas assez japonais.

> That day, I went to a film production facility trying to get financing for a screenplay with a one-sentence pitch: "Paris, 1983: a Japanese college student asks a girl up to his apartment and then eats her." Right off they told me that this project was unlikely to amount to anything because on one hand *it was too literary* and on the other my treatment was not Japanese enough.[7]

---

5. See the last chapter of this book.

6. Smolders, *La Part de l'ombre*. For more details on Olivier Smolders, born in 1956 and auteur of some ten short subjects before the 2005 full-length feature *Nuit noire*, see: www.smolderscarabee.be/oli_bio.php (last accessed 9 June 2017).

7. Smolders, *La Part de l'ombre*, 5, italics by this study's author.

De commissions en commissions, de dossiers en dossiers, de réécritures en
réécritures, je m'efforçai de faire ressembler le scénario de *Nuit noire* à un
modèle connu, le film de genre fantastique, espérant rassurer ainsi les par-
tenaires potentiels. Ils restèrent cependant tous sur leur réserve. . . . Le pro-
ducteur avec qui je m'étais associé ne voyait plus d'autres portes où frapper
(alors même que la télévision nationale venait de refuser le scénario avec un
argument qui eût ravi Ozu: "*ce film n'est pas cinématographique* car le per-
sonnage n'évolue pas.")

Meeting after meeting, draft after draft, I kept trying to make *Nuit noire* fit
a familiar model, a fantasy film, hoping to attract potential partners. But no
one came forward. . . . The producer I was working with didn't know where
else to look for funding (once the Belgian national television company had
turned down the script with a critique that Ozu would have loved: "*this film
is not cinematic* because the character doesn't develop.")[8]

These firsthand assertions paint a backhanded portrait of what literary
cinema is thought to be: something *deprived* of what is basic to the never-ending literary adaptations found onscreen. This means plot and action leading
toward an end, that is, a climax and conclusion, characters with recognizable motivation, and a believable setting, even if it is pure science fiction.
Bizarre and paradoxical as it may seem, a "literary" film would thus end up
as "non-novelistic," even "anti-novelistic," or to put it more positively, strictly
"cinematic."

A similar approach toward literature in cinema corresponds fairly well to
Olivier Smolders's own ideas, since he has always been opposed to reducing
literary cinema to the practice of adaptation. Not because he rejects adaptation, but through a stronger conviction about the connections between text
and image: image *shows,* while text *suggests* (or to use more technical terminology, image relies on *denotation* and text on *connotation*). For Smolders,
this difference is so great that transposing a text into image or vice versa is
meaningless; putting images into words strips them of their directness, while
visualizing a text removes the evocative power of words. Smolders draws the
conclusion not that an author should avoid combining text and image, due
to their lack of common attributes, but rather play up the contrast between
them, mining the possibilities offered by fitting film and image together. In
Smolders's eyes, film *ought to become more literary,* pursuing new combina-

8. Ibid., 146–47, italics by this study's author.

tions that surpass or counterbalance the sterile exchanges of adaptation from one media to another.

In Smolders's work, the strategy of a "literary" cinema translates to a series of formal or semantic choices that the label "fantasy" or even "Surrealist" cinema associated with his work may belie. Before returning to this question at the end of this chapter, let us try to give an overview of Olivier Smolders's "literary" poetics as a director, recalling the artistic strategy of Chris Marker, the implicit role model of many contemporary filmmakers. Three elements are worth emphasizing here: first, the choice of the short subject form and its marginal distribution system, limited to festivals and film archives, allowing the author to steer clear of the narrative demands of full-length films; next, the attempt to integrate true literary texts into the cinematic work, whether this be through quotations or original creations, in collage mode, that is, contrasted in a manner that is intentional, calculated, careful; and finally, the acceptance of certain dead zones, that is, images or words that are lost, impossible, invisible, inaudible, unreadable. . . . The overall effect of this kind of cinema is a tribute to the imagination: the best films are those we only imagine—beginning with what we are shown. From this point of view, there is something of Marcel Duchamp's *anti-retinal* stance in Smolders, however else conceptual and fantasy art may diverge.

The question of novelization, with Olivier Smolders conceiving a book of self-commentary and self-analysis as an adjunct to the launch of his first feature film (*Nuit noire*), is not simply a technical one. Confronted with his own "literary" poetics, the genre's classic strategies are utterly meaningless: novelization can no longer be the pathway from film to book, since such a procedure, fundamentally a transmedia passage from filmic to fictional narrative, would be a death sentence for Smolders's core vision of literary cinema: appealing to the imagination through the collision of words and images in a structure mostly unmoored from narrative concerns.

In fact, the problem presents two intertwined aspects. The first is that of novelization itself: can one, must one, novelize? Smolders answers in the affirmative, even if he takes off in quite a different direction from standard novelization and further rejects a totally "freehand" style (his solution, examined in detail below, is rather to novelize by tweaking the conventional format of the director's commentary). The second aspect, generally unrecognized but crucial, is that of novelization in book form over any other format that might be more suitable (a bonus commentary added to a DVD version, for instance). For Olivier Smolders, the choice of book format appears less problematic than novelization, per se: the book's structure guarantees a slower, more reflective, more convenient reading environment, allowing for a better understanding of the work's dense collage of combined effects, while offering new approaches to the interchange of image and text so characteristic of literary cinema. It is certain that the multiplication and diversification of the work's "margins" found in current DVD format influenced the general composition of *La Part de l'ombre,* beginning with the book's unconventional dimensions, corresponding to the size of a DVD. But Olivier Smolders's fundamental approach is tied to the material nature of the book-object, used to more direct advantage in his treatment of novelization. The question of novelization is not uniquely framed in terms of relationships between film and novel forms, but also and perhaps crucially in terms of the book-object.

## FROM ANTINOVELIZATION TO
## REINVENTING THE GENRE

No reader with even a glancing knowledge of Olivier Smolders's work will be surprised to note that *La Part de l'ombre* bears little resemblance to a commercial novelization. However, a rapid comparison to an outline of the genre's conventional forms will help us more readily grasp how *Nuit noire* was turned into a book.

To begin with, like other chapters of *La Part de l'ombre,* "Nuit noire"[9] is not a true novel. If certain parts of the book evidence a more or less novelistic development, considerations and reviews of the original text plus Olivier Smolders's cinematic work take up the larger part of the book. The genuinely novelistic or narrative piece thus becomes a backdrop for musings on the film's reception, notes from the set, additional script ideas. One might even say that "Nuit noire" is not presented as a work of fiction at all, and the first-person voice is that of the filmmaker, not a character or other narrator.

Similarly, a second noteworthy difference from the conventional model is that the larger text incorporating "Nuit noire," meaning *La Part de l'ombre,* is not made of one piece. Far from containing material relevant only to the film *Nuit noire,* on which the book is supposedly based, *La Part de l'ombre* resolutely adopts the heterogeneous form of a *collection,* emphasizing its breaks in style and tone. It goes over the bulk of Olivier Smolders's film work, but from one film to the next, there are radical shifts (furthermore, which bears further scrutiny, not all his short subjects are included in the book, nor are they presented in chronological order, or in a manner proportional to their

---

9. For purposes of clarity, we will follow the typographical convention of placing the title of an independent work in italics (the film *Nuit noire,* in the present case) and in quotations the title of part of a work (herein the chapter "Nuit noire," the final section of *La Part de l'ombre*).

length). From this point of view, rewriting happens, tweaking film reality, with relationships reinvented through the book process. As regards *Nuit noire,* this rewriting represents a break with the filmic material, since Olivier Smolders inserts an intentionally ambivalent section entitled "Oscar et Marie-Neige" ahead of "Nuit noire." On one hand, "Oscar et Marie Neige" is presented as the first, unrealized version of what would become *Nuit noire.* On the other, these two parts of the book, which follow each other chronologically but have a different ontological status (since the first corresponds to a screenplay never made into a movie and the second did result in one), are brought together in terms of illustrations, thus becoming two panels of the same diptych, with no distinction in status or precedence.

Finally, it is noteworthy that unlike what happens in a standard novelization, the film *Nuit noire* is not retold but shown. Put another way, something is missing (narrative, to use shorthand) and something else fills in for it (a series of images that obviously constitute a narrative, given the knowing selection and composition of film stills). Most of all, there is a very clear relationship between the missing and compensating elements: the extent to which Smolders rejects textual narrative is what paves the way for meaningful image sequences. Classical novelization, as we have seen, often does without images (except in the book's perigraphic material, and then only for commercial reasons). Smolders, however, relates his film, or at least "a" film, *through intermediary images.*

## THE DOCUMENT AS NARRATIVE TOOL

Studying these three major characteristics of "Nuit noire," or more exactly, of *La Part de l'ombre* (for it seems absurd to separate this section from the work as a whole), the first problem to address is indisputably that of novelization itself. The absence of the genre's conventional signs, on one hand, and reliance on analysis and commentary, on the other, might lead to the conclusion that Olivier Smolders's book is well outside any form of classic novelization. This too-swift assessment, in my opinion, misses out on the author's very original take on the form.

If there is indeed novelization in this new version of *Nuit noire,* it is primarily due to the very singular reuse of the screenplay. Unlike the rather technical format film scholars prefer for the publication and study of screenplays, Olivier Smolders opts for an eminently *written* presentation of his material. He completely abandons the idea of a scene-by-scene exposition (whether dealing with material that was shot or not). The organizing principle tends instead toward a thematic-type structure and does not shy away from a highly literary style (the exact opposite of a dry cinematic approach). On one hand, replacing chronological order with a thematic approach stresses how greatly this film work resists being categorized in conventional narrative terms. On the other, maintaining a consistent and distinctive style throughout the book adds to its literary quality. The effect of these two rules is anything but identical: on one hand, narration is avoided; on the other, literature wins out. At first glance, neither of these techniques brings the text closer to novelization. Still, on closer examination, each reinforces the idea that "Nuit noire" is truly the double, or a double, of the film by the same name. Rejecting narrative does not turn the text into a document, but rather means faithfully rendering a film that defies traditional narration. From this standpoint, the antinovelization dimension of "Nuit noire" is one possible way to translate the antinarrative stance of *Nuit noire* the film. And the intentionally literary tone of the self-analysis demonstrates an attempt to grant the text independence from the film on which it is based. On this point, "Nuit noire" differs little from other novelizations, which also strive to be read as separate works despite the legal and institutional strangleholds affecting them.

Moreover, and this is a second reason we can truly refer to novelization, Olivier Smolders does not simply rework his screenplay; he includes drafts of scenes that were never shot (to wit, "Oscar et Marie Neige") as well as scenes cut in the final edit. These additions, with their indisputable narrative orientation, undergird the novel-like tenor of the "Oscar et Marie Neige" / "Nuit noire" diptych. Smolders may actively resist the pitfalls of traditional novelization, yet he is quick to novelize the "impossible" and "absent" parts of his film: he fills in what could not be done due to lack of financing, just as he rescues parts of his film that were left in the cutting room. There is nothing really new in this twofold approach: commercial novelizations also favor add-ons (for instance, including "prequels" to the novelized diegesis; especially in serial novelizations, amplification—of time, places, characters—has become the rule rather than the exception), while paranovelizations emerging from the DVD format phenomenon rely on providing "deleted scenes" (which seem more and more likely to have been filmed only with an eye toward an "enhanced" version: purchasing the wide-release version thus becomes almost a given). In the case of *La Part de l'ombre*, the way it deals with the impossible and the missing does not yield to this line of reasoning. In Smolders, what the book manages to salvage in terms of the "impossible" seems crucial. The transposition of *Nuit noire* is as much the reconstruction of what could not be made as the echo, with variants, of what did make it to completion. At the same time, the limits of the film's distribution to some extent blur the distinction between the novelization of the nonfilm (meaning the novelization of all that had to be sacrificed) and a commentary on the film that was produced but was never in wide release. This uncertainty makes "Oscar et Marie Neige" / "Nuit noire" a novelization that is certainly unorthodox, yet not unacceptable as such: the story of the final film may not be told, but the fact that Smolders also shows us a film that was never made is more than compensation, the mixture of the two being in fact one of the book's principal issues.

## NEITHER LONG FORM NOR SHORT: THE COLLECTION

The argument in favor of *La Part de l'ombre* as a novelization, however, exceeds mere story line considerations. One of the essential points of Olivier Smolders's artistic strategy is its reticence regarding the cinematic equivalent of the novel: the full-length feature. Of course, the difference between full-length film and short subject is not in the least quantitative. If the long form is problematic, it is because, unlike the novel, it forces the author to use a series of tools that he or she would sooner be free of: action leading to the resolution of a problem, characters acting in a "believable" and "motivated" manner, a spatiotemporal universe governed by the laws of reason and common sense, and so forth. *Nuit noire,* which Olivier Smolders conceived as an attempt to stretch the boundaries of the long form by introducing ten-odd short films with their own complex visual and narrative viewpoints, raises quite an exciting problem from this perspective: should he or shouldn't he provide a verbal equivalent the length of a novel? Or, less anecdotally speaking: how should the length of a novelization be managed?

The traditional narrative is *paraphrasable.* This is furthermore one of the reasons why visual filmmakers like Olivier Smolders are so reluctant to be storytellers. But the possibility of paraphrase also implies a purely quantitative dimension: paraphrase can mean to *abridge* or the contrary to *lengthen.* As Hollywood-type cinema amply demonstrates, this can mean churning out a 90-minute film from a science fiction novella as easily as from a lengthy historical saga, and equally, reducing any commercial movie to a tag line or "pitch." Olivier Smolders's solution naturally runs counter to these practices, not for the sake of being different but because the modifications he uses are in line with the cinematic work. "Nuit noire," which may well function as the summary of a film (note that I say *film* rather than *narrative*), is of a length that defies the novelistic norm. However, the objective of this reduction is not so much to create an antinovel or nonnovel as to pave the way for an unprecedented structure within the novel form: a collection of linked short stories.

Novelization, which sides instinctively with the long-form narrative, meaning a minimum number of signs and pages, is fundamentally incompatible with the textual regime of the short story and the linked collection.

As it happens, Olivier Smolders draws maximal benefit from this opening to the collection form, since its less conventional status is more in line with his critique of the traditional narrative. Three main tactics work together to intensify the antinarrative effects of the short story—the short subject of the textual realm. To begin with, reducing *Nuit noire*'s "material" to about twenty pages frees up space for other texts, allowing for the inclusion of "Oscar et Marie Neige." In splitting up the scenario, consequently, the novelization reinforces the collage esthetic that Smolders has always sought. In addition, the diptych "Oscar et Marie Neige" / "Nuit noire" creates an internal contrast to the film, baring its "virtual" component (*Nuit noire* could have been something quite different, and the reader could have necessarily become a spectator for whom the onscreen experience is only a suggestion). It becomes equally possible to multiply points of contact with other sections and other chapters, each part of the book having its own special, irreducible style. Finally, and this is a capital point, the dissociation of novelization and volume, meaning the lack of connection between film narrative and book structure, also opens the way for significant temporal shifts. For this book synthesizing Olivier Smolders's visual production does not do so in chronological fashion. A new structure is invented, with an opening text on *Mort à Vignole* [*Death in Vignole*], the work preceding Smolders's most recent film, *Nuit noire*. Just as *Nuit noire*'s cinematic narrative is not transposed in a way that follows the chronological chain of shots and sequences, but instead lays bare the film's vehemently nontemporal thematic framework. *La Part de l'ombre* proceeds through a complete restructuring of Olivier Smolders's career, revealing different meanings, or more precisely, the most profound workings of his mind. The book as a whole obeys a narrative organization that is like a mirror or a funnel: the book opens with a double autobiographical twist; it ends with a no less revealing look at the author's ambitions and dreams; both parts bracket attempts to project this "personal" material onto outside characters. A structure like this, which prioritizes the first-person point of view, also subtly undermines it: the autobiographical opening quickly sweeps the filmmaker's ego aside, even while putting it forward (father-figures and the question of paternity instead come to the fore); the conclusion, which seems to relate a crowning achievement (graduating from obscure short films to a full-length feature aimed for wide release), strips the author of command over his film, which is framed as a collective, impersonal object. The resultant gap is full of disjunctions: "je est un autre [I is another]," as Rimbaud said, but the other is also myself. Without its short-story format, *La Part de l'ombre* would never have produced such effects. Yet these effects enrich the practice of novelization more than they vandalize it, as a quick run-through might suggest, far as this book is from the genre's baseline.

## A "VISUAL" NOVELIZATION?

An even more radical innovation is at work in *La Part de l'ombre*'s illustrations, the third way in which Olivier Smolders's book breaks the traditional mold of novelization. Here again, a superficial reading of the volume would fail to reveal its breakthroughs. Does the author limit the role of images to that of simple illustration, as is the case for commercial novelizations where film stills or set photos are sprinkled through the text? At first glance, neither the sort of images selected nor their placement in the book is particularly spectacular. However, the interweaving of words and photographs explores territory rarely encountered in the domain of novelization.

One of the decisive aspects regarding the combination of words and images is the degree to which they are similar or divergent. In light of Olivier Smolders's ideas on "literary cinema," *La Part de l'ombre* would be likely to avoid, as an example of what might be qualified as a "visual novelization," any *redundant* articulation of the two types of signs. The novelization should not be uniquely visual because of the importance given to the description of things to see—an aspect generally stifled in contemporary novelization—or again, more flatly, because of the inclusion of stills or set photos, but also and most important because of the possibility of an "unreconciled" montage between text and image. This is in fact how "Oscar et Marie Neige" / "Nuit noire" proceeds, contrasting sharply with the more conventional use of images in the preceding sections, going far beyond abandoning black and white. In the book's final diptych, Smolders moves toward a skillful montage of the two classes of signs, leading them to communicate in an active and productive way, exactly as in his films. To establish such a dialogue, a crucial point is for the book to operate independently from the written realm. In *La Part de l'ombre*, this declaration of independence takes several forms. Negatively, at first, through the systematic proscription of any captions as well as ignoring the respective borders of text and image: the stills from *Nuit noire* inscribe a visual chain that eliminates the divide between "Oscar et Marie Neige" on one hand and "Nuit noire" on the other, as if the images from the film indiscriminately accompany the film that was actually made as well as the one that exists only through the book's description of it, and then positively, through the synthetic and thematic coherence of the stills selected, which in themselves constitute both a visual whole, plate by plate and double-page by double-page, and also throughout the "Oscar et Marie Neige" / "Nuit noire" section, a consistent visual sequence that can be paged through—and mentally transformed into a narrative—without reliance on the printed word. Moving on to the text, it is clear that neither the ascendancy nor the autonomy of the images loses ground. Just as the text does something besides simply retelling the plot of the film, the pictures are tasked with carrying the narrative weight of the novelization. Here, the images do not refer back to a text reproducing the film: they instead allow the reader to sketch out the narrative of a film he or she may not have seen. The existence of this *structural* contrast between the written and iconographic parts of the book buttresses the profoundly visual character of the novelization, the particular care taken in the choice and layout of illustrated pages representing a sort of explanation of the book's openness to a nonredundant contribution from photo stills.

There is yet more, since *La Part de l'ombre* also contains an ironic but acute reflection on the relationship between the book's photographic images and the film work from which they derive. In this regard, the primordial difference is evidently between the mobility of the cinematic images, at least at the level of their projection, arousing an illusion of movement, and the fixed nature of the photographic images, which seems inalterable. Olivier Smolders does not rework this distinction in the manner of Chris Marker in *La Jetée* [*The Jetty*], for instance, or other directors intrigued by photomontage. He rethinks the photographic tool in attaching it to the theme of taxidermy, one of the guiding threads in *Nuit noire*. The film sways between action and fixity on several levels: the narrative takes off, then stalls (or stops and starts before getting under way); the humans and animals populating the story are alternately natural and naturalized; as for the images, they are not confined to a single state, but go back and forth between the stability of the photograph and the mobility of film. What counts here are the constant exchanges: the photographic images do not pin the moving image like a technological taxidermist, but instead try to generate stories in the mind of the audience; photography is not simply used to mirror taxidermy but also as a springboard for the imagination. A novelization's visual quality likewise involves the capacity to make the reader conjure invisible films: "Les plus beaux films sont ceux qu'on imagine sans les avoir jamais vus" [The most beautiful films are those we imagine without ever seeing them].[10]

---

10. Smolders, *La Part de l'ombre*, 8.

## CODA: RETURN TO SURREALISM?

It may seem incongruous to reconcile novelization with Surrealism, a literary movement that certainly had a visual bent but was openly hostile toward the novel and its humanistic wiles. And yet *La Part de l'ombre* is the kind of work that readily brings Surrealism to mind, not the least because the filmmaker himself, and critics as well, make repeated mention of the fantastic. For Smolders, it seems that the appeal of Surrealism is less in its supposed fantastic or even fantasy side, but more rooted in a precise narrative technique. Discussing his initial outline of *Nuit noire,* he remarks:

> J'imaginai alors recourir à un modèle narratif inspiré des films surréalistes, alternant effets de collage, citations détournées, lieux communs, obsessions personnelles et provocations tragi-comiques.

> I imagined modeling my narrative on Surrealist film, alternating collage effects, roundabout quotations, platitudes, personal obsessions and tragi-comic provocations.[11]

Surrealism's concentration on the photographic medium, claimed by some even to unite the twin poles of literature and cinema in a "writing of the real,"[12] admits such a derivation. In a certain way, *La Part de l'ombre* also promotes the same medium: photography plays more of a part than simply illustrating the text or deriving from the filmic image; it becomes a full-fledged medium, establishing connections between the written and the cinematic poles. In a certain way, one might even say that it takes their place and that the other media present within or around novelization all tend toward the mode of photography, a stable narrative tool and visual representation of a world still only partially imagined.

However, this sort of synthesis, relocating a work in the Surrealist camp while neutralizing the split between text and image, with a nod to a certain idea of photography, does not fully account for Surrealism as practiced by Olivier Smolders; we know he derives more from Paul Nougé than André

---

11. Ibid., 128.

12. According to Rosalind Krauss's analysis in *Du photographique,* 1990, photography is writing in that it repeats while dissociating, which for Krauss, in line with Jacques Derrida, is the very essence of writing, with its literary (automatic writing), pictorial (symbols as reflections of the unconscious), and cinematic (montage-collage) versions being mere variations. From Krauss's viewpoint, endorsing photography as the ultimate Surrealist technique overcomes the apparent contradictions between the movement's revolutionary character in literary terms and its often academic outlook in pictorial terms.

Breton. As Nougé's biographer,[13] Smolders incorporated two key points of the writer's esthetic for a novelizing collection like *La Part de l'ombre*: on one hand, mistrust of the nonconstructed (the arbitrary nature of the *found* object prized by Breton, which Nougé consistently countered with the notion of the "objet bouleversant," or the subversive or *upsetting* object) and the scrupulous avoidance of anything that eases the internal tension of a work; on the other hand, the primacy given to mental projection rather than intellectual reasoning, to sensations rather than feelings, to the imaginary rather than entertainment. From this perspective, why not consider that *La Part de l'ombre* may represent a later example of fiction writing that the Surrealists themselves, for whatever reason, were never able or willing to produce in all good conscience?

---

13. Smolders, *Paul Nougé.*

# PART III

# The Poem-Novelization

# CHAPTER 10

# The Poem-Novelization,
# A Sub-Genre?

## PRESENCE AND PERSISTENCE OF POETRY

One of the great surprises in the historical study of novelization, a surprise purposely set aside up to this point, is no doubt uncovering a poetic variant of the genre. This poetic form exists; it is old and varied, encompassing the classic domains of poetry in verse as well as prose poetry, even if it seems richer in the English-speaking world than in French literature. But perhaps this impression is distorted by the existence of anthological work in English, like that of Philip French and Ken Wlaschin,[1] with an extremely broad reach, while French historiography focuses more on a single period, that of Surrealism. Most of the time, however, whether in French or English, this poetic output does not connect to novelization.

Alongside novelizations in verse, an example of which we will examine more closely below, quite another tradition exists, recently brought to light by cinema scholars, wherein the relationship between poetic writing and novel-

---

1. French and Wlaschin, *Faber Book*. Examples of novelization are scattered throughout the volume, though novelization does not fall within any of its part-historical, part-thematic categories ("The Silent Camera," "Hollywood," "Movie Houses and Moviegoing," "The Stars and the Supporting Cast," "Behind the Camera," "Films and Genres," "Movies as Metaphor," "TV and the Afterlife of Movies"). Of course, there are any number of French anthologies on the theme of "writers at the movies," but none specifically concerned with poetry about cinema.

ization is much more obvious. In an article on the novelizing practices at the end of the silent era, Viva Paci starts from the following observation:

> La France, on le sait, connaît au cœur de ces années vingt une démultiplication de publications sur le cinéma, dont des rubriques consacrées au cinéma dans les quotidiens et diverses sortes de publications périodiques spécialisés de cinéma: grand public, corporatifs et pour cinéphiles avertis. Et chacune offre des niveaux différents de "récits écrits de films," et par-là, si on veut, différentes formes de novellisation.

> France, as we know, saw a wealth of publications on cinema during the 1920s, with movie-oriented columns in daily papers and a wide variety of specialized periodicals: for the general audience, the trade, and for dedicated cinephiles. Each offered different levels of "written accounts of films," resulting, if you will, in different forms of novelization.[2]

Within this nebula of textual accounts, the author points out a very particular case, which notably broadens the domain of what might be called "poetry-novelization." Rereading the critical work of writers such as Louis Delluc, Germaine Dulac, or Jean Epstein, proponents of the "École de la Photogénie [The Photo Genius School]," Viva Paci brings short analytical texts to the foreground, texts that strive to make the reader *see,* rather than simply describing images from French avant-garde cinema at the time:

> Mais alors que la novellisation, *au sens strict,* consiste à traduire par l'écriture l'agencement d'actions que le film propose, redoublant et valorisant l'intrigue . . . *les récits de films* inscrits dans ces textes vont valoriser une nature du cinéma qui échappe à la narration, fondant la spécificité du cinéma sur les éclats de photogénie, des courts moments d'émotion, des visions défamiliarisées. Ce que ces textes tentent de faire c'est plutôt de nous laisser voir les images grâce à la qualité et au style de l'écriture, qui fait la part belle aux effets de grossissement, de surenchère, d'amplification, de répétitions, de ralenti, afin d'épuiser tous les aspects de la visualité à laquelle les auteurs des textes ont été confrontés en regardant le film.

> But while novelization, in the strict sense, consists of translating into written form the configuration of action a film proposes, reinforcing the plot . . . *the accounts of films* within these texts will enhance a variety of cinema that defies narration, founding cinema's specificity on bursts of "photogénie,"

---

2. Paci, "Pas d'histoires," 206.

short moments of emotion, de-familiarized visions. What these texts attempt
to do is rather to let us see images thanks to the quality or style of writing,
giving top billing to blowups, excess, amplification, repetition, slow motion,
as a way of using up every aspect of visuality the authors encountered while
viewing the film.[3]

Here is one such *récit de film,* cited by Paci, from a text by Jean Epstein:

Les ombres se déplacent, tremblent, hésitent. Quelque chose se décide. Un
vent d'émotion souligne la bouche des nuages. L'orographie du visage vacille.
Secousses sismiques. Des rides capillaires cherchent où cliver la faille. Une
vague les emporte. Crescendo. Un muscle piaffe. La lèvre est arrosée de
tics comme un rideau de théâtre. Tout est mouvement, déséquilibre, crise.
Déclic. La bouche cède comme une déhiscence de fruit mûr. Une commis-
sure littéralement effile au bistouri l'orgue du sourire.

The shadows shift, tremble, waver. Something is decided. A gust of emotion
pulls at the mouths of clouds. The face's orography lurches. Seismic trem-
ors. Capillary wrinkles try for a gap in the fault. A wave sweeps them away.
Crescendo. A muscle bucks. The lip is ruffled with tics like a theater curtain.
Everything is movement, imbalance, crisis. Click. The mouth gives way like
the splitting seed pod of a ripe fruit. A sliver of lip cuts through the organ
fugue of a smile.[4]

The border between *récit de film* and "novelization-poem" is very porous
here. Be that as it may, the corpus on which Viva Paci has shone a new light
seems closer to novelization-poetry than to standard novelization. The "École
de Photogénie's" *récits de film* remain nonfiction narratives, based on a filmgoer's visual experience. They do not reject the original medium's parentage.
As journalistic or documentary writing, they do not go much beyond what
Marion and Gaudreault term "protonovelization." But these limitations do not
prevent them from functioning in a poetic register. Finally, insofar as their
aim is to bring images back to life in the reader's mind, these *récits de films*
make a clean break with the nonvisual stance of narrative novelizations, thus
moving closer to the world of poetry.

---

3. Ibid. Paci's italics.
4. Epstein, "Grossissement," in *Écrits sur le cinéma,* 93.

# THE IMAGE AS AN OBJECT OF DESIRE
## OR AN OBJECT OF FEAR

Poetry has a longstanding partnership with the art world, especially the visual arts. From Homer describing Achilles' shield to John Ashbery's *Self-Portrait in a Convex Mirror,* among a thousand and one other examples from every culture and era, poetry has always been concerned with evoking works of art, some that certainly do exist, others imaginary. How these encounters play out proves as varied as the possibilities of writing itself. Poetry can describe a work of art, placing us squarely in the realm of visual poetry or *ekphrasis,* as a noteworthy study by Robert Heffernan would have it.[5] But it can also strive to *become* the image, increasing what Jean Gérard Lapacherie calls its *grammatextual*[6] content, and to imitate spatial and visual properties through verbal means. Finally, poetry can also choose to transpose the work that serves as its model or springboard, that is, to use the image as a *generator.*[7] Whether it *describes, imitates,* or indeed *transposes* an image, poetry is never without a hidden agenda. It uses the image to take a position, for example, to gain legitimacy at a historical moment when the text feels threatened by the force of the image. This attempt at legitimization is liable to rely on very different strategies: poetry may enter into a coalition with the image to take advantage of its prestige, but it is just as likely to take strong exception to the image. If for instance an unknown or minor poet writes about Picasso or Beuys, one might suppose that this stance is halfway between admiration and self-promotion.

Often when poetry comes into contact with images a veiled tension between the two arises. Their encounter often implies a sort of competition, as if poetry only measures itself against the image in order to suggest its own superiority. Fear of the image, whose meaning always exceeds verbal description, is a historic leitmotiv of this literary genre.[8] Hence the multiple attempts to maintain a strict separation between the possible applications of the two mediums. Ever since Lessing's *Laocoon* (1766), which remains a benchmark, it has been customary to attach the image to spatial arts and the text to temporal ones, creating a divide between the two great branches of artistic expression: simultaneity and linearity.

With the advent of cinema, this division between temporal and spatial arts is breached. Moving picture, image sequence, and film has as much to do

---

5. Heffernan, *Museum of Words.*

6. Lapacherie, "De la grammatextualité."

7. Good examples of this procedure are found in the collection "Les Chemins de la création" [The Roads of Creation] (Éditions Albert Skira).

8. For more details, see Mitchell, *Iconology.*

with space as with time. With the cinema, visual art begins to consider itself a form of *writing* (thus a temporal art). But there is more: the specificity of the film image is to be an object that considers itself *not as poetry but as prose*. Any generalization is of course dangerous, but we can risk hypothesizing that visual poetry seems linked to the fixed images of painting or sculpture, while literary works arising from the cinema's moving pictures[9] fall on the side of fiction writing. To put it bluntly: to transpose painting or sculpture, the choice is poetry; and to transpose film, choose the novel. This opposition may seem abstract, but it clearly defines how we think about the literary transposition of different image classifications. In this sense, cinema exposes a certain idea of poetry. Poem-novelization, for its part, moves well beyond this notion.

But how to explain the spontaneous painting/poetry association, on one hand, and cinema/novel, on the other? The cultural value of the visual object figures into this equation: in general, painting is considered *nobler* and cinema more *common*. Hence their almost natural alliances with poetry and prose, respectively, further distinguishing themselves by the objects to which they attach. But even more decisive is the relationship of continuity or discontinuity on the material level: painting and sculpture are *spatial* arts, while cinema is an essentially *temporal* medium. From these general ideas, very decided conclusions are often drawn, for example, the conviction that poetry is more closely aligned with space than time, which becomes cinema's purview.

Poetry, apparently more legitimate as to the visual objects it describes and closer to being "beyond time," is clearly idealized. Through its object, more prestigious and seemingly more durable, less hemmed in by temporal constraints, in contemporary culture, poetry emerges as a haven of eternity, a practice less polluted by the fleeting futilities of time and narrative, in short as the eternal "monument" of Horace's dreams. . . . Poetry's trivialization, which will be discussed later on, can be fully understood only in this idealistic context.

## WHY THE POEM-NOVELIZATION?

In the domain of novelization, choosing poetry rather than the novel does not mean choosing poetry over the novel, but rather choosing one form of poetry over another, and this is where the fundamental interest of the poem-novelization resides. Indeed, the poem-novelization upends many a literary commonplace. While novelization "in prose" often sticks to preexisting for-

---

9. This is the case in the generally accepted use of the term, which minimizes, for instance, the contributions of short films or experimental cinema.

mats (serialization, popular fiction, screenplay, photo-novel), the poem-novelization instead strikes out on its own. The choice of poem-novelization is
almost tantamount to a manifesto, and the genre is inseparable from poetics.
This is not unique or monolithic. The way the Surrealists seized on silent film
and the world of "serials" is far from the way Allen Ginsberg wrote about
Marlene Dietrich, for instance. That said, a rapid survey of the field of poem-
novelizations will highlight several guiding principles.

First of all, rewriting a film in poem-novelization form is an attempt to
reconnect with the present, the contemporary, the *hic et nunc,* which is often
lacking in modern French poetry. The excessive seriousness of this poetry;
its tendency to consider itself an adjuvant to, if not a competitor with, phi-
losophy; its half-hieratic, half-apodictic tone; its conception of the poet as
thinker[10]; all of this is certainly admirable, as long as such a concept of poetry
does not become hegemonic, as is unfortunately the case in France today. The
interaction between poetry and cinema is one way to make large thematic
sections and stylistic tones that are missing in French, more accessible in a
certain kind of American poetry: the wish to bring mass culture and private
life into the mix; openness to "the world we live in;" and a more direct way of
addressing things, for instance, a stay in rehab, a dull evening in front of the
TV, mounds of filth or even . . . yesterday's movie, or today's.

Second, the poem-novelization proves close (and this is an added advantage) to constrained literature, that is, any form of writing that starts from
a predetermined rule or set of rules, then tries to elaborate a text without
"cheating," that is, without deviating from the rule or rules formulated at the
outset.[11] Constrained literature, which takes exception to romantic notions of
"spontaneous" inspiration, provides a very useful framework for understanding many aspects of a poem-novelization, which quite often approaches the
film as a *reservoir of constraints.*

A third aspect is that any poem-novelization implies a certain idea of
poetic form. The very expression "to novelize in poetry" is something of a
contradiction in terms, but the contradiction is intentional. The attempt to
create "unmarked poetry," as one might speak of an unmarked police car
(which still is nothing but a police car) by sending it headlong into the realm
of mass culture, skirting poetry's traditional concerns and questions, poses
some tricky writing problems. There can be no question of maintaining a hier-
atic style, even though such an impossibility is far from absolute (still, the
risk of an awkward pastiche is always on the horizon: approaching Buster

---

10. Essentially, this is found in the so-called "minimalist" poetry that has dominated the
avant-garde for several decades, see Baetens, "Enough."

11. For further details, see work in *Formules, revue des littératures à contraintes.*

Keaton through the style of, say, André Du Bouchet would be quite a feat). Yet the form's major problems cannot be ignored, either. The poem-novelization thus serves as the research laboratory for writers seeking to "unpoeticize," to breathe new life into, poetry.

The fourth and final point is that associating cinema and poetry does not create a level playing field: the proximity of the filmic image sheds light on the *specificity* of the poetic text. Even readers who have not seen the film on which a poem-novelization is based know that it is a cinematic work; this inevitably leads to a "contrasted" reading of the text. Such a comparison leads to questions about the properties of its writing. In this way, mobilizing the filmic infratext will prevent poetry, even when intentionally "unmarked" due to its subject and its rejection of a certain poetic style, from becoming "natural." Added to the care for constraint, the management of writing in an environment where media come into contact can help reformulate, in a different way, the question of the antistereotype. How to evade clichés, platitudes, repetitions? How to act as if one is not seeking a solution by pressing the problem to its logical end (something that would be perfectly feasible and even exciting from a literary standpoint), and working within the stereotype?[12] The poem-novelization is an opportunity to invent a form of poetry that accepts the trivial in all its guises, except for the writing itself.

## THE POEM-NOVELIZATION, AN ANTINOVELIZATION?

The poem-novelization must take some notice, however brief, of novelization in the realm of fiction. Does it then follow that novelization in prose acts as a foil to poetic novelization? That would seem to be the case. The poem-novelization, as explained by Gaudreault and Marion, does not shy away from the presence of the original medium: the great majority of poem-novelizations do not pretend to be original works. Likewise, the poem-novelization does not in any way pose as an antiadaptation: the poem arises from an image, not from a film's verbal, scripted subject, and from this standpoint, the effort of converting one medium into another is omnipresent, unlike what happens in many fiction novelizations. A similar strategy can be noted concerning the problem of "remediation," which is a high-stakes issue for the poem-novelization. Unlike the fictional novelization, which tries very hard not to compete with the force and impact of film images, the poem-novelization does not flinch when facing the cinema's challenge. Proposing a text that not only

12. This solution is somewhat related to what Jean-Benoît Puech calls "literary suicide." See Puech, *Du vivant*.

shows things, but shows them in a manner just as lively, direct, and vivid as the original film did, is part of the contract between writer and reader of a poem-novelization.

Once such definitions are accepted, it is clear that in an even more general way prose novelization appears as almost the exact opposite of what we call poetry. Inversely, the poem-novelization is scarcely a canonic illustration of the genre. Novelization is a narrative: poetry, as normally envisioned, is not. Novelization is moreover an especially classic kind of narrative, where clichés abound, something that true poetry would leave far behind. Novelization is a narrative that tries to be *the least "literary" possible,* light-years from the received poetic ideal. It is no stretch of the imagination, then, to conclude that novelization is a prime genre for poetry. The poem-novelization provides a chance not to move beyond poetry but rather to rethink it, via a practice theoretically *resistant* to the idea of poetry as well as its outward forms.

This is the framework within which the poem-novelization must be considered. Novelizing in poetry must be conceived as a way of intervening in the literary and media landscape of our times, through the very subtle means deployed by contemporary poetry. The poem-novelization is a form of writing *against. Against the novel,* whose monopoly on cinematic adaptation it wants to break. *Against the cinema* or rather against a certain idea of the cinema, to which it opposes, unlike documentary or avant-garde cinema, a less essentially narrative conception of the medium.

~

# CHAPTER 11

# Jean-Luc Godard 1, 2, Infinity . . .

In the domain of novelization, Jean-Luc Godard has a legacy as rich and varied as his cinematic work. Novelized in fiction when *À bout de souffle*[1] was
new, then in the poetry of Adrienne Rich, author of a famous contemplation
of *Pierrot le Fou* [*Pierrot the Madman*],[2] and a handful of others,[3] eventually
self-novelized in books like *JLG/JLG* or *For Ever Mozart*,[4] which blur the borders between poetry and prose, while remaining within the genre of novelization—all this makes Godard the logical choice for the final part of this section.
Concentrating on his French-language novelizations alone, it is tempting to
contrast the classic novelistic version of *À bout de souffle* by Claude Francolin
with the poetic and iconoclastic works by Godard himself. But with Godard,
one must be wary of easy dichotomies.

---

1. Francolin, *À bout de souffle*.

2. The poem by the same name was collected in Adrienne Rich's sixth book, *The Will to
Change*, 1971.

3. This includes the author of the present study, who published a verse novelization of
*Vivre sa vie* with Impressions Nouvelles in 2005.

4. Both from Éditions P. O. L. in 1996.

## NEW WAVE "AUTEURS"

Let us begin by pointing out that Francolin's adaptation, one of the many novelizations from the early years of the New Wave, participated fully in the movement's literary and cinephile culture. In fact, the New Wave not only represented the substitution of "auteur" cinema (with the director in charge of the film like a writer responsible for a book) for a cinema of adaptation (where filmmakers are beholden to screenwriters and actors, following the theatrical model). Nor did it simply signify the passage from an outmoded cinema, the so-called "cinema of quality," with its largely patrimonial outlook, to a more modern, fast-paced, "American" model with a minimum of technical and institutional constraints and a pared-down screenplay. The great revolution in the second half of the 1950s was how a French-style cinema culture[5] formed around a few key films; according to Antoine de Baecque,[6] this was in fact a literary culture. Though Godard and his friends may have argued against a flatly literary conception of filmmaking as "adapting a masterpiece" (the Aurenche-Bost screenwriting team's notorious "dialogue-adaptation"), their films were imbued with a literary sensibility, and they dubbed their efforts "screenwriting."[7] A passion for cinema went hand in hand with a passion for writing: for a cinephile, love or hate a film, you had to write about it, particularly in your own specialty publication; and writing about movies inevitably meant being bitten by the filmmaking bug. This passion for writing is quite evident in Francolin's work; his *À bout de souffle* aptly melded the film and the literary world that inspired it, yet avoided the pitfalls of the "Romans-choc" collection that had commissioned the book. Francolin was able to keep his distance from the "high style" and make good use of what he learned from "hard-boiled" fiction.

New Wave novelization appeared almost instantaneously. Truffaut, quite logically, since he was closest to the classic status of novelist, wrote his own novelizations. More precisely, he and his screenwriter, Marcel Moussy, published a joint novelization of *The 400 Blows* on the heels of the film release.[8]

---

5. French cinephile culture was quite distinct from its Hollywood counterpart, which meant that a film buff could reel off film credits from memory or tell you what color gloves the supporting actor was wearing in a certain scene.

6. De Baecque, *La Cinéphilie.*

7. Film historians often cite Alexandre Astruc's article "Naissance d'une nouvelle avant-garde. La caméra-stylo" as a turning point; it appeared in *Écran français* on 30 March 1948.

8. As Ann Miller writes: "A novelization of François Truffaut's *Les 400 coups* was published by Gallimard in 1959 shortly after the film came out, and was attributed to Marcel Moussy, the television screenwriter who had collaborated with Truffaut on the dialogues. It was reissued by Gallimard in 1998 (by which time the film was enshrined on the lower secondary school syl-

This text, which later somewhat strangely slipped from the adult category into children's literature, is a faithful transposition of a cinematic work, though exaggerating the already very ambivalent attitude toward the mother figure and women in general.[9]

In Godard's case, things happened even more suddenly. With the success of his début film, Seghers, the leading publishing house (along with France-Empire) for commercial novelizations of French films, seems to have commissioned an "express" version of *À bout de souffle* (at the end of 1959), which came out a few months later (the colophon reads February 17, 1960) under the name of Claude Francolin.[10] Unlike Truffaut and Moussy's book, which gave every appearance of being a "serious" work, from its style to its publishing pedigree, the novelization of *À bout de souffle*, more quickly produced and above all faster-paced, was intended for a very different audience. Dialogue prevails, and one might suspect that the novelizer, working under a deadline, was mainly concerned with getting the plot right (a concern for most commercial novelizations). At the same time, while it fails to render Godard's images, Claude Francolin's text does resist the temptation to sanitize the dialogue, retaining some of the film's edgy quality. The author delivers a good sense of the action and has the intelligence not to try matching the effects of film montage. What novelization of *À bout de souffle* loses in regard to the filmic model, failing to translate its formidable energy, it undoubtedly makes up for through its literary intertext, the "Série noire," mainstay of French detective fiction at the time. The novel relies on crime fiction's brutality, with the fortunate addition of a fresh and poignant love story, helping it break through the strictures of the "Romans-choc" collection.

The reasons why the New Wave's critics-turned-filmmakers paid so little attention to novelization is unclear. Were they afraid that association with the "Romans-choc," the existent genre fiction powerhouse, would diminish their cultural credibility? Were they overtaken by the "film-novel" that reappeared on the cusp of the 1960s, with new writers exploring the cinema? Or was their own conception of the cinema beginning to change? Alongside experiments like Marguerite Duras's *Hiroshima mon amour* in 1960 (based on her

---

labus in France) in a children's edition, this time attributed to both Moussy and Truffaut, with a peritext that emphasizes the fact that the book is a "real novel": "François Truffaut et Marcel Moussy ont écrit le récit d'Antoine Doinel, l'histoire des *400 coups*, non pas comme un film raconté, mais comme un vrai roman" (Miller, "*Les 400 coups*," 111).

9. Miller, "*Les 400 coups*," 117–19.

10. The Bibliothèque Nationale's online database does not list any entries for this author. One cannot rule out the hypothesis that this may have been an ad hoc pen name. The work-for-hire world of novelization did attract real writers, but they were loath to compromise their reputation by putting their own name (or their usual pen name) on these works.

work for Alain Resnais) or Alain Robbe-Grillet's *Last Year at Marienbad* in 1961 (also written with Resnais, though he did not cosign the book), Truffaut's work as a novelizer is disappointing in its academic bent, however fine his writing may be. He does not go beyond fictional versions of the shooting script, widely reprinted in numerous film journals at the time (publishing a "bare bones" screenplay, replete with technical specifications, was a sign of artistic recognition, while novelization remained stigmatized as a subgenre). After *The 400 Blows*, Truffaut published several screenplays from his Antoine Doinel cycle. With *The Man Who Loved Women* (1977), he returned to a more traditional form of novelization, meaning one less oriented toward screenplay. As for Godard, he turned toward films that were either increasingly free of any book ties, even if almost all were published as screenplays; or else grappling with a literary infratext, as in *Le Mépris,* based on a fairly conventional novel by Moravia. In neither case, however, did a real novelization result. Jean-Luc Godard would return to novelization only through his venture into *Histoire(s) du cinéma* (1988–98), where it can be assumed to play a role in a brand-new form of poem-novelization that he calls "phrases."

## "PHRASES" [SENTENCES], AN UNCLASSIFIABLE NOVELIZATION

What to make of the novelization examples Jean-Luc Godard himself proposed, publishing several texts drawn from film like *JLG/JLG* or *For Ever Mozart,* with the generic title "Phrases" on the front cover? These volumes might be called *ready-mades.* They consist of snippets of film dialogue with almost no graphic enhancement: no dashes, no stage directions, no mention of characters, no elaborate fonts (the author opted for sans serif, deemed more modern and less literary than the Times font family), nor changes in the body of the text, nor indents, nor other visual effects other than the occasional skipped page or a few blank lines. By way of example, here are the opening lines of *For Ever Mozart*:

> T'es en retard
> Embrasse-moi
> Aïe
> Sabine, s'il te plaît
> Sabine, plus
> Penalty
> Monsieur, monsieur, monsieur,

Sabine

Alors

Boka, on vous attend

Le franc français a encore baissé, monsieur

Le baron

Quatre, quatre

Allons-y Boka


You're late

Kiss me

Ow

Sabine, please

Sabine, more

Penalty

Monsieur, monsieur, monsieur

So

Boka, we're waiting

The French franc has gone down again, monsieur

The baron

Four, four

Let's go Boka[11]


This is undeniably the poets of free verse, more concretely "classic" free verse in the Cendrars mold: *one idea per line, one line per idea.*[12] The one slight difference is that the tone is hardly poetic; furthermore, the text relies heavily on discontinuity. The editing is not "invisible" as in big Hollywood productions or the transcription of café conversations in Brassaï's *Paroles en l'air,*[13] verbal snapshots that seem somewhat dated and mawkish next to Godard's. Close to the cut-up, but never going quite that far, Godard's "phrases" are truly what they claim to be: phrases, that is, very short utterances that interact with one another but also remain independent, managing to keep their distance from the poetic and narrative binding agent. The way they function recalls found objects: plucked from their original context of enunciation, these

---

11. Godard, *For Ever Mozart,* 7–8.

12. Contemporary free verse is more radical, as theorized by Jacques Roubaud, defined by line breaks (see *La Vieillesse d'Alexandre*). In poets like Denis Roche, among others, the semantic unity and cohesion of free verse fall apart. This is clearly not the case in Godard (but it is true that Godard does not consider himself a poet and that today's "liberated" free verse probably represents the worst of clichés).

13. Paris, Jean-Claude Simoën, 1977. The texts in the collection were written during the Occupation.

phrases are so many small surprises (mini-bombs?) whose eye-opening effect is not neutralized by their sequencing. Without inventing anything, Godard creates an entirely new text, sometimes unnerving, which should be considered more an autonomous text than a true novelization.

Godard achieved something "outside" the genre without moving completely beyond it. In his unique way, he makes the strongest case for the poem-novelization.

# PART IV

# From Novelization to Adaptation

# CHAPTER 12

~

# New Readings of the Genre

Although it tries to cover a whole field—and probably also because of that—the limits of this book cannot be denied. Some of these limits have to do with linguistic issues: the corpus of its close readings is Francophone. Others are due to chronological restrictions: the original version of this work was written in 2007–08, and the history of novelization and its scholarship did of course not stop in those years. Still other problems can be explained by the somewhat tight definition of the genre, which I tried to distinguish as clearly as possible from similar practices such as, for instance, the published script (which, as we all know, is never the "real" script but the version that best reflects the final cut of the movie) or the narrative transpositions of the plot as retold in "the making of" (equally a genre that comes very close to novelization), not to speak of the subgenre of the self-novelization, underrepresented in the French version of this work. Finally, crucial elements are also put between brackets by the rather restrictive interpretation of the genre's medium, in the manifold meanings this term can bear. Novelizations in book format receive the absolute priority, as if they were the natural horizon of all valuable novelization work. True, nonverbal novelizations were mentioned once in a while, but readers may rightfully have felt the lack of a special chapter on, for instance, novelizations in comics or videogames (academic research in this field is often very inspiring[1]). One can only acknowledge

---

1. See Boillat, "Des Films en cases."

these many lacunas, although it is also a pleasure to notice that the first edition of this book has proved capable of making some small contributions to a larger awareness of the novelization genre and its many possibilities for narrative and transmedia studies.

The generous invitation to complement the English version of the book with a chapter that looks back at the last decade and addresses some questions that may set the agenda for the coming years can undoubtedly remediate some of the many absences of this work. It is however a slightly different path that I have chosen for these concluding remarks. Instead of trying to fill in all the gaps—an impossible task for an individual researcher—I rather propose a global reframing of the novelization genre in light of some current debates in adaptation and transmedia studies (both fields have strongly tended to converge in recent studies). This discussion will however not be purely abstract or theoretical, but take as its starting point an example that is perhaps illustrative of everything that was left out in the French version of the book. The example in question, Kim Deitch's *Alias the Cat,*[2] contains the comics novelization of an invented movie, whose narrative use and treatment will help reopen the debate on novelization and adaptation.

## BATCAT STORIES

An important figure of the comics underground scene of the 1960s, Kim Deitch has developed in later decades a very personal way of comics making that perfectly blends the old and the new. In his work, which smartly plays with page layout structures and the intertwining of different times, places, voices, perspectives, and styles, is often thematically centered on the world of animation and early cinema of the silent era. Deitch's most intriguing character is a mysterious cat named Waldo, which appears in countless roles and forms in his work, including in that of the creator himself. Deitch's production, which always first appears in serialized comic book format is gathered nowadays in hard cover graphic novels published by Pantheon, as is the case of other artists such as Art Spiegelman and Chris Ware. *Alias the Cat,* serialized under the name of "The Stuff of Dreams" in 2002, 2004, and 2005, is the collection that perhaps represents Deitch's altogether fictional, autobiographical, and autofictional universe in its purest, that is its most radical form. The central volume of the trilogy, "Part 2: Alias the Cat," contains a special type of visual novelization, which is both a story within a story and the pivot of a diz-

---

2. Deitch, *Alias.*

zying play of metalepsis, that is, of the blurring of boundaries between embedding story and embedded story, which blend one into another. The general context of the story—for in Deitch's world all stories build on each other, each new creation being a new form given to what is finally a moving target—is the author's twofold fascination with the figure of the cat and the culture of early cinema. Pamela, Kim Deitch's wife, is a collector of old cat dolls, and one day she buys on eBay an antique cat costume. Some days later, Deitch himself discovers in an old movie magazine ("Moving Picture World," September 21, 1915) an ad for "Alias the Cat," a movie serial being filmed in Matesak, New Jersey, and featuring a costumed character (a masked superhero revenger *avant la lettre,* the villains here being clandestine munition and weapon producers making big money thanks to the war in Europe). This is Deitch's comment:

> Almost as fascinating to me was the announcement of a comic strip version of the story running simultaneously in a New Jersey newspaper!
>
> This keenly interested me for two reasons. First: the film stock early movies were shot on decomposes over time so the chances of a print of this serial still existing were pretty close to nil.
>
> Second: while it was quite common to publish serials concurrently in publications as serialized fiction, I had never before heard of it being done as a comic strip!
>
> And, while the film might be gone forever, finding that comic was at least possible.[3]

Nothing being, of course, impossible in Deitch's world, the narrator rapidly finds the edition of the *Fairmont Democrat* that issued the novelization and immediately starts including the successive chapters in his own story, where each of the fifteen chapters occupies more or less half of the page, except for the weekend episodes that ran full page in the weekend color comics sections. The rest of the page is first devoted to insightful comments on the structure of the film business of that period, more specifically the full-scale national craze of the movies serials from 1914 to 1917. Very soon, however, things get more complicated. The comics novelization is indeed quite unusual. Visually speaking it adopts exactly the same style as the rest of the comics, but even more surprising is its narrative treatment. After a couple of pages, it appears that the mutual mirroring of the movie episodes shown at the local "Bijou" theater and comics novelization serialized in the *Fairmont Democrat* is just the beginning of a more radical mirroring of fiction and reality, which Deitch's graphic novel

---

3. Ibid., n.p.

reconstructs via a subtle web of shifting perspectives, testimonies, shocking revelations, and plot twists that not only bridge the gap between the real and the fictional characters of 1915 but also that between the historical figures of these years and the present of the storytelling. The final wrapping up of the story is however but an excuse allowing Deitch to invent new chapters and developments in the never-ending building of his idiosyncratic narratives.

But what is the place of this strange novelization in recent debates on novelization and adaptation studies? If we take Linda Hutcheon and Siobhan O'Flynn's 2012 *A Theory of Adaptation*[4] as a yardstick for what is going on in the field, one easily sees that *Alias the Cat* corroborates certain tendencies in this domain, but not all of them. Deitch's work exemplifies first of all the two majors aims pursued by Hutcheon in the first edition of the book (2006; the book was not rewritten but expanded for the 2012 version). To start with, Deitch shows the extreme variety of the phenomenon: "If you think adaptation can be understood by using novels and films alone, you're wrong."[5] By inventing a posteriori a type of novelization that was absent in the period of its historical setting, Deitch noticeably enlarges the range of the novelization genre (the importance of which has been courageously stressed by Hutcheon). At the same time, and this is the second point, *Alias the Cat* equally underlines the interest of Hutcheon's special take on adaptation, which she studies "as adaptation," that is, as not just as an independent object—this is often the perspective of those eager to get rid of the allegedly old-fashioned fidelity issue—but as a process that acknowledges the transposition of a recognizable work. *Alias the Cat* is presented as a kind of "novelization" in action, both in the past (a masked revenger produces the movie and its accompanying comics novelization in order to charge the villains in real life) and the present (the search for the hidden treasure helps Deitch give a new twist to his ever-expanding comics universe). In other words, Deitch's novelization is a creative answer to each of these evolutions. It opens the gamut of what can count as adaptation (no other example of a comics novelization of 1914–17 has ever been identified by film scholars), while emphasizing the "work" done by a wide range of agents all of them pursuing sometimes very different objectives.

The major change foregrounded by the second edition of Hutcheon's book is the impact of new media. I already quoted the opening sentence of the preface to the first edition, it is time now to quote as well that of the preface to the second edition:

---

4. Hutcheon and O'Flynn, *Theory of Adaptation*.
5. Ibid., xii.

No, things *do not* stay the same, not always, and certainly not since the last six years *A Theory of Adaptation* was published. The proliferation of adaptations has continued apace, of course; our thirst for retelling stories has not been quenched in the least. But what *has* changed is the availability of many new forms and platforms. New digital media have burgeoned in these last years.[6]

In this regard, it cannot be denied that Deitch's work is to a certain extent rather anachronistic. Its fiction looks back to the past (the era of silent cinema). Its format is that of the classic publication host media, namely comic books and graphic novels (which does not mean that it can't be sold or read as an e-book, although this is not yet an option). However, the relative absence of new media (for it goes without saying that the whole process of editing, printing, publishing, promoting, and distributing a book has become unthinkable without digital means) is not a feature of Deitch, but a common feature of the graphic novel in general, an art form famously known for its love of paper and ink as well as its strong resistance to digitization.[7] And as *Alias the Cat* makes very clear, the skepticism toward the digital turn is more complex than it seems to be. Indeed, Deitch may reject some material aspects of digital culture, but he does not stay away from the broader context of participatory culture that Hutcheon and O'Flynn rightly stress as key aspects of transmedial digitization. Questions of copyright, ownership, distribution, and more generally creative appropriation and participatory culture are not all ignored, on the contrary. After all, the sociological setting of Deitch's adventures is that of fan culture, the importance of cultural mediation and the creative interaction between maker and consumer. In that sense, Deitch enlarges the notion of user's creativity outside the sole domain of digital culture (it is tempting to rephrase thus Hutcheon's claim: "If you think participatory culture can be understood by looking at computer screens alone, you're wrong").

Hutcheon's and many others' work[8] have been paramount in resetting the agenda of the field and solving some of the problems that have long hindered the development of adaptation studies: the narrow focus on book to film transpositions; the shallow contextualization of adaptations "as adaptations"; the cluster of difficulties created by the returning fidelity questions, for example. Novelization studies of the last five years have undoubtedly taken advantage of these evolutions, as shown in the work of Neil Archer, among others.[9]

---

6. Ibid., xix.

7. Groensteen, *Comics and Narration*; Dozo and Crucifix, "E-Graphic Novels."

8. See the portal site of the journal *Adaptation*: academic.oup.com/adaptation

9. Archer, "Novel Experience."

Two recent publications have introduced however rather different perspectives on adaptation, which will prove crucial to the further development of novelization studies. The first is Simone Murray's *The Adaptation Industry*, which proposes a radical shift in scope and focus of all existing adaptation research:

> The premise of this book is that considering contemporary literary adaptions through the prism of the adaptation industry throws new light on the processes by which adaptations come to be made, the forms they take, and the audiences who encounter them. The incorporation of the phrase "cultural economy" in my book's subtitle, yoking together two terms often considered antithetical, is designed to distance this book from adaptations studies' previous over-easy association of commerce with cultural taint. . . . *The Adaptation Industry* is designed to showcase a broadly sociological approach to adaptation, foregrounding those issues usually pushed to the margins of adaptations studies work: the industrial structures, interdependent networks of agents, commercial contexts, and legal and policy regimes within which adaptations come to be.[10]

The decision to concentrate on literary adaptations, either print or online, gives of course the possibility of an in-depth examination of the novelization genre (repeatedly mentioned by Hutcheon, yet not studied in much detail). Murray underscores the limits of the classic analysis of novelization (either disdain, the novelizing writer being seen as the victim of a money-hungry system, or superficiality, via the "relentlessly descriptive, rather than critical 'how to' guides,"[11] while making room for fresh views by insisting on the legal and commercial analogies between novelizations and published scripts.[12] The many very concrete examples discussed in the book make it a real eye-opener for novelization studies, whose strategic position in the film and literature field comes strongly to the fore. For obvious reasons, Murray's study does not include textual analyses of the novelizations under scrutiny. One of the major challenges of novelization and adaptation studies of the upcoming years is therefore to examine the mutual influence of text and context, or if one prefers, of the autonomous view of the work (the novelization as a work to be read as an independent work, always in relationship with the work it transforms) and the heteronomous view of the same (the novelization as the result of external constraints that determine any cultural industry whatsoever.[13]

10. Murray, *Adaptation Industry,* 6.

11. Ibid., 23.

12. Ibid., 152–53.

13. See for instance Van Parys, "Commercial Novelization," and "A Fantastic Voyage" as well as Mahlknecht, "Hollywood Novelization."

Building upon the work by Murray, the French specialist of filmic adaptations, Jean-Louis Jeannelle, proposes an even more radical paradigm shift:

> The conceptual displacement wrought by Simone Murray has not, however, resulted in the hoped-for effects, particularly because it has not led to a reexamination of concepts currently in use. Of course, it has been essential to replace adaptation within the questioning of the institutional, social and economic forces that govern the logic of production. Yet the *theoretical,* and more precisely *poetic,* consequences remain to be explored, that is to say, reconsidering adaptation no longer as an *end product* but as a *process* bringing together multiple agents with diverging interests. In this article, I propose to substitute the notion of *adaptability* for that of adaptation.[14]

The fundamental objective of Jeannelle's intervention is to replace the inevitably binary analysis of adaptation "as adaptation"—for even if one insists on the limitless possibilities of transforming a work into another work, one will always be bound by the dialectics of source and target—it is to make a plea for a radically forward-looking approach that tries to understand from three different but complementary perspectives: economic, script-related, and critical, that is the "adaptability quotient"[15] of a given work. This approach is crossmedial as well as transmedial. It also offers a new autonomy to the adapted work. Jeannelle gives great weight to the fact that most readers or spectators do not always care to inform themselves on the adaptation's source, let alone take the time to have a closer look at it. Jeannelle's approach enables a new reading of the work's genesis. Instead of just studying the relationship between source and target, Jeannelle is keen to emphasize the decisive position of "failures" in the adaptation process: the roads not taken, the rewritings that were abandoned halfway or not even initiated, the rejected adaptations, for example. Finally this approach underscores the necessity to also study "inadaptability."[16]

Just like Simone Murray's book, Jeannelle's article opens many new windows to adaptation studies, which moreover have the advantage of being compatible with the results and perspectives of previously elaborated models and methodologies. Concerning more precisely the subfield of novelization, to cross the insights of Murray and Jeannelle, may offer opportunities for the combination of close reading and cultural-economical readings, two perspectives that are only rarely intertwined. Concurrently, the combination

---

14. Jeannelle, "Adapatability," 96.
15. Ibid., 97.
16. Ibid., 99.

of Jeannelle and Murray can reposition the novelization genre in unexplored ways. It is one thing indeed to make a plea for the study of novelization as a genre worth analyzing, it is another one to both stress its specific aspects and consider it in the larger context of the published and unpublished film script. Novelizations are not only often based on scripts, which they rewrite in order to dissimulate their supposedly nonliterary aspects, they are also often taking a form that can be easily confused with them. One of the future assignments of novelization studies will certainly be to enlarge the corpus in order to include forms of writing that have been excluded—paradoxical as this term may sound in the case of a genre that has itself been systematically marginalized—from the field of novelization: rough scripts, for instance, of book adaptations of filmic material that do not respect the ideal of sequential storytelling. Quite a few film adaptations adopt a model whose logic is less syntagmatic than paradigmatic: instead of retelling the plot, they offer the reader a set of images and accompanying texts that are no longer arranged as a story that is progressively unfolded, but as the elements of a story world or imaginary construction, according to a purely visual logic that reinterprets—often in a very faithful and illuminating way—the basic components of a work. Another crucial innovation is that of the partial or integrated novelization. It often occurs that the rewriting of a filmic source does not translate into an independent work, but appears within other works, which have themselves not always much to do with the world of novelization and adaptation. This fragmentation concerns both sides of the adaptive relationship: instead of reworking a complete film (and the notion of "film" includes here every cinematographic work, from video clips, short movie, and TV serials to various types of archives), the novelizing author can select one single scene, character, or setting, if not a single shot or even image, and the same applies of course to the soundtrack (it is reasonable to suppose that it is no longer possible to have even the faintest idea of all literary and nonliterary texts doing something with *Taxi Driver*'s famous line: "You talkin' to me?"). The notion of "transfictionalization,"[17] which studies the migrations from fiction "elements" from one universe to another, will prove dramatically helpful in this regard. It also establishes a healthy and necessary counterpart to the notion of transmedia storytelling à la Jenkins,[18] which goes in a completely different direction (actually a direction that can only be taken by big media conglomerates like Disney, which is of course not the only future of adaptation and novelization studies).[19] Finally, but this description does not claim to be exhaustive, the

17. Saint-Gelais, *Fictions transfuges.*
18. Jenkins, "Transmedia 202."
19. See also Peeters, "Multimodality."

multiple suggestions made by Murray and Jeannelle also invite the rereading
of previous analyses, for instance those gathered in this book, which clearly
remains too silent on the practice of self-novelization.

## FINAL POST: BERGMAN BY BERGMAN

*Through a Glass Darkly* (1961) is the first of Ingmar Bergman's "Faith Trilogy
Films," which also contains *Winter Light* and *The Silence* (both released 1963).[20]
Like many other films by Bergman, they have been published in book form by
the director himself (this analysis will use the English translation by Paul Britten Austin, then Bergman's brother-in-law, whose contribution to the director's bibliography can therefore be seen as perfectly authorized). This double
production, that of filmmaker and that of writer, is anything but exceptional
in European art house cinema around 1960. The dominating *auteur* approach
of film does not only foreground the leading role of the director—instead of
that of the movie star, the producer, or the scriptwriter, the latter a key role in
French cinema. It stresses above all his (and less frequently her) position as
similar and equivalent to that of the writer, with cinema progressively taking
over the prevailing place of literature in the cultural hierarchy. The writing of
the director takes however two different forms. It is "new" when it concerns
the actual shooting and editing of a movie—and here the essential ambition of
the director is to communicate an original worldview or *Weltanschauung*. It is
"old" when it translates into the publication of actual texts in print, generally
reviews, speeches, interviews, or scripts, either in specialized film-connoisseur
magazines or in book format. Most French New Wave directors were avid
book writers (some of them had started as critics and novelists). In publishing their screenplays, however, they do not only cater to an emerging market,
that of the blossoming cinephilia as well as that of the emerging academic
interest in film studies. They also made a complex authorial statement, for in
these years, to publish one's screenplay is not an abstract gesture. The publication of a book is in the first way an attempt to break away from the multiple
forms of narrating cinema in popular magazines. As seen above, films were
very actively issued in print beginning in the 1910s, and after the First World
War, this production was ubiquitous. Next to often very detailed and illustrated summaries in all kinds of general magazines, comparable to what we
would call today the "readers' digest" way of telling, all theatrically released
movies were rapidly reprinted in different popular novelization formats, either

---

20. Bergman, *Three Films.*

as "narrated films" (see the chapter on Dreyer's *Joan of Arc*) or as "film photo-novels," that is, as complete stories in *fumetti* or photo-story magazines retelling the movie's plot with the help of approximatively two hundred to three hundred pictures (film stills or publicity photos) in page layouts that closely resemble that of a comic book, including the use of speech balloons.[21] Both types, narrated films and film photo-novels, were generally anonymous productions, commissioned by magazine editors eager to cash in on the success of both movies and photo-novels. Publishing an authorized screenplay in book form, if possible, with a serious publisher or in a film magazine targeting an intellectual audience, is in the first place an attempt to position oneself at the complete opposite of these immensely popular and unashamedly cheap novelizations. Next to this concern, that is, the fear of being confused with the most commercial and thus decidedly nonauteur segment of the film business,[22] there was also a positive motivation, namely the desire to take advantage of print to shape one's profile as a truly literary writer.

In most cases, this strategy was strongly related to genre. Writer-directors such as Alain Robbe-Grillet, Jean-Luc Godard, Marguerite Duras, or Alain Resnais, tried to establish a new genre one could call the "new film novel," an innovative merger of screenplay and novelization, complemented with new ways of editing illustrations (the simple paraphrase of the new genre does not signify however that there existed a single genre label: terminologically speaking, many different terms were concurrently in use). The film novels made by Ingmar Bergman can fruitfully be analyzed in light of this broader context, of which there is one of the most representative as well as the most long-running examples (for most readers, the best-known work of this series is probably *Scenes of a Marriage,* first published in 1973).

*Through a Glass Darkly* is one of the numerous Bergman films that testify to the obsession with God. It is the story of a father, a writer suffering from a severe writer's block, who is tortured by his daughter's madness, which at the same time he also tries to exploit for his new novel. Contrary to this strong but painful relationship with his (married) daughter, the father is indifferent

---

21. Baetens, *Film Photo Novel.* The "film photo novel" is virtually unknown in the United States, at least in the 1960s. The only magazine that published photographic novelizations using the *fumetti* technique was *Famous Films,* one of the many horror magazines published by James Warren. *Famous Films* was however very short-lived and had only three issues (1964–65). Its cultural impact and afterlife are very limited, in spite of the truly original contribution to the evolution of the genre.

22. This fear was anything but imaginary, as the work of many New Wave filmmakers was as systematically recycled in commercial novelization outlets as any other movie. Even a filmmaker as "pure" as Ingmar Bergman was adapted in *fumetti* magazines (the rights of these lowbrow adaptations were handled by local distributors).

to the psychological demands of his son, a young boy of fifteen, who develops an incestuous fascination with his sister. The fourth character of this drama, composed as a three-act play offering three different perspectives on the same topic, is the daughter's husband, a character that is as much included in the family's tragedy as he stays outside of it. As the title of the film already suggests, a truncated quotation of 1 Corinthians 13:12: "For now we see in a mirror, darkly, but then face to face. Now I know in part, but then I shall know just as I also am known" (New King James Version), the existential dimension of the human relationship is framed by religious interrogations and concerns. During her schizophrenic crises, the daughter believes that she is really seeing and meeting God, who appears to her in the form of a monstrous spider. The religious skepticism of the son as well as the husband are counterbalanced by the final confession of the father, who expresses his belief in the existence and goodness of God, more precisely of God as love and love as God (this interpretation is in perfect correspondence with Corinthians 13, but the rest of the Faith trilogy will criticize it as an illusion).

*Through a Glass Darkly* appeared in book format as part of the trilogy in the volume *Three Films,* first in Swedish in 1963, then in other languages, including English (1967). The form and content of the movie are so downright Bergmanian,[23] and its meaning, although open-ended, is so strong that the director's novelization seems to fulfill a purely strategical function, that of increasing the status of Ingmar Bergman as a real auteur and that of confirming the status of his work as high art, a key contribution to the cultural and intellectual life of its times and beyond. Self-novelization and canonization are two sides of the same medal. Relevant as it may be, this interpretation does not however do justice to the complexity of Bergman's writing, and it is therefore important to have a closer look at what the text actually looks like.

What strikes first is of course what is missing. The text is completely deprived of all technical didascalia (camera position, camera movements, camera angles, timing, stage indications, sound, etc.). On the one hand, it rejects everything that refers to a traditional film script of a screenplay, as if *Through a Glass Darkly* was not meant to be filmed; as if, in other words, the text we are reading was not really a script, that is, to quote the famous definition by Pier Paolo Pasolini, "a structure designed to become another structure."[24] This policy is rather different from that of many other auteur-directors, who do not refrain from these technical details even if they try to rethink and rewrite them in a more literary form (the inclusion of these ele-

---

23. Readers who have never seen the movie, may think of it as a work bridging the gap between *Joan of Arc* (Dreyer, 1927) and, for instance, *Stalker* (Tarkovsky, 1979).

24. Pasolini, "Scenario."

ments is also a way of stressing the novelty effect of the text, for traditional literary text refrains from using them, even when the author makes an effort to copy the language of cinema). In the case of Ingmar Bergman, this antifilmic stance seems to have troubled some of his publishers, for in certain editions one finds a detailed introductory note stating for instance:

> The script in itself amply conveys the continuity of the film by its sheer literary quality. However, it contains no technical details of camera position and movement, and for this reason a shot-by-shot cutting continuity is included in this edition which, together with the stills keyed to the text, should help the reader to visualise the action. In this cutting continuity, the camera position is indicated by initials: CU for close-up, MCU for medium close-up; MS for medium shot; MLS for medium long shot; LS for long shot.[25]

On the other hand, *Through a Glass Darkly* also refuses all references to another model, that of the published theater play. In spite of the fact that the three-act structure is repeatedly hinted at by Bergman himself, the text of the book does not bear stage indications or voice instructions. It also lacks the classic initial presentation of the characters. It thus starts in medias res, and much is left to the imagination of the reader, who is invited to immerse herself into a dramatic setting that raises unique and unconventional ethical and existential questions.

The reader's imagination, however, and this is the second major characteristic of all Bergman's self-novelizations, is not free to seize the works as it pleases. For if *Through a Glass Darkly* faithfully reproduces the movie's dialogues, the book frequently interrupts these lines with detailed narratorial comments, separated from the dialogues by their typographical presentation (in italics). All these comments are in the third person and initially they seem to offer a rather neutral, yet willingly literary rewriting of all that the movie is telling us by just showing it. This is, for instance, how the book starts:

> The house, strongly marked by its exposed position, stands by itself on a long sandy promontory. Built in two stories, it is a dark green color, except where sun and wind have burnished its timbers to a lighter silky hue. At the back it looks out over a large wild garden, all run to seed and partly screened from prying eyes by a high paling.
>
> People are living in the house. Washing flaps on the line, and underneath ragged and wind-blown awnings the windows are wide open.

---

25. Bergman, *Wild Strawberries*, 5.

Out of heaving waves, half-dark in the gloaming, arise shouts and laughter. Suddenly four heads are bobbing on the waves, and after a moment four people begin struggling in through the shallows, toward the shore. They are breathing hard, as if after a long swim, and laugh helplessly as they walk side by side—four black figures against the sunset.[26]

Yet the tone and scope of these narrative intermezzi, which tend to occupy as much space as the dialogues themselves, rapidly change. The more or less objective description of settings, gestures, and events morphs into the analysis of an omniscient narrator, who explains what the movie is apparently not capable of telling us by just showing it. Some omniscient passages also contain fragments in free indirect style, which further prove that no secret remains hidden to the narrative voice:

Minus (= *the son*, JB) is sitting somewhere in eternity with his sick sister in his arms. He is empty, exhausted, frozen. Reality, as he has known it until now, has been shattered, ceased to exit. Neither in his dreams nor his fantasies has he known anything to correspond to this moment of weightlessness and grief. His mind has forced its way through the membrane of merciful ignorance. From this moment on his senses will change and harden, his receptivity will become sharpened, as he goes from the make-believe world of innocence to the torment of insight. His world of contingency and chance has been transformed into a universe of law.[27]

He (= *David, the father,* JB) leans his head against a windowpane and feels his pulse. Yes, he must have a temperature, he'd better take a couple of aspirins. He searches on the bookshelf, above the washstand, among pillboxes and bottles.[28]

The logical conclusion of this writing strategy seems very simple: novelization is necessary to communicate the "real" meaning of the movie, as if the latter's language did not suffice to establish a satisfying and unambiguous relationship with the spectator. In spite of its newly won status as high art and the newest form of literature, film can still not compete with traditional writing, hence the revenge of literature and the book, which strike back in a format that, while directly referring to the movie, wipes out all allusions to the film set as well as the theater stage. Yet here as well this interpretation is much too naïve. First of all, it should be stressed that Bergman, perhaps with an irony

---

26. Bergman, *Three Films*, 15.
27. Ibid., 51.
28. Ibid., 33.

that is completely absent from the movie, takes the incredible risk of being confused with the character of the father, the novelist suffering from a writer's block who after the failed attempts to exploit his daughter's illness to find inspiration for his new book will end up burning his papers, finally choosing the authenticity of real human contact to the slick but deceiving fictionality of his novels, which he writes for his own glory and as an excuse to hide away from the illness of his first wife and the suffering of his daughter. In the movie, the contrast between literature's high stakes and literature's false achievements is crystal clear, and one can read this as a metaphor of the cultural shift from literature to cinema, given the fact that as a movie *Through a Glass Darkly* has the ambition to suggest that, contrary to literature, it has the capacity to produce actual and positive changes in real life. The director suggests that he helps us think about the most important issues of our life and we as spectators are invited to continue this discussion after we have left the theater. In the book, however, the situation is completely different. Here, we don't see images (the illustrations of the three movies are gathered in the middle of the book and their intention is less to tell a story than to highlight the correspondences between the characters of the three parts of the Faith trilogy), we read words, and these words do not necessarily differ from the allegedly ridiculous words of the novel the father does not succeed in finishing:

DAVID (READS): She came toward him, panting with expectation, scarlet-faced in the keen wind . . . (*sighs*) Oh my God, oh my God.
*He thrusts his spectacles up on his brow and hides his grey face in his hands. But after a few moments he resumes work.*
DAVID (READS): She came toward him, panting with expectation . . .
*He runs a long thin line through the rest of the sentence, and contemplates his work. Then he strikes out all the rest, too.*
DAVID: She came running toward him, her face scarlet in the keen wind . . .
*He shakes his head and leans forward over his sheets of paper, and in capital letters, in red ink, writes the following: SHE CAME RUNNING TOWARD HIM. Then he gives a sigh, shakes his head, runs a thick line through what he has written in capital letters and resolutely writes: "They met on the beach."*[29]

To a certain extent, it is not absurd to think that the style of Bergman's proper text, which never manages to achieve the sobriety of David's final version ("They met on the beach"), falls prey to the same critique that slowly disintegrates the style of the novel in the making. This hypothesis is crucial,

29. Ibid., 33–34.

for it reveals that the writer-director Ingmar Bergman is perfectly aware of the paradoxical and thus highly ambivalent status of his self-novelization. Structurally and philosophically speaking, a novelization is a "supplement," that is, in the Derridean sense of the word,[30] the addition of a "detail" that reveals a lack or flaw in an existing "whole." Supplementing the movie, which in auteur theory supplants writing and literature as the culturally dominant form, the book discloses the insufficiencies of cinema, incapable of delivering a full and complete meaning without the help of an additional literary text. Yet this text is not just a text, it is supposed to be the previous and underlying version of the film, which thus appears itself as the visual supplement of the text, that is, of a previous whole whose lack and incompleteness are revealed through the visual shooting and editing of a verbal script. Bergman's textual irony, the suggestion that the book version of *Through a Glass Darkly* could be as ridiculous as the unauthentic novel written and eventually destroyed by the father, exposes the director's awareness of the limits of his own text. At the same time, however, the very existence of this text reveals a similar awareness of the limits of the movie.

From this point of view, Bergman's literary production can be considered a complex, nuanced, and radically open-ended intervention in the field of novelization in particular and of adaptation in general. The "mirror" the title of his movie refers to is a two-way as well as a two-step mechanism. In *Through a Glass Darkly*, film and book are inextricably linked. The movie reflects the script and vice versa. Both supplement each other and by doing so reveal each other's lacunas. Since the published script is both the text used during the shooting and made public after it (several publications of Ingmar Bergman make this point very clear in their editorial paratext), it is impossible to say which comes first, the movie or the film. The script precedes the film just as the film precedes the script. All we know is that *Through a Glass Darkly* is a work, more precisely a network, that illustrates both the cultural economy turn and the adaptability turn of recent adaptation studies. The self-novelization exists because it plays a key role in the global economy of cinema and literature. The paradoxical intertwining of book and movie, which eternally morph into one another as the sides of a Möbius strip, demonstrate the cultural dynamism of great works of art, whose reading always takes the form of new creative appropriations.

---

30. Derrida, *Of Grammatology*.

# CONCLUSION

~

In 1946 (the colophon notes December 28), the journalist Pierre Lapierre published a singular work, *Aux Portes de la nuit* [*Gates of the Night*], with the front cover proclaiming it "the novel from Marcel Carné's film," what we would call today a "making of" account.[1] Written by an insider who tells everything he saw and heard, on and off the set, and ending with a report on the first screenings for industry professionals shortly before Lapierre's text went to press, this documentary work is also a novelization. In its own fashion, it is part reportage, part fiction, written on the fly, from a point of view that is not retrospective but up to the minute and forward-looking. Lapierre does not tell how the film was made, but how it came into being and where it might be going, even if in no particular direction. The book thus contains many accounts of scenes that were definitely filmed, but with no guarantee, even as he was describing them, that they would end up one day in a Marcel Carné film (as Lapierre tells it, the filming was full of drama, the production disjointed and rushed). Little by little, what started out as the "novel" of a film's shooting turned into the story of a film that might never have seen the light of day. It is easy enough to imagine how the only remnant of Carné's film might have been Lapierre's book.

---

1. Lapierre, *Aux Portes.*

What does this example teach us, aside from being about Carné's film? Essentially this: that novelization is never a gratuitous exercise; that it fulfills a need, modest as its function may be in the highly complex web of connections between book and film within cinematic culture. *Aux Portes de la nuit* is a useful text: Lapierre wants to support the film and its creator; but also, along the way, to save the film from potential doom; or even, after the negative audience reaction at the first showings, to bolster critical reception. As the book's final entry puts it:

Samedi 14 décembre
Depuis deux semaines, la presse en raconte de toutes les couleurs.

Le film est chahuté par une partie du public. Des gens qui ont encaissé, sur les écrans des Champs-Elysées, les pires coyonnades, voudraient faire croire, par un réveil soudain et bruyant, qu'ils y connaissent quelque chose.

Jadis, on a sifflé *Caligari* et la *Roue*.

Il y a moins longtemps, on a fait la moue devant *Sous les toits de Paris* et devant *Drôle de drame*.

D'ici quelque temps, on revendiquera l'honneur d'avoir découvert du premier coup les beautés des *Portes de la nuit*.

Saturday December 14
For two weeks now, the press has been printing all sorts of wild tales.

The film was booed by some audiences. People who watch pure junk on screens along the Champs-Elysées would have us believe that they know something about cinema, as if they'd had a sudden and noisy wake-up call,

Once they booed *The Cabinet of Dr. Caligari* and *The Wheel.*

Not so long ago, *Sous les toits de Paris* and *Drôle de drame* got a cool reception, too. And not too long from now, some will brag about being the first to recognize how beautiful *Les Portes de la nuit* is.[2]

Lapierre's example may be marginal, but less than one might think. The novelizations analyzed in this book demonstrate that the genre has as many rules as exceptions. But what constantly recurs is the idea of *necessity*. No matter what the authors' motives are, novelization almost always appears as a book that *must* be written, that has important implications, that, in short is relevant. And that is basically an enviable destiny.

Moreover, one can posit that research into novelization, while in its early phase, has many surprises in store (and regretfully the present work is limited to only a few case studies, with so many others that would also have war-

---

2. Ibid., 246.

ranted careful and contextual examination). Likewise, we need not fear that the genre of novelization will disappear in the new cinematic culture currently emerging. One might get the sense that all art forms are melding together into a new *hybridized* and *globalized* structure: hybridized because the borders between different art forms—between media, genres, registers—are becoming fluid; globalized because everything is supported by a single system, since digital infrastructure allows for the production, registration, archiving, circulation, and ultimately the transformation of signs. In fact, a third and different situation now prevails. Practically speaking, various media preserve their identities, ever-changing as they are, but instead of existing separately, or in isolation, they constantly appear and function in intermedia networks. This pluralization of media, which all rely on other frameworks, will necessarily generate new forms of novelization, even if it is impossible to predict exactly what they will be.

In this progression, DVDs, downloads, and streaming play a capital role. Far from merely offering a new distribution platform for cinematic works, DVD technology in fact plays a role in a film's content and perception. First of all, the DVD replaces the former collective viewing environment (the darkened theater and the big screen) with an individual, domestic, small-screen environment, much like television, but with interactive and multiple-viewing capacities (meaning that viewing time is no longer predicated on screening time). This new technology further produces a fusion of several "textual" domains that were heretofore distinct: the film "text" is no longer complemented by some kind of "peritext" (for instance, the trailer or an interview with the director), or "metatext" (such as the director's scene-by-scene voiceover commentary), or a "foretext" (such as outtakes or deleted scenes). Today, a film's "text" in the DVD version by rights includes all these elements, which are often planned from the beginning for inclusion in the "final product." The multiplication of alternative endings or the simultaneous release of "short" and "long" versions of a work have become a standard feature of film-making, with the result that one film may exist in widely varying formats: theatrical release, DVD, broadcast TV, streaming, as well as video game or television spinoffs. It would be unfortunate to exclude novelization from this new media panorama, but the history of the genre and the examples analyzed in this book amply demonstrate how much we can trust in novelization's power to adapt.

# APPENDICES

# APPENDIX 1

## Éditions Gallimard: "Le Cinéma Romanesque" series

Berritz, Sabine. *Solitude,* 1929, preface by Paul Morand, 96 pages.

Bost, Pierre. *La Passion et la mort de Jeanne d'Arc,* 1928, prefaces by Jean Cocteau, Valentine Hugo, Jacques de Lacretelle, and Paul Morand, 94 pages.

Bouissounouse, Janine. *L'Opérateur,* 1929, 96 pages.

Bousquet, Marina. *En vitesse,* 1929, 96 pages.

Duchâteau, R. *Un homme en habit,* 1928, 96 pages.

Falbet, J.-L. *La petite marchande d'allumettes,* 1928, 96 pages.

Feuillant, Étienne. *L'invincible Spaventa,* 1929, preface by Fratellini bros., 96 pages.

Fornairon, Ernest. *L'enfer de l'amour,* 1928, 96 pages.

Idem. *La République des jeunes filles,* 1929, 96 pages.

Frauberg, J., and G. Kosenzoff. *Neiges sanglantes,* 1929, 96 pages.

Gratias, L., and O. Lévy. *La grande passion,* 1929, 96 pages.

von Harbou, Théa. *Métropolis,* 1928, trans. by Alain Laubreaux and Serge Plaute, preface by Jules Romains, 96 pages.

Holman, Russel. *En vitesse,* 1929, unknown translator, 96 pages.

Humbourg, Pierre. *Chang,* 1928, preface by Paul Morand, 96 pages.

Jacob, Manu. *La Vie privée d'Hélène de Troie,* 1928, preface by Maurice Bedel, 96 pages.

Joannon, Léo. *Nostalgie,* 1928, 96 pages.

Kessel, Joseph. *L'Équipage,* 1928, 96 pages.

Loos, Anita. *Les Hommes préfèrent les blondes,* 1928, trans. by Harry Morgan and Lucie Saint-Elme.

Marin, Jean. *Vengeance posthume,* 1929, 96 pages.

Mitry, Jean. *Poings de fer, cœurs d'or,* 1929, 96 pages.

Ploquin, Raoul. *Le Chant du prisonnier,* 1929, preface by René Clair, 96 pages.

Righelli, G. *Le Rouge et le noir,* 1929, 96 pages.

# APPENDIX 2

## ÉDITIONS GALLIMARD: "CINARIO" SERIES

Beculer, André. *Un suicide,* 1925, 124 pages.

Bizet, René. *Dans la peau du rôle,* 1926, 118 pages.

Boutet, Frédéric. *Gribiche,* 1925, 128 pages.

Cartoux, Paul, and Henry Decoin. *Le Roi de la pédale,* 1925, 128 pages.

Gheusi, P.-B. *Les Tueurs de rois. Charles IX et Marie Touchet,* 1926, 190 pages.

# APPENDIX 3

## ÉDITIONS SEGHERS: "ROMANS-CHOC" COLLECTION

D'Eaubonne, Françoise. *Les tricheurs, d'après le film de Marcel Carné,* 1959, 255 pages.

Jean-Charles, Jehanne. *Les Cousins. D'après le film de Claude Chabrol,* 1959, 236 pages.

D'Eaubonne, Françoise. *J'irai cracher sur vos tombes. D'après les travaux cinématographiques de Boris Vian et Jacques Dopagne,* 1959, 254 pages.

Do Canto, Violante. *Orfeu negro. D'après le film de Marcel Camus et la pièce de Vinicius de Morães,* 1959, 224 pages.

Rousselot, Jean. *Les Tripes au soleil. D'après le film de Claude Bernard-Aubert,* 1959, 250 pages.

Francolin, Claude. *À bout de souffle. D'après le film de Jean-Luc Godard,* 1960, 235 pages.

Marsan, Robert. *Le Beau Serge. D'après le film de Claude Chabrol,* 1960, 235 pages.

Marsan, Robert. *Les Mordus. D'après le film de René Jolivet,* 1960, 245 pages.

## TRANSLATIONS (COPUBLISHED WITH GÉRARD & CIE, VERVIERS)

Ray, Nicholas. *La Fureur de vivre* [*Rebel without a Cause*], 1956, 1956 (trans. by Anne Mesritz), 217 pages.

Cobb, Humphrey. *Les Sentiers de la gloire* [*Paths of Glory*], 1958, 256 pages.

# BIBLIOGRAPHY

Albera, François. "*La Roue* roman de Ricciotto Canudo d'après *La Roue* d'Abel Gance," in *Il Racconto del film/Narrating the Film. La Novellizzazione: del catalogo al trailer/Novelization: From the Catalogue to the Trailer,* ed. Alice Autelitano and Valentina Re (Udine: Forum Edizioni, 2006), 87–102.

Apollinaire, Guillaume. "L'Esprit nouveau et les poëtes," in *Œuvres complètes.* Tome 3 (Paris: Gallimard, 1966), 900–910.

Archer, Neil. "A Novel Experience in Crime Narrative: Watching and Reading *The Killing,*" *Adaptation* 7:2 (2014), 212–27.

Arnaud, Noël. *Dossier de l'affaire "J'irai cracher sur vos tombes"* (Paris: Bourgois, 2006 [1974]).

Arnoldy, Édouard, and Laurent Le Forestier. "Cinéma, histoire, novellisation: considérations autour d'écritures en miroir," in *Il Racconto del film/Narrating the Film. La Novellizzazione: del catalogo al trailer/Novelization: From the Catalogue to the Trailer,* ed. Alice Autelitano and Valentina Re (Udine: Forum Edizioni, 2006), 139–58.

Ashcroft, Bill, Gareth Griffiths, and Helen Tiffin, eds. *The Empire Writes Back* (London: Routledge, 1989).

Assouline, Pierre. *Gaston Gallimard, un demi-siècle d'édition française* (Paris: Balland, 1984).

August, John. "Where to Find *Natural Born Killers* Novelization," online: http://johnaugust.com/archives/2004/where-to-find-natural-born-killers-novelization (last accessed 14 June 2017).

Autelitano, Alice, and Valentina Re, eds. *Il Racconto del film/Narrating the Film. La Novellizzazione: del catalogo al trailer/Novelization: From the Catalogue to the Trailer* (Udine: Forum Edizioni, 2006).

Baetens, Jan. ". . . aboutir à un livre, " *Écritures* 13 (2002), 13–14.

———. "A Critique of Cyberhybrid-hype," in *The Future of Cultural Studies,* ed. Jan Baetens and José Lambert (Leuven: Leuven UP, 2000), 153–71.

———. "Enough of this So-Called Minimalist Poetry," *Substance* 107 (2005), 66–74.

———. *The Film Photo Novel* (forthcoming with Texas UP).

———. *Vivre sa vie. Une novellisation en vers du film de Jean-Luc Godard* (Brussels: Les Impressions Nouvelles, 2006).

Baetens, Jan, and Marc Lits, eds. *La Novellisation. Du film au livre/Novelization: From Film to Novel* (Leuven: Leuven UP, 2003).

Baetens, Jan, and Hilde Van Gelder. "Petite poétique de la photographie mise en roman (1970–1990)," in *Photographie et romanesque*, ed. Danièle Méaux (Caen: Lettres Modernes Minard, 2006), 257–71.

Barthes, Roland. "The Third Meaning," in *Image Music Text: Essays Selected and Translated by Stephen Heath* (Hammersmith: Fontana Press, 1977), 52–68.

Bazin, André. "Pour un cinéma impur," in *Qu'est-ce que le cinéma?* (Paris: Cerf, 1987), 81–106.

Bellos, David. *Jacques Tati, sa vie et son art* (Paris: Seuil, 2002).

Benvéniste, Emile. "Sémiologie de la langue," in *Problèmes de linguistique générale 2* (Paris: Gallimard, 1974), 43–66.

Berenboom, Alain. *Le Goût amer de l'Amérique* (Paris: Bernard Pascuito, 2006).

———. "Les pratiques virtuelles du romancier," in *La Novellisation. Du Film au livre/Novelization: From Film to Novel*, ed. Jan Baetens and Marc Lits (Leuven: Leuven UP, 2003), 163–73.

Bergman, Ingmar. *Three Films: Through A Glass Darkly. Winter Light. The Silence*, trans. Paul Britten Austin (New York: Evergreen, 1970 [1967]).

———. *Wild Strawberries*, trans. Lars Malmström and David Kushner (London: Lorrimer Publishing, 1970 [1960]).

Boillat, Alain. "Des Films en cases: l'adaptation de longs métrages en feuilletons dessinés," in *Case, Strip, Action!*, ed. Alain Boillat, Marine Borel, Raphaël Oesterlé, and Françoise Revaz (Gollion, CH: Infolio, 2016), 157–234.

Bolter, Jay David. "Critical Theory and the Challenge of New Media," in *Eloquent Images*, ed. Mary E. Hocks and Michelle Kendrick (Cambridge, MA: MIT Press, 2003), 19–36.

Bolter, Jay David, and Richard Grusin. *Remediation: Understanding New Media* (Cambridge, MA: MIT Press, 1999).

Bost, Pierre. *La Passion et la mort de Jeanne d'Arc* (Paris: Gallimard, 1928).

Brangé, Mireille, "Le Cinéma chez Jean Prévost et les écrivains de la NRF," in *Jean Prévost aux avant-postes*, ed. Jean-Pierre Longre and William Marx (Brussels: Les Impressions Nouvelles, 2006), 43–56.

Burch, Noël. *Une Praxis du cinéma* (Paris: Gallimard, 1986).

Burgin, Victor. *Indifferent Spaces: Place and Memory in Visual Culture* (Berkeley: California UP, 1995).

Calinescu, Matei. *Rereading* (New Haven, CT: Yale UP, 1993).

Canudo, Ricciotto. *La Roue* (Paris: Ferenczi, 1923).

Carrière, Jean-Claude. *Mon Oncle* (Paris: Laffont, 1958).

———. *Les Vacances de Monsieur Hulot* (Paris: Laffont, 1958).

Cartmell, Deborah, and Imelda Whelehan, eds. *Adaptations* (New York: Routledge, 2000).

Clerc, Jeanne-Marie. *Littérature et cinéma* (Paris: Nathan, 1993).

Clerc, Jeanne-Marie, and Monique Carcaud-Macaire. *L'Adaptation cinématographique et littéraire* (Paris: Klincksieck, 2004).

Couégnas, Daniel. *Introduction à la paralittérature* (Paris: Seuil, 1992).

Daily, Nicholas. *Literature, Technology, and Modernity, 1860–2000* (Cambridge: Cambridge UP, 2004).

Damisch, Hubert. *Ruptures, Cultures* (Paris: Minuit, 1976).

D'Eaubonne, Françoise. *J'irai cracher sur vos tombes* (Paris: Inter, 1972 [1959]).

De Baecque, Antoine. *La Cinéphilie. Invention d'un regard, histoire d'une culture. 1944–1968* (Paris: Fayard, 2003).

De Berti, Raffaele. "'King Vidor Comes to Italy': dai film alle trasposizioni in romanzo di *The Big Parade* e *The Crowd*," in *Il Racconto del film/Narrating the Film. La Novellizzazione: del catalogo al trailer/Novelization: From the Catalogue to the Trailer*, ed. Alice Autelitano and Valentina Re (Udine: Forum Edizioni, 2006), 123–38.

Debord, Guy. *Œuvres cinématographiques complètes, 1952–1978* (Paris: Gallimard, 1994).

Debray, Régis. *Vie et mort de l'image* (Paris: Gallimard, 1992).

Deitch, Kim. *Alias the Cat* (New York: Pantheon, 2007).

Dellisse, Luc. *L'Invention du scénario* (Paris-Brussels: Les Impressions Nouvelles, 2006).

Delteil, Joseph. *Jeanne d'Arc* (Paris: Grasset, 1925).

Derrida, Jacques. *Of Grammatology*, trans. by Gayatri Chakravorty Spivak (Baltimore: Johns Hopkins UP, 1976 [1967]).

Des Forêts, Louis-René. *Le Malheur au Lido* (Saint-Clément: Fata Morgana, 1987).

Deville, Patrick. *La Tentation des armes à feu* (Paris: Seuil, 2006).

Dozo, Björn-Olav, and Benoît Crucifix. "E-Graphic Novels," in *The Cambridge History of the Graphic Novel*, ed. Jan Baetens, Hugo Frey, and Steve Tabachnick (New York: Cambridge UP, forthcoming).

Dumont, Bruno. *L'Humanité* (Paris: Florence Massot, 2001).

———. *La Vie de Jésus* (Paris: Dis-Voir, 2001).

Edmond-Magny, Claude. *L'Âge d'or du roman américain* (Paris: Seuil, 1949).

Eleftériou-Perrin, Véronique. "Film-feuilleton, guerres et propagande aux États-Unis," in *Au bonheur du feuilleton*, ed. Marie-Françoise Cachin et al. (Paris: Créaphis, 2007), 297–311.

Enzensberger, Hans Maria. "La Culture considérée comme bien de consommation. Analyse de la production du livre de poche," in *Culture ou mise en condition?* (Paris: UGE, coll. 10/18), 161–201.

Epstein, Jean. *Écrits sur le cinéma. 1921–1947*, vol. I (Paris: Seghers, 1974).

Feuillade, Louis, and Georges Meirs. *Les Vampires: Vol. 1: La tête coupée* (Paris: Librairie contemporaine, 1916).

Film-TV Tie-ins: http://www.film-tvtieins.com/ (last accessed 14 June 2017).

Fiorentino, Giovanni. *Luci del Sud. Sorrento un set per Sofia* (Naples: Eidos, 1995).

Fleischer, Leonore. *À bout de souffle Made in USA*, trans. Michel Darroux and Bernadette Emerich (Paris: J'ai Lu, 2001).

———. *Breathless* (New York: Dell, 1983).

*Formules, revue des littératures à contraintes*: www.formules.net (last accessed 12 June 2017).

Francolin, Claude. *À bout de souffle* (Paris: Seghers, 1960).

French, Patrick, and Ken Wlaschin, eds. *The Faber Book of Movie Verse* (London: Faber and Faber, 2000).

Gaudreault, André. *Du littéraire au filmique* (Montréal: Nota Bene, 2005).

Gaudreault, André, and Philippe Marion. "Les Catalogues des premiers fabricants de vues animées: une première forme de novellisation," in *La Novellisation. Du film au livre/ Novelization: From Film to Novel*, ed. Jan Baetens and Marc Lits (Leuven: Leuven UP, 2003), 41–60.

Gauthier, Michel. "Christopher Reeve. Les coulisses du réenchantement," in *Fresh Théorie*, ed. Mark Alizart (Paris: Léo Scheer, 2005), 63–78.

Genette, Gérard. *Palimpsests: Literature in the Second Degree*, trans. by Channa Newman (Lincoln: U of Nebraska P, 1997 [1982]).

Godard, Jean-Luc. *JLG/JLG* (Paris: P. O. L., 1996).

———. *For Ever Mozart* (Paris: P. O. L., 1996).

Grivel, Charles. "Photocinématographication de l'écrit romanesque," in *La Novellisation. Du film au livre/Novelization: From Film to Novel*, ed. Jan Baetens and Marc Lits (Leuven: Leuven UP, 2003), 21–39.

———. *La Production de l'intérêt romanesque* (The Hague: Mouton, 1970).

Groensteen, Thierry. *Comics and Narration*, trans. by Ann Miller (Jackson: UP of Mississippi, 2013 [2009]).

Groupe Mu, *Rhétorique générale* (Paris: Larousse, 1970).

Heffernan, James. *Museum of Words: The Poetics of Ekphrasis from Homer to Ashbery* (Chicago: Chicago UP, 1993).

Hutcheon, Linda. *A Theory of Adaptation* (New York: Routledge, 2006).

Hutcheon, Linda, and Siobhan O'Flynn. *A Theory of Adaptation* (New York: Routledge, 2012).

Jeancolas, Jean, Jean-Jacques Meusy, and Vincent Pinet. *L'Auteur du film. Description d'un combat* (Lyon/Arles: Institut Lumière/Actes Sud, 1996).

Jeannelle, Jean-Louis. "Adaptability: Literature and Cinema Redux," trans. by Margaret C. Flinn. *Studies in French Cinema* 1:2 (2016 [2013]), 95–105.

Jenkins, Henry. "Transmedia 202: Further Reflections. Confessions of an Aca-Fan" (2011). Online: http://henryjenkins.org/2011/08/defining_transmedia_further_re.html (last accessed 14 June 2017).

Kalifa, Dominique. *La Culture de masse en France 1. 1860–1930* (Paris: Complexe, 2001).

Krauss, Rosalind. *Du photographique* (Paris: Macula, 1990).

Kyrou, Ado. *Le Surréalisme au cinéma* (Paris: Ramsay, Poche/Cinéma, 1999 [1953]).

Lacassin, Francis. *Georges Feuillade* (Paris: Gallimard, 2005).

———. *Mémoires. Sur les chemins qui marchent* (Paris: Le Rocher, 2006).

———. *Pour une contre-histoire du cinéma* (Paris: UGE, coll. 10/18, 1972).

Lapacherie, Jean Gérard. "De la grammatextualité," *Poétique* 59 (1985), 283–94.

Lapierre, Pierre. *Aux Portes de la nuit* (Paris: La Nouvelle Édition, 1946).

Larson, Randall D. *Film into Books: An Analytical Bibliography of Film Novelizations, Movie, and TV Tie-Ins* (Metuchen, NJ: Scarecrow Press, 1995).

Leonardi, Francesca. "La Vie passionnée des *Cousins*, les avatars d'un film Nouvelle Vague," in *Il Racconto del film/Narrating the film. La Novellizzazione: del catalogo al trailer/Novelization: From the Catalogue to the Trailer*, ed. Alice Autelitano and Valentina Re (Udine: Forum Edizioni, 2006), 179–95.

Levie, Françoise. *L'Homme qui voulait classer le monde* (Brussels: Les Impressions Nouvelles, 2006).

Mahlknecht, Johannes. "The Hollywood Novelization: Film as Literature or Literature as Film Promotion?" *Poetics Today* 33:2 (2012), 137–68.

Marker, Chris, and Bruce Mau. *The Jetty* (New York: Zone Books, 1992).

McFarlane, Brian. *Novel to Film* (New York: Oxford UP, 1996).

Mélon, Marc. "Cinéma," in *Dictionnaire des termes littéraires*, eds. Paul Aron, Denis Saint-Jacques, and Alain Viala (Paris: PUF, 2002).

Meneghelli, Andrea. "La bellezza facile del *Romanzo film*," in *Il Racconto del film/Narrating the film. La Novellizzazione: del catalogo al trailer/Novelization: From the Catalogue to the Trailer*, ed. Alice Autelitano and Valentina Re (Udine: Forum Edizioni, 2006), 223–30.

Miller, Ann. "*Les 400 coups*, From Film to Novelization," in *La Novellisation. Du film au livre/ Novelization: From Film to Novel*, ed. Jan Baetens and Marc Lits (Leuven: Leuven UP, 2003), 111–20.

Mitchell, W. J. T. *Iconology* (Chicago: Chicago UP, 1985).

———. *Picture Theory* (Chicago: Chicago UP, 1994).

Morin, Edgar. *L'Esprit du temps* (Paris: Grasset, 1962).

Morreale, Emiliano, ed. *Lo Schermo di Carta. Storia et Storie dei cineromanzi* (Turin: Il Castoro, 2007).

Murray, Simone. *The Adaptation Industry: The Cultural Economy of Contemporary Literary Adaptation* (London: Routledge, 2012).

Musser, Charles. "The Devil's Parody: Horace McCoy's Appropriation and Refiguration of Two Hollywood Musicals," in *A Companion to Literature and Film*, ed. Robert Stam and Patricia Raengo (Cambridge: Blackwell, 2005), 229–57.

Nacache, Jacqueline. *L'Acteur de cinéma* (Paris: Nathan, 2003).

Noli, Jean. *La Banquière* (Paris, Ramsay, 1980).

North, Michael. *Camera Works: Photography and the Twentieth-Century Works* (Oxford: Oxford UP, 2005).

Odin, Rober. "La novellisation du théoricien," in *Il Racconto del film/Narrating the film. La Novellizzazione: del catalogo al trailer/Novelization: From the Catalogue to the Trailer*, ed. Alice Autelitano and Valentina Re (Udine: Forum Edizioni, 2006), 397–407.

Paci, Viva. "Pas d'histoires, il faut que le cinéma vive," in *Il Racconto del film/Narrating the Film. La Novellizzazione: del catalogo al trailer/Novelization: From the Catalogue to the Trailer*, ed. Alice Autelitano and Valentina Re (Udine: Forum Edizioni, 2006), 205–12.

Pasolini, Pier Paolo. "The Scenario as a Structure Designed to Become Another Structure," *Wide Angle* 2:1 (1966), 40–47.

Peeters, Heidi. "Multimodality and Its Modes in Novelizations," *Image (&) Narrative* 11:1 (2010), 118–29.

Pellerin, Jean. *Le Copiste indiscret* (Paris: Albin Michel, 1919).

Puech, Jean-Benoît. *Du vivant de l'auteur* (Seyssel: Champ Vallon, 1990).

Raynaud, Isabelle. "Dialogue in Early Silent Screenplays: What Actors Really Said," in *The Sounds of Early Cinema*, ed. Richard Abel and Rick Altman (Bloomington: Indiana UP, 2001), 69–78.

Ricardou, Jean. *Problèmes du nouveau roman* (Paris: Seuil, 1967).

———. *Une Maladie chronique. Problèmes de la représentation écrite du simultané* (Paris-Bruxelles: Les Impressions Nouvelles, 1989).

Robbe-Grillet, Alain. *For a New Novel*, trans. Richard Howard (Evenston, IL: Northwestern UP, 1972).

Roubaud, Jacques. *La Vieillesse d'Alexandre* (Paris: Maspéro, 1978).

Saint-Gelais, Richard. *Fictions transfuges. La transfictionnalité et ses enjeux* (Paris: Éditions du Seuil, 2011).

———. "La novellisation en régime polytextuel. Le cas *Blade Runner,*" in *La Novellisation. Du film au livre/Novelization: From Film to Novel,* ed. Jan Baetens and Marc Lits (Leuven: Leuven UP, 2003), 131–40.

Schatz, T. "The New Hollywood," in *Film Theory Goes to the Movies,* ed. Jim Collins, Hillary Radner, and Ava Preacher Collins (New York: Routledge, 1993), 8–36.

Smolders, Olivier. *La Part de l'ombre* (Brussels: Les Impressions Nouvelles, 2005).

———. *Paul Nougé. Ecriture et caractère à l'école de la ruse* (Brussels: Labor, 1995).

Souchier, Emmanuel. "Formes et pouvoirs de l'énonciation éditoriale," *Communications et langages,* 154 (2007), 23–38.

Storey, John. *Inventing Popular Culture* (Malden, MA: Blackwell, 2003).

Sullivan, Vernon (pseudonym of Boris Vian). *J'irai cracher sur vos tombes [I Spit on Your Graves]* (Paris: Le Scorpion, 1946).

Thiesse, Anne-Marie. *Le Roman du quotidien* (Paris: Le Chemin vert, 1984).

Truffaut, François. "A Certain Tendency of the French Cinema," in *New Wave Film.com* (first published in French in 1954), online: http://www.newwavefilm.com/about/a-certain-tendency-of-french-cinema-truffaut.shtml (last accessed 14 June 2017).

Truffaut, François, and Marcel Moussy. *Les 400 coups* (Paris: Gallimard, 1959).

Tsala Effa, Didier. "La Novellisation du film *Rencontres du troisième type* par Steven Spielberg. D'une forme schématique à l'autre," in *La Novellisation. Du film au livre/Novelization: From Film to Novel,* ed. Jan Baetens and Marc Lits (Leuven: Leuven UP, 2004), 121–30.

Van Parys, Thomas. "The Commercial Novelization: Research, History, Differentiation." *Literature/Film Quarterly* 37:4 (2009), 305–17.

———. "A Fantastic Voyage into Inner Space: Description in Science-Fiction Novelizations." *Science Fiction Studies* 38:2 (2011), 288–303.

Van Parys, Thomas, Lien Jansen, and Elisabeth Vanhoutte. "*eXistenZ*: A Different Novelization?," *Image (&) Narrative* 9 (2004): http://www.imageandnarrative.be/performance/vanparys.htm (last accessed 14 June 2017).

Varinot, Raymond. *La Règle du jeu* (Paris: Tallandier, 1940).

Vercier, Bruno, and Dominique Viart. *La Littérature française au présent* (Paris: Bordas, 2005).

Vian, Boris (under the pseudonym Vernon Sullivan). *J'irai cracher sur vos tombes [I Spit on Your Graves]* (Paris: éd. du Scorpion, 1946).

Viel, Tanguy. *Cinéma* (Paris: Minuit, 1999).

Virmaux, Alain, and Odette Virmaux. *Le Ciné-roman* (Paris: Edilig, 1984).

———. *Du film à l'écrit. Du roman cinéma au roman cinéoptique* (Perpignan: Institut Jean Vigo, 1998).

———. *Les Surréalistes et le cinéma* (Paris: Ramsay, Poche/Cinéma, 1988 [1976]).

Vouilloux, Bernard. "L' 'Impressionnisme littéraire': une révision," *Poétique* 121 (2000), 61–92.

# INDEX

*This index contains three types of items: names of authors and scholars, titles of books and films, and concepts. In order to distinguish between novelizer (the primary focus of this book) and film director in the case of a novelized movie, the latter's name is introduced by an asterisk. In the case of a self-novelization, only the name of the director-as-novelizer appears.*

# THEORY AND INTERPRETATION OF NARRATIVE

*James Phelan, Peter J. Rabinowitz, and Katra Byram, Series Editors*

Because the series editors believe that the most significant work in narrative studies today contributes both to our knowledge of specific narratives and to our understanding of narrative in general, studies in the series typically offer interpretations of individual narratives and address significant theoretical issues underlying those interpretations. The series does not privilege one critical perspective but is open to work from any strong theoretical position.